# Anatomy
# of
# Film

# Anatomy of Film

## Bernard F. Dick

St. Martin's Press

New York

Library of Congress Catalog Card Number: 76–28140
Copyright © 1978 by St. Martin's Press, Inc.
All Rights Reserved.
Manufactured in the United States of America.
21098
fedcba
For information, write St. Martin's Press, Inc.,
175 Fifth Avenue, New York, N.Y. 10010


cover design: Mies Hora


cloth ISBN: 0-312-03360-5
paper ISBN: 0-312-03395-8

# Preface

*Anatomy of Film* examines the exterior and the interior of the narrative film—its outer form and its inner structure—in order to isolate its parts and study their functions, to explore what happens on the screen of the theater and on the screen of the imagination, and to determine what critical approaches should be taken to the medium.

Since film knowledge varies from individual to individual, a context is supplied for every film reference made in this book. In choosing examples, I have drawn upon four categories of films that are customarily taught in film courses and periodically revived (e.g., *The Birth of a Nation, Potemkin, The Grapes of Wrath, Citizen Kane, Wild Strawberries*); films that are commonly shown on television (Hitchcock's films, *Double Indemnity, The Best Years of Our Lives, Cat People, Shane*); films for which published screenplays are available (*The Third Man, The Seventh Seal, The Passenger, The Story of Adele H.*); and recent films that have had critical and popular appeal (e.g., *Last Tango in Paris, Nashville, Taxi Driver, One Flew over the Cuckoo's Nest, All the President's Men*).

There will always be differences of opinion about the way films should be cited. Some writers merely give the name of the film *(Casablanca)*; others add the release date *(Casablanca, 1943)*; still others preface the title with the director's name (Michael Curtiz's *Casablanca,* 1943). This book uses the last-named method of citation.

Film is a subject to be studied and an art form to be enjoyed. *Anatomy of Film* attempts to provide a similar combination of instruction and pleasure.

I would like to thank my wife for accompanying me to the urban netherworld in pursuit of a forgotten film; my former student Martin Nocente for sharing his awesome knowledge of movies with me; Billy Wilder for allowing me to interview him at a time when he was preparing for a new film, and his secretary Kay Taylor for making the arrangements; the staff of the Margaret Herrick Library of the Academy of Motion Picture Arts and Sciences in Los Angeles, a film scholar's paradise; Thomas Broadbent, Ellen Wynn, Peter Phelps, and Edward Cone of St. Martin's Press for encouraging this project; the indispensable Mary Corliss of The Museum of Modern Art's Stills Archive; Rose Marie Kenney for helping me type the manuscript; Bob Dorfman, head of publicity at Warner Brothers; Stanley Forman for sending me his Pulitzer Prize-winning photos of Diana Bryant's tragic fall from a Boston fire escape; and Fairleigh Dickinson University, where I am able to teach the two disciplines I love most—literature and film.

I would like to acknowledge the University of California Press for permission to quote from Rudolf Arnheim's *Film as Art* (Copyright © 1957 by The Regents of the University of California); Oxford University Press for permission to quote from Siegfried Kracauer's *Theory of Film* (Copyright © 1960 by Oxford University Press); Grosset & Dunlap, Inc., for permission to quote from *Agee on Film* (Copyright © 1969 by Grosset & Dunlap, Inc.); and Dwight Macdonald for permission to quote from *Dwight Macdonald on Movies* (Copyright © 1969 by Dwight Macdonald).

No one is impervious to influence. My major influence is acknowledged in the dedication.

Teaneck, New Jersey
January 13, 1977

# Contents

IN MEMORIAM
PARKER TYLER
(1904–1974)

# Anatomy
## of
# Film

# 1
# The Nature of Film

On July 23, 1975, in Boston, an aerial ladder deposited a fireman on the balcony of a burning building. Robert O'Neill had come to the rescue of nineteen-year-old Diana Bryant and her two-year-old goddaughter, Tiare Jones. Suddenly the balcony gave way. The fireman grasped the ladder, but Diana fell to her death; Tiare was seriously injured although she survived. The next day the *New York Times* ran four pictures of the incident, which won Stanley Forman a Pulitzer Prize in 1976 for spot news photography. The pictures look like stills from a disaster film. In the first Diana is gripping the railing while the fireman stands alongside her, his arm raised as if he were acknowledging an ovation. In the second the balcony collapses; the fireman grabs the ladder, and Diana begins her plunge with the eerie grace of a slow-motion death. The third shows Diana moving through the air like a swimmer and Tiare balancing herself in the void like a tightrope walker. In the last of the four photos, three figures like the three fates of Greek mythology, are seen bending over a body.

Most people would find these photos fascinating because they

*1–1a   Diana and fireman on the balcony.*

*1–1b   The collapse of the balcony.*

capture the suddenness with which life turns into death and a human being into a mere object. But the student of film might be drawn to them for other reasons. The pictures tell a four-part story that could be entitled "The Fall of Diana Bryant." Yet they break up her fall into separate stages, giving the impression that it occurred in four discrete steps, whereas it was really a single, uninterrupted

1–1c   *The fall of Diana and Tiare.*

1–1d   *The aftermath.*

action. By taking individual pictures of a continuous action, Forman has fragmented it the way a film maker does; and by fragmenting the fall, he has made it seem longer than it actually was. If we understand what Stanley Forman achieved in these photos, we understand one of the basic elements of film: that film can expand or contract time.

# FILMIC TIME

Filmic time is arbitrary. Film makers can compress a whole day into a few minutes, or they can prolong a few minutes into what seems to be a whole day. In the famous Odessa Steps sequence in *Potemkin* (1925), Russian director Sergei Eisenstein distorts real time: He makes the massacre on the steps seem longer than it normally would have been because he wants to emphasize the atrocities that czarist troops committed against the citizens of Odessa. Toward the end of the sequence, a czarist soldier swings his saber, striking an old woman who is wearing a pince-nez, in her right eye. In reality, the soldier would have slashed her eye with one movement of his arm. Eisenstein fragments the act: first we see the soldier, his arm raised with the blade behind his head; then we see his savage face but not the saber; now his face dominates the screen; next he shouts something as his raised arm begins to descend; finally, we see the woman—her mouth gaping, the right lens of her pince-nez shattered, blood spurting from her eye and running down her face.

In *Notorious* (1946), Alfred Hitchcock compresses a party that would have lasted an entire evening into eight minutes. The climax of Peter Bogdanovich's *Nickelodeon* (1976) is the premiere of D. W. Griffith's *The Birth of a Nation* (1915). To make the premiere as credible as possible, Bogdanovich used clips from the actual film. The setting is so authentic and the audience reaction so natural that we do not realize a three-hour epic has been reduced to a few minutes.

Time is not peculiar to film, yet filmic time is unique. Similarly, sound, color, and lighting are properties of other media, yet film uses them in an original way.

# SOUND

Although we call the first thirty years of the motion-picture industry "the silent period," the movies were never really silent. Usually there were commentators, musicians, sound-effects machines, and phonograph recordings to provide some kind of synchronization of sound and image.

*Synchronous sound*, sound that originates in the image, is the kind with which we are most familiar. As characters speak, we see them and hear what they are saying. *Asynchronous sound*, on the other hand, does not originate in the image. John Schlesinger's *Marathon Man* (1976) opens with the sound of heavy breathing but we do not see the person making it. Gradually we discover the source of the sound: Babe Levy (Dustin Hoffman), who is running through Central Park in New York City. It is a provocative opening, for it implies *Marathon Man* will be the kind of movie that requires the audience to make certain connections for itself.

Asynchronous sound can be considerably more imaginative than synchronous sound because (1) it allows film makers to substitute a sound for an image; (2) it enables them to contrast sound and image; and (3) it encourages them to juxtapose sounds and images that would not normally occur at the same time.

In Fritz Lang's *M* (1931), Mrs. Beckmann is waiting anxiously for her daughter Elsie to return from school. She leans out the window, calling "Elsie! Elsie!" On the screen we do not see Elsie but rather a series of images: an empty stairwell, an empty attic, Elsie's place setting at the dinner table, her ball on the grass, and, finally, a balloon that is momentarily caught in some telephone wires and then floats away.

The asynchronization is remarkably subtle. Ironically, Mrs. Beckmann's call is heard: Images denoting absence and emptiness answer her. Elsie will never return. Like the balloon that was caught in the wires and then blown skyward by the wind, Elsie was enticed by a child murderer and led away to death.

Sound may also be categorized as actual or commentative. *Actual sound* comes from a visible or identifiable source. The breathing at the opening of *Marathon Man* is an actual sound although the audience does not yet know its source. *Commentative*

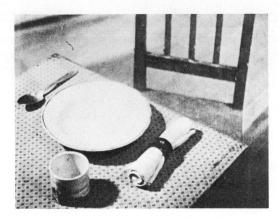

1-2 *Asynchronization in Fritz Lang's* M *(1931). When Mrs. Beckmann calls "Elsie!," the response is not verbal but visual: a place setting never to be used again. Courtesy Janus Films. Photo courtesy Museum of Modern Art/Film Stills Archive.*

*sound,* on the other hand, does not come from a visible source; it is added for dramatic effect. Background music is usually commentative. The dark, brooding music heard at the beginning of Orson Welles's *Citizen Kane* (1941) while the camera scans Kane's vast estate is commentative.

## COLOR

Although color can certainly embellish a film, it should serve more than a decorative function. Color can have a direct bearing on character, plot, and setting. Alfred Hitchcock, Federico Fellini, and Brian De Palma, for instance, have made interesting use of the color red to enhance films they have directed.

Although the heroine of Hitchcock's *Marnie* (1964) has suppressed all memory of a murder she committed as a child, the guilt persists in the form of an intense aversion to red. Instinctively, she removes red gladioli from a vase and replaces them with white chrysanthemums. A drop of red ink on her white blouse sends her rushing to the washroom; the red polka dots on a jockey's uniform petrify her. Not until the end of the film do we learn that Marnie's reaction to red was the result of her having killed a sailor with a poker to protect her prostitute-mother from possible harm.

The title character of Fellini's *Juliet of the Spirits* (1965) is a housewife whose fantasies are dominated by erotic reds. When we first see Juliet, she is trying on a red wig; then she sets the table with red candles. When she visits a clairvoyant, she wears a red scarf. Yet red is not her color; it is the color of the women of her fantasies. At the end of the film Juliet reverts to white, the color that typifies the ordinary person that she is.

The title character of De Palma's *Carrie* (1976) is a high-school senior with telekinetic powers. Her mother is a religious fanatic, and both have reddish hair. When Carrie menstruates for the first time, she thinks she is bleeding to death. Her naïveté makes her an object of derision to her classmates, who cajole her into attending the senior prom where they humiliate her publicly by dropping a bucket of blood on her. Carrie literally sees red. Her revenge, as one might suspect, is appropriately bloody.

No rule exists that dictates when a film should be made in color and when it should be made in black and white. A movie about Depression America can be as effective in color (e.g., Hal Ashby's *Bound for Glory,* 1976) as in black and white (e.g., John Ford's *The Grapes of Wrath,* 1940). Nor is it accurate to say that color is better than black and white for westerns and musicals. Several of John Ford's classic westerns were photographed in black and white: *Stagecoach* (1939), *My Darling Clementine* (1946), *Fort Apache* (1948), *Wagon Master* (1950), *The Man Who Shot Liberty Valance* (1962). And the great musicals of the 1930s—Lloyd Bacon's *42nd Street*(1933), Mervyn LeRoy's *Gold Diggers of 1933*, Busby Berkeley's *Gold Diggers of 1935*, George Stevens's *Swing Time* (1936), and so forth—did not need color to be effective entertainment.

Color is, however, widely used today. Although sometimes it is merely ornamental, often it serves a specific function, and the job of the student of film is to discern the film maker's intention in using it. Does he use it to underscore the film's theme, the way Stanley Kubrick does in *A Clockwork Orange* (1971) by dressing Alex and his gang in gleaming white that grows progressively dirtier? Does he use it as a means of characterization, as Hitchcock does in *Marnie*, where the heroine's aversion to red is the result of a childhood trauma? Is it part of the setting, as in Victor Fleming's *The Wizard of Oz* (1939), where the Kansas scenes are photographed in sepia and the Oz scenes in color to convey the disparity between the colorless real world and the colorful world of the imagination? Or does the film maker relate color to the reality he wishes to depict, as Kubrick does in *2001: A Space Odyssey* (1968), where oceans are pink, waves are purple, and mountains orange?

Even a black and white film can use color creatively. Throughout Orson Welles's *Citizen Kane* (1941) white is an ambivalent symbol. It suggests innocence as well as loss of innocence; it is the color of the real snow that Kane knew as a boy in Colorado and the color of the artificial snow in the glass paperweight he keeps as a memento of his lost childhood. White is a symbol of freedom; when Susan leaves Kane, a white cockatoo screeches and flies away. But white also evokes sterility and death: Xanadu, Kane's palatial home, is decorated with useless statues and white marble, and the nurse who enters Kane's room at the moment of his death is clad in a white uniform. The possibilities for the creative use of color are unlimited, as the discerning student soon realizes.

## LIGHTING

Lighting can also express subtleties of character, plot, and setting. In *high-key lighting* the key light (the chief source of light) supplies most of the illumination, while the fill light (an auxiliary light of lesser intensity) "fills in" areas left unlit by the key light and softens the shadows cast by it. Since high-key lighting provides almost uniform brightness, it is the kind most often used for comedies and musicals and for scenes of tranquillity and peace. In *low-key lighting,* the key light supplies much less illumination, leaving a large part of the setting in shadow. Such lighting may be used to illuminate a face on an otherwise dark screen; the effect is one of eerie contrast between intense brightness and extreme darkness. Low-key lighting is ideally suited to horror films and melodramas, and was extensively used in that type of film of the forties known as *film noir* (literally, "black" film), where passions ran high in urban settings that were grimy or fogbound.

In addition to these two general categories of lighting, there are five other types distinguished by the angle from which the light source illuminates an object: front, back, top, side, and bottom. *Front lighting* has a softening effect and thus makes the object we are viewing more attractive than it actually is. Front lighting imparts a feeling of pastoral tranquillity to the meal of wild strawberries and milk that Mia offers the Knight in Ingmar Bergman's *The Seventh Seal* (1957). *Back lighting* omits details but adds depth. At the beginning of Bergman's *The Magician* (1958), a wagon is silhouetted against the sky. The details are obscured, but a feeling of depth is achieved. When a character is backlit, as Esther (Barbra Streisand) is when she sings "Evergreen" at the end of Frank Pierson's *A Star Is Born* (1976), a halo-like effect is produced that gives the character an ethereal quality. Similarly, *top lighting* is used to create an aura of youthfulness or spirituality, as it was in Henry King's *The Song of Bernadette* (1943) to suggest Bernadette's saintliness. *Side lighting* puts the object half in light, half in shadow; thus it can denote a split personality, a morally ambiguous character, or a *femme fatale.* Greta Garbo and Marlene Dietrich were often photographed in this fashion. *Bottom lighting* gives the object a sinister air; it was the kind of lighting D. W. Griffith employed in *Dream Street* (1921) to emphasize the villainy of Sway Wan.

In a black and white film, the contrast or interplay of light and darkness can produce visual symbolism. Throughout *Citizen Kane,* Thompson, the reporter trying to decipher the meaning of Kane's dying word ("Rosebud"), is always seen in shadow. He is literally in the dark and remains in that state throughout the film. Just as darkness can denote ignorance, so light can intimate knowledge. When Thompson enters the Thatcher Memorial Library to read the

1–3  *Note how the lighting imparts a feeling of serenity to the meal of wild strawberries and milk in Ingmar Bergman's* The Seventh Seal *(1957). Courtesy Janus Films. Photo courtesy Museum of Modern Art/Film Stills Archive.*

memoirs of Kane's guardian, shafts of light illuminate the mausoleum-like room. Perhaps the memoirs will explain the meaning of "Rosebud." But the light is deceptive, and Thompson leaves the library as much in the dark as ever.

But Thompson is not the only character who suffers from ignorance. Although Thompson is ignorant of the meaning of "Rosebud," Kane is ignorant of himself. When Kane delivers his Declaration of Principles, promising to be a "fighting and tireless champion" of the people, his face is in darkness. Kane does not know that he will never live up to his declaration, and the lighting states as much.

Lighting is also used effectively in Preston Sturges's *Sullivan's Travels* (1941). In that film some black parishoners invite the white prisoners of a local chain gang to their church to watch a movie. When we see the prisoners making their way to the church, they are in darkness; for a moment they look like black men. The lighting establishes a bond between the black congregation and the prisoners; it also reinforces the film's theme that moviegoing is a form of brotherhood that erases all distinctions, including racial ones. Movies are the great leveler; in the dark everyone is equal.

## THE BLENDING OF FILM ELEMENTS

Thus far we have been discussing time, sound, color, and lighting as individual elements of a movie. The skillful film maker, however, works with all of these elements simultaneously to create a harmonious mix, each element underlining some aspect of plot, character, or setting. In two sequences—one from Hitchcock's *Notorious* (1946), a black and white film, and one from John Guillermin's color remake of *King Kong* (1976)—one can see this kind of creative directorship at work.

### The "Key Episode" in "Notorious"

In *Notorious*, Alicia Huberman (Ingrid Bergman) is an American intelligence agent whose mission has required her to marry Alexander Sebastian (Claude Rains), a top-ranking Nazi residing in Brazil after Germany's defeat in World War II. Since Sebastian has given her a key to every room in the house except the wine cellar, she suspects it may contain more than wine. Gaining access to the cellar poses a problem, however, because Sebastian carries his key ring with him at all times. On the evening of a party they are giving, Alicia notices that Sebastian has left the key ring on his dressing table. While he is in the bathroom, she decides to remove the key to the wine cellar. In such a situation in real life, she would have taken it in a matter of seconds. But to create suspense, Hitchcock prolongs the action. He fragments the scene, showing us Alicia's tense face, the bathroom door, the key ring, and, finally, the removal of the crucial key. The lighting is low key—shadowy and sinister, as if anything might happen. Throughout the scene commentative sound in the form of eerie background music is more significant than the actual sound of Sebastian's voice. Thus, the effectiveness of the scene is directly related to Hitchcock's blending of fragmented time, commentative sound, and low-key lighting.

### The Death of Kong

At the climax of Guillermin's *King Kong*, the giant ape is on top of New York's World Trade Center with his captive-turned-sympathizer, Dwan (Jessica Lange). Although she begs him to hold her up as a shield and thus save himself from the helicopters that are firing at him, Kong refuses to endanger her. Bullets rip through his body, and Kong crashes to the pavement. As he is about to die, his heartbeat grows progressively fainter until it stops. But we hear more than just a heartbeat; complementing it is a tender motif from John Barry's musical score, one that evokes the love Kong felt for Dwan. There is something tragically human about Kong in this scene: He bleeds, his heart beats, and his eyes finally close in death. By contrast Dwan looks like a tinsel queen in her silver lamé gown. No sooner does Kong's heart stop beating than Dwan is surrounded by reporters and fans. The death of Kong has made a star of Dwan in record time. The impact of the final scene can be attributed to the successful coordination of

1. *Sound*—diminishing heartbeat (actual) juxtaposed with poignant background music (commentative)
2. *Color*—Kong's natural color (black spotted with red) contrasted with Dwan's artificial color (tinsel-like silver)
3. *Time*—foreshortened because Kong's death means instant stardom for Dwan

The four elements we have been discussing—time, sound, color, and lighting—are not peculiar to film. A novel not only takes a certain amount of time to read but is also generally set in a particular time period. However, a film can reduce a 400-page novel to 90 minutes, it can compress an entire decade into a few images, or it can extend an action beyond its normal time span. In the theater, it is the actors who speak the dialogue; in a film, a character may say something and the camera, rather than another character, will answer with an image. The theater relies on lighting to illuminate the action and to create moods; film lighting can go one step further and characterize a person as vapid or complex, good or evil, saint or sinner. A painter uses color, but to a film maker color is part of the moving image; no longer a static phenomenon, color is a dynamic feature of reality.

What is unique about film is that it can draw on the other arts and still be one itself.

# 2
# Film Language I:
## Shot, Scene, and Sequence

Ancient Greek seems a formidable language to most beginners; but once they adjust to the alphabet and master the grammar, it ceases to be inaccessible. It is not an easy language, but it can be learned. Similarly, in an anatomy textbook, the human body at first appears to be a confusing mass of organs, each labeled with strange Latin and Greek derivatives. When the parts are studied separately and in terms of their functions, however, the body begins to disclose some of its mysteries. It is the same with film: before the art of film can be fully appreciated, students must first acquire a working knowledge of how that art is communicated. In short, film language must be learned.

A film is made up of shots, scenes, and sequences. A *shot* is what is recorded by a single operation of the camera, from the time the camera starts to the time it stops. A *scene* is a group of shots with continuous action. A *sequence* is a group of scenes forming a self-contained unit that is often intelligible in itself. Each of these has a distinctive function within a film, and each can be composed in a variety of ways.

# THE SHOT

A shot can make a factual or a symbolic statement, but it cannot tell a story. If someone who had never seen William Wellman's *Beau Geste* (1939) were shown a publicity still of the bugle in the sand and asked to explain the image, he or she would probably say "death," "loss," or "a voice silenced"—and that answer would be substantially correct. Similarly, someone viewing a still of the watch without hands in Ingmar Bergman's *Wild Strawberries* (1957) would probably say that it signified "time that has stopped" or "death." Certain images not only carry their symbolism with them, but they convey that symbolism independently of a context. It is the same with certain lines of poetry that can communicate their meaning even to those who have never read the complete poem.

A shot can therefore impart information, but of an elementary sort. The first shot of Mamie (Jane Russell) in Raoul Walsh's *The Revolt of Mamie Stover* (1956) as she looks straight at us while the credits appear immediately identifies her as a woman of dubious virtue: We know what she is from the way she looks. A bugle in the sand or a watch without a dial or a face in the night can only tell us what they represent: without the context we do not know to whom the bugle or the watch belongs or who the woman is whose eyes meet ours. A *long take*, or sequence shot, a shot of more than usual duration, is more informative, yet it too is incomplete by itself. The opening of Orson Welles's *Touch of Evil* (1958) is an uninterrupted three-minute shot that starts with the credits. Someone puts a time bomb into the trunk of a car. Two people get into the car and proceed down the street of a Mexican border town, past Mr. and Mrs. Vargas (Charlton Heston and Janet Leigh). The car stops at the customs booth, continues a short distance, then explodes into flames. Besides being magnificently atmospheric, this shot also introduces the leading characters and establishes the mood of the film, but it does not tell us why someone planted a bomb in the car of the ill-fated couple. Even the long take needs a context.

Although shots convey only bits of information and are therefore a relatively elementary part of film language, they can be quite complex, because film makers are free to compose their shots in a number of ways. Shots are distinguished by the distance of the camera from a subject, the camera's angle, whether it is stationary or movable, and other such considerations.

# The Range of Shots

The *range* of a shot refers to the distance of the camera from its subject. In a *close-up* (CU), sometimes also called simply a "close shot" (CS), the camera is actually or apparently close to the subject; in anatomical terms, it is a shot of the head or of the area from the shoulders to the top of the head. A variation of this shot is the *extreme close-up* (ECU), or big close-up (BCU), in which the camera comes in much closer, shooting perhaps a part of the head or face. In contrast, a *long shot* (LS) is one taken by the camera at a considerable distance from the subject, at least fifty yards. In between is the *medium shot* (MS), in which the camera is nearer to its subject than it would be for a LS, but not so near as it would be for a CU; in the American sense, it is a shot covering the area from the knees to the head. As with the close-up shot, film makers use variations on both medium and long shots (the so-called medium close shots and medium long shots). Whereas medium shots are used to present a subject impartially, both close-ups and long shots comment more pointedly on their subjects and therefore deserve further consideration.

## The Close-up

French director Jean-Luc Godard is fond of saying that the close-up was invented for tragedy, the long shot for comedy. Certainly there are few sights more poignant than the close-up of Lucy's face in D. W. Griffith's *Broken Blossoms* (1919), when her father denounces her. Yet if her face is photographed in close-up, her father's should be also. The close-up is perfect for intense emotion of any sort; it has the impact of a crescendo in a symphony or a sudden question in a lyric poem. ("Where are the songs of Spring?" Keats asks abruptly in "To Autumn.") Thus the confrontation between father and daughter in *Broken Blossoms* achieves its tragic effectiveness through two close-ups: one of a face disfigured with hatred, the other of a face transfigured with innocence.

Alfred Hitchcock finds the close-up ideal for objects like a suspicious glass of milk (*Suspicion*, 1941), a wine bottle filled with uranium ore (*Notorious*, 1946), or an envelope dropped by a Nazi agent (*Saboteur*, 1942). These objects are so crucial to the plot that Hitchcock cannot assume the audience will pay attention to them unless their presence is emphasized.

The close-up can be as valid as an italicized word or phrase; however, its cousin, the extreme close-up, should live up to its name and be used only in extreme cases. Too many extreme close-ups can create an imbalance in the film; the effect would be like the speech pattern of a person who stresses every work he utters including "a" and "the." An ECU can be used when the plot hinges on some detail that is so important that the camera must get as close as possible to it. If a scar identifies a murderer, as it does in Johan Jacobsen's *A Stranger Knocks* (1963), the scar should be photographed in ECU.

One exception to this general rule is the use of extreme close-ups in horror films. There a director may use an ECU, even though the plot does not require it, in order to sustain terror and send the proverbial chill up the audience's spine. Hitchcock's extreme close-ups of Marion Crane's screaming mouth and staring eye in *Psycho* (1960) are justified on this ground; his purpose was not to fill the screen with a woman's anatomy as she is being stabbed to death in a shower, but to make shots of the body an integral part of fifty seconds of nerve-racking horror.

A close-up can be as commonplace as Magic Marker underlining or as esthetic as a Richard Avedon photograph. Two close-ups with the pictorial quality of great art come to mind. In Rouben Mamoulian's *Queen Christina* (1933), Christina (Greta Garbo) stands against the prow of the ship that carries the body of her dead lover—her gaze fixed ahead, her face impenetrable; thinking of absolutely nothing as the story goes. The close-up of her face shows the most agonized absence of thought one is likely to see. In William Wyler's *Mrs. Miniver* (1942), Kay Miniver (Greer Garson) opens a window and looks up at the planes overhead. With a breathless onrush, the camera meets her face as the sky forms the background for her close-up.

## The Long Shot

If a close-up can be compared to a portrait, a long shot is the film maker's means of composing a landscape. The western is especially noted for its long shots: a deer lapping water from a stream with snow-fringed mountains in the background (George

Stevens's *Shane*, 1953), a man bidding farewell to a woman who merges with the landscape as he rides off (John Ford's *My Darling Clementine*, 1946). Many of Ford's long shots in *Clementine* are, in fact, evocative of a lonely masculine world: We are shown a bar thronged by men, seen sometimes in silhouette, sometimes illuminated by the kerosene lamps hanging overhead, or we see a stretch of sky brooding over a desolate street.

When death is photographed in long shot, it is less painful to watch. In *The Naked Dawn* (1955), Edgar G. Ulmer chose a long shot for the shooting of Santiago (Arthur Kennedy). Santiago is on horseback when the bullet strikes him; we see neither paralyzed eyes nor spurting blood. The shot has a formalized beauty about it that reminds one of a painting such as Breughel's *Fall of Icarus*, where, as poet W. H. Auden describes it, "everything turns away/Quite leisurely from the disaster."

The position of the camera is like word order in Latin, where the two most important places in a sentence are the beginning and the end. The camera, like Latin syntax, can shift the positions of subject and object depending on which it cares to emphasize. Latin can "jumble" the words of a sentence, putting the verb at the end, a phrase at the beginning, and the subject in the middle. The camera can do the same: It can stress the subject in CU and ignore it in LS. It can also alter the significance of the subject by shooting it from different angles.

## The Angle of Shots

In a *low-angle shot* the camera shoots up at the subject, making it seem larger than it actually is. Such a shot can suggest dominance or power, as it does in Orson Welles's *Citizen Kane* (1941), when one character early in the film hovers over the young Kane as he presents him with a sled. In a *high-angle shot* the camera shoots down at the subject, making it seem smaller than it is. When a female member of the French underground interrogates Bill Kluggs (Dan Dailey) in John Ford's *When Willie Comes Marching Home* (1950), the high angle from which he is photographed represents the diminution of the self a person feels under cross-examination. The high-angle shot of the president pacing the floor in Griffith's *Abraham Lincoln* (1930) reminds us that the burdens of office dwarf even the great.

2–1  *Orson Welles prepares for a low-angle shot, below floor level, in* Citizen Kane *(1941). Courtesy Janus Films. Photo courtesy Museum of Modern Art/Film Stills Archives.*

In Alan J. Pakula's *All the President's Men* (1976), as reporters Bob Woodward and Carl Bernstein (Robert Redford and Dustin Hoffman) are sorting out library slips, the camera watches them from above; they, in turn, grow smaller as they realize the enormity of their task. The scene ends with the camera's peering down at the reading room of the Library of Congress, which looks like a magnified snowflake.

Sometimes the script requires a high-angle shot for reasons that have nothing to do with symbolism or imagery. In George Marshall's *The Blue Dahlia* (1946), Mrs. Harwood (Veronica Lake), who is on the mezzanine of a hotel, phones down to Johnny Morrison (Alan Ladd), who is standing by the registration desk in the lobby below. Marshall had to shoot down at Morrison to match the angle from which Mrs. Harwood saw him. Thus the nature of the material dictated the nature of the shot.

2–2 *Robert Redford (Bob Woodward) and Dustin Hoffman (Carl Bernstein) prepare for the Library of Congress scene in Alan J. Pakula's* All the President's Men *(1976). The camera is set for a high-angle shot. Courtesy Warner Bros. Inc., copyright © 1976.*

## Shots from Stationary Camera Positions

When the camera moves, it leaves meaning in a state of abeyance until it sees what the director wants to see. The moving camera is rather like the periodic sentence, where the sense is suspended until the very end.

When the phrase "moving camera" is used, it can mean two things. The whole camera may be on a moving vehicle, such as a dolly or a truck, or it may stand stationary on a device such as a tripod but have the freedom to rotate. The direction of its rotation—left or right, up or down—determines whether the shot is a pan or a tilt. Both can be used to add emphasis to a subject.

### The Pan Shot

When the camera *pans*, it rotates horizontally on a fixed axis. Panning is the closest film can come to imitating the natural movement of our eyes as we read. Generally, a pan shot moves from left to right, but it can also move from right to left, recalling the back-to-front way some people read magazines. As we read, we learn; it is the same with the pan shot. At the beginning of Griffith's *Ab-*

*raham Lincoln,* for example, a pan shot guides us through the bare woods to the cabin where Lincoln was born. (The same shot, incidentally, occurs at the end, thus bringing both the film and Lincoln's life full circle.) A pan shot can also comment on a situation: As David Locke (Jack Nicholson) of Michelangelo Antonioni's *The Passenger* (1975) cries aloud in desperation because his Land Rover is stalled in the sand, the camera answers by panning the indifferent desert. Sometimes a pan shot can be quite witty. There is a delicious one in Woody Van Dyke's *The Thin Man* (1934). As Nora Charles (Myrna Loy) opens a door on the right, the camera pans right to left, from the doorway to the interior where her husband is comforting a weeping girl. When he catches sight of his wife, the camera pans left to right, back to Nora in the doorway, as if it too were embarrassed at being found in a compromising situation.

Two variations on pan shots can also produce interesting effects. In a *circular pan,* the camera rotates 360 degrees. François Truffaut used this device in *Jules and Jim* (1961), where the camera shoots Thérèse from the center of a room while she moves rapidly around the room imitating a steam engine by puffing on a cigarette. A *swish pan* is an unusually rapid pan that produces a momentary blur. Mamoulian swish pans immediately after Dr. Jekyll becomes Mr. Hyde for the first time (*Dr. Jekyll and Mr. Hyde,* 1932).

## The Tilt Shot

When the camera *tilts,* it rotates vertically on its axis. Like panning, tilting can also add to a viewer's knowledge of an object or a person. In Robert Stevenson's *Jane Eyre* (1944), the camera tilts down from a plaque that reads "Lowood Institution" to the sleeping Jane who is being carried into it. In *Citizen Kane* the camera tilts up the entrance gate of Kane's estate, Xanadu, past the No Trespassing sign, reminding us that the warning applies to everyone but itself. At the end of the film, the camera tilts *down* the gate to the No Trespassing sign as it returns to its starting point.

The tilt shot is especially good at suggesting horror. As the female vampire (Gloria Holden) is about to sink her teeth into a victim's neck in Lambert Hillyer's *Dracula's Daughter* (1936), the camera begins climbing the wall, leaving the rest to our imagination. The tilt shot is also adept at generating suspense. In Antonioni's *The Passenger*, the camera is in the process of tracing the curve of a surface wire up the wall of a hotel room when a sudden knock at the door interrupts its ascent, causing it to backtrack and swing over to the doorway to see who is there. (It is only a waiter!) A tilt shot can suggest the actual or potential fate of a character. When Phillip Vandamm (James Mason) in Hitchcock's *North by Northwest* (1959) discovers his mistress is an American agent, he decides to kill her aboard a plane. "This matter is something that is disposed of at great height—over the water," he remarks. At the mention of "height," the camera tilts up—to nothing but empty space.

As it pans or tilts, the camera guides the eye horizontally or vertically, determining both the direction and the object of our vision. Sometimes the camera will pan, then tilt, as it directs the viewer's gaze or the character's across one surface and up another. There is a notorious flashback in Hitchcock's *Stage Fright* (1950), which is later revealed to be a complete lie. Jonathan Cooper (Richard Todd) is explaining to his bewildered girlfriend how Charlotte Inwood (Marlene Dietrich) begged him to go to her flat and bring her a new dress; it seems the one she was wearing was stained with her husband's blood. As Cooper enters the flat, the camera pans across the room to Mr. Inwood's body and then tilts up a closet door. At first the camera's tilting seems inexplicable; but as Cooper opens the door and removes the dress, the camera reveals that it is a clothes closet. Although tilting up a clothes closet may seem trivial or even unnecessary, it is part of Hitchcock's plan to make Cooper's story plausible. Thus Hitchcock has the camera guide Cooper to the closet as if he did not know where it was. If Cooper headed straight for the closet, the audience would sense that he was more familiar with Charlotte's flat than he should be and therefore might not accept his story.

## Shots from a Mobile Camera

Instead of merely rotating on a pivot, some cameras can actually move with, toward, or away from their subject. The phrase *moving shot* is properly applied to this kind of camera action, and there are several varieties of such shots, depending on the means by which the camera moves. If the camera moves on tracks, it is a *tracking shot*; if it is mounted on a dolly (a small wheeled platform), it is a *dolly shot*; if it moves up and down, in and out of a scene on a crane, it is a *crane shot*.

Today most writers on film use dolly shot and tracking shot interchangeably; the camera dollies in (tracks in) when it moves toward the subject, dollies out (tracks out) when it moves away from the subject. Others simply call any shot in which the camera is moving on a vehicle (a truck, a dolly, a bicycle, even roller skates*) a "tracking shot." Thus they will speak of a "forward tracking shot," a "vertical tracking shot," a "diagonal tracking shot," and so forth.

"Tracking shot" is a good synonym for "moving shot" because it is a good description of what the camera actually does and because it is often impossible to tell whether a camera is on tracks that have been laid on the set or on a dolly. A crane shot, on the other hand, is identifiable from the ascending or descending movement.

Tracking shots have certain advantages over other shots. Because tracking shots can cover a greater area and supply more detail than other types, they can sustain a mood for a longer period of time. Equally significant, tracking shots can become a character's alter ego or unseen companion. Max Ophuls was a master of mobile camera techniques. In an Ophuls film the camera seems to waltz and glide; it sometimes rushes up the stairs with the breathless lovers or accompanies them demurely on a stroll, occasionally slipping behind a fountain so as not to be conspicuous. In Ophuls's *Letter from an Unknown Woman* (1948), the camera is listening to a provincial band ruin the "Song to the Evening Star" from Richard Wagner's *Tannhäuser*. Unable to bear the tinny orchestration, it rises up fastidiously and leaves the square to join Lisa and her boorish suitor. At the opera it escorts the ticket holders up the grand staircase; since the camera knows its place, it does not use the stairs but moves up the marble railing.

Mobile camera work can draw spectators physically into the action, but it can also lure them into a character's mind as it does in Sidney Lumet's *Long Day's Journey into Night* (1962). The crane shot that ends that picture is one of the great feats of film making, for in it Lumet manages to incorporate almost all of Mary Tyrone's monologue. Mary (Katharine Hepburn) is in her parlor with her husband and two sons. She recalls how a nun had dissuaded her from entering the convent because of her claim to have had visions of Our Lady of Lourdes. If regression could be visualized, it would consist of gradual diminution. Almost as soon as Mary begins her monologue, the camera starts backing away from her; then it rises

---

*Cameraman James Wong Howe became a human dolly when he photographed a boxing scene in Robert Rossen's *Body and Soul* (1947) on roller skates.

up as her thoughts leave this world. As Mary grows smaller, so do her husband and sons. As the monologue draws to a close, we see Mary's face in close-up as she speaks the final lines: "That was in the winter of senior year. Then in the spring something happened to me. Yes, I remember. I fell in love with James Tyrone and was so happy for a time." Lumet follows Mary's close-up with close-ups of the other Tyrones. Then he returns once more to Mary's face, no longer ethereally mad or blazing with recriminations, but tragically inscrutable.

## Other Types of Shots

One of the most common ways of suggesting movement today is through the *zoom* shot. Strictly speaking, it is not a moving shot because the camera does not move by means of some conveyance, but the impression of movement close to or far away from the subject is given because the cameraman is using an adjustable lens. There are occasions when a film maker may wish to use a zoom shot: to single out a man in a crowd, to point out a criminal's hiding place in the woods, to capture a facial expression without the person's being aware of the camera's presence, and so forth. But excessive zooming in and out of scenes can affect the spectator adversely. Whereas a tracking shot allows spectators to move with the camera, zooming tends to hurl them into or pull them out of the action. Because of its potentially disorienting effects, the zoom shot should never be used when a tracking shot would be more appropriate.

The opposite of the zoom, which represents deceptive motion, is the freeze, a form of stopped motion. In a *freeze* all movement suddenly halts and the image "freezes" as it turns into a still photograph. At the end of Truffaut's *The 400 Blows* (1959), Antoine Doinel (Jean-Pierre Léaud) escapes from a reformatory and heads toward the ocean. When he reaches the water's edge, he briefly walks in the shallows; then he turns and faces the shore. At that instant Truffaut freezes the frame, trapping Antoine between the reformatory and the ocean, between the past and the future. The freeze implies immobility, helplessness, or indecision.

The zoom and the freeze are similar in the sense that they can call attention to details more dramatically than other devices. Because of their strong underscoring power, it is easy to misuse them the way young writers misuse italics. Many theatrical films (e.g., *Fellini Satyricon*, 1970; Milton Katselas's *Report to the Commissioner*,

1975; John Avildsen's *Rocky*, 1976; and Frank Pierson's *A Star Is Born*, 1976) as well as many made-for-TV movies end with a freeze, so it would be well to clarify what functions the freeze actually serves.

A great director will freeze the action for a reason; a mediocre one will freeze for effect. A good example of a freeze well used is Ken Russell's *Women in Love* (1970), a film version of D. H. Lawrence's novel. The novel comes to no real resolution. Toward the end Birkin tells Ursula that he wants an "eternal" union with a man. Ursula, who cannot conceive of such a relationship, says, "You can't have it, because it's false, impossible." "I don't believe that," Birkin replies, and with these words the novel ends. Russell's last shot is a freeze of Ursula's (Jennie Linden's) face caught in a state of utter bafflement. Birkin's (Alan Bates's) words leave her speechless, and what conveys speechlessness better than the freeze?

The freeze can also suggest timelessness, as it does at the close of George Roy Hill's *Butch Cassidy and the Sundance Kid* (1969). We never see Butch and Sundance die; instead we watch them freeze into myth as they change from men into legends.

## THE SCENE

A shot is limited by the amount of reality it can encompass and the amount of knowledge it can impart. But what would happen if two shots, each of which was part of the same action, were joined and shown in succession? Each shot by itself would make a factual statement; together they would make a narrative statement.

In Griffith's *Broken Blossoms* (1919) the Yellow Man (Richard Barthelmess) takes in Lucy (Lillian Gish) after her father has expelled her from home. She is in the rear of her benefactor's shop one day when the Spying One enters at the very moment she drops a cup. Griffith films the action by following a shot of Lucy dropping the cup with a shot of the Spying One reacting to the sound. Together these shots constitute the rudiments of a *scene:* a series of interrelated shots taken at the same location. Their joining actually establishes a cause-effect relationship, which has implications for the outcome of the film. After the Spying One becomes aware of Lucy's presence, he informs her father, who not only terminates her involvement with the Yellow Man but her life as well. Thus the two shots constitute the pivotal point of the film. The dropped cup observed by the Spying One causes Lucy's detection and, indirectly Lucy's death at her father's hands; this in turn effects her father's death at the Yellow Man's hands and the Yellow Man's ultimate suicide.

## THE SEQUENCE

Whereas a director may think in terms of "shooting a scene" or an actor of "playing a scene," a filmgoer usually is not conscious of watching a scene. What we recall from most movies are individual shots or *sequences*, groups of scenes that become autonomous in their ability to form a miniature film within the film. We remember a shot because of its incisive brevity, a sequence because of its dramatic unity. But it is extremely difficult to remember a scene because it is neither a striking image nor a self-contained drama. Furthermore, scenes grow into sequences so rapidly that it is difficult to know exactly where they occurred in the film without the aid of a shooting script. The film maker can connect shots or scenes in one of three ways to produce a linear, associative, or episodic sequence.

### The Linear Sequence

In a *linear sequence* one action links up with another, creating a miniature drama with a beginning, a middle, and an end. Let us return to the "key sequence" in Hitchcock's *Notorious* discussed in chapter 1. The beginning of that sequence initiates the action: Alicia removes the key to the wine cellar. The middle then adds something to the action: (1) Alicia slips the key to her co-worker, Harry Devlin (Cary Grant), during a party; (2) they proceed to the wine cellar, where they discover that some of the bottles contain uranium ore; (3) meanwhile the champagne supply dwindles, and Alicia's husband and the wine steward go down to the cellar. The end follows from what has gone before and completes the action: The husband discovers his wife and Devlin together. In a linear sequence then, the connection between scenes seems to follow from the action itself.

### The Associative Sequence

Hitchcock is also a master at unifying a sequence associatively. In an *associative sequence* the beginning, middle, and end are linked together by an object or a series of objects. In another sequence

2–3  *Harry Devlin (Cary Grant) on the verge of forgetting the bottle of champagne in Hitchcock's* Notorious *(1946). Hitchcock ends the scene with a close-up of the bottle, the object that unifies the entire sequence. Courtesy ABC Picture Holdings, Inc.*

from *Notorious,* Alicia, who is working for American intelligence to unmask a Nazi colony in postwar Rio de Janeiro, falls in love with her contact, Harry Devlin. She plans an intimate dinner for the two of them. As Devlin leaves for headquarters, Alicia asks him to pick up some wine. In the next scene Devlin enters his supervisor's office with a bottle of champagne, which he leaves on a desk. When he discovers that Alicia's assignment will require her to seduce a leading Nazi figure, he is so disturbed that he forgets the champagne. Scene 2 ends with a close-up of the bottle. In the third scene Devlin is back in Alicia's apartment, where the dinner is burned and there is not even any wine to salvage the evening. Devlin looks around for the champagne; "I guess I left it somewhere," he mutters. These three scenes actually coalesce into a sequence that might be entitled "The Ruined Dinner," a playlet in three parts: "The Bottle Suggested," "The Bottle Purchased,"

"The Bottle Forgotten." Yet it is an object that unifies the sequence: the CU of the bottle in scene 2 that links scenes 1 and 3, bringing them into dramatic focus.

There is a similar sequence in Hitchcock's *Rebecca* (1940). Maxim de Winter's new bride lives in the shadow of her husband's first wife, Rebecca. Rebecca's presence is everywhere. In a sequence that might be called "The Ubiquitous Rebecca de Winter," we first see a shot of Rebecca's room, closed since her death and guarded by her dog; then a napkin with Rebecca's initials; finally, Maxim de Winter (Laurence Olivier) and his young bride (Joan Fontaine) at opposite ends of a long table. What separates them is not just distance but the spirit of Rebecca, who is present even in the napkins on the table. Hitchcock has fashioned a sequence out of three different shots, each dominated by an object associated with the late Rebecca de Winter: a bedroom door, an embroidered napkin, and a dining room table.

In the sequence that ends still another Hitchcock film, *North by Northwest*, Eve Kendall (Eva Marie Saint) is holding on to the hand of Roger Thornhill (Cary Grant) to keep from sliding off Mt. Rushmore. Thornhill encourages her to "hang in there" and, as an added incentive, proposes marriage. In one of the smoothest transitions in film history, the hand to which Eve was just clinging is now helping her climb to the upper birth of a compartment on the Twentieth Century Limited. Without the audience's suspecting it, the scene changed from Mt. Rushmore to a train compartment. Thornhill's hand was the unifying object: It rescued Eve from death and saved her for marriage.

## The Episodic Sequence

An *episodic sequence* does not spell out all the details of an action or the reasons for a character's behavior; it expects the audience to make the connections for itself. The wedding of Angharad in John Ford's *How Green Was My Valley* (1941) comprises three scenes that appear, on the surface, to be loosely related: "The Courting of Angharad," "The Visit to Gruffydd," and "The Wedding." In "The Courting," the young Evans (Marten Lamont), a mine owner's son, comes to court Angharad (Maureen O'Hara) after his pompous father has made the initial arrangements. Since Angharad is such a spirited and honest woman, there is little likelihood that Evans will win her despite his wealth. Thus we do not take the courting seriously. In the second scene Angharad calls on

Mr. Gruffydd (Walter Pidgeon), the minister, whom she really loves. There is something disturbing about this episode: It has an air of fatalism, of love never to be consummated. Angharad speaks guardedly of her affection for Gruffydd to discover if he feels the same toward her. But Gruffydd's only concern is his low salary that makes marriage impossible. In the third scene Angharad steps wraithlike into a carriage, her bridal veil billowing in the breeze.

The three episodes become linked only by the impressions they have created in the audience's mind. Initially there seemed to be no connection between the courting and Angharad's visit to Gruffydd, but the link becomes clear with the final episode: Money, which initially meant nothing to Angharad, means a great deal to the minister. In choosing Evans she chose what Gruffydd considered the prerequisite for marriage. The folly of her choice is a mirthless wedding where the wind makes sport of her veil as if it were a kite. The tragedy of her choice is mirrored in the minister's face as he watches the wedding party wend its funereal way.

Throughout this chapter we have been speaking of film in terms of its most basic components—shots, scenes, and sequences. As disconcerting as it may be to think in such piecemeal terms, it is necessary to do so. No lover of poetry enjoys seeing a favorite poem dissected for images and mined for symbols. But unless one knows how imagery and symbolism operate in a poem, one will never be able to appreciate the art of poetry. Images are to poetry what shots are to film—means to an end. A poet can work one image through a poem, move from one image to another, or create image clusters. Similarly a film maker has various ways of combining shots and moving from one shot to another, as we will see in the next chapter.

# 3
# Film
# LanguageII:
## Cuts and
## Transitions

## CUTS

"Cut" is one of the most commonly used terms in film. It can be a verb a director shouts to terminate a shot ("Cut!"); it can be a synonym for edit ("to cut" a movie); it can also be a strip of film or a joint between two separate shots. In the context of this chapter, a *cut* is the joining of two separate shots so that the first is instantaneously replaced by the second. A film maker uses a cut to show something the preceding shot did not. The way one shot replaces another when we view a film is analogous to the way one sentence replaces another as we read a paragraph. While we read, one sentence yields to the next, so that at the end we have not read five or six isolated sentences but one complete thought. There are four basic kinds of cuts: simple, contrast, parallel (cross), and jump cuts.

### The Simple Cut

In the *simple*, or *straight*, *cut* one image instantaneously replaces another. The simple cut is the equivalent of a declarative sentence. In *The Lady Eve* (1941), Preston Sturges cuts from Charles Pike (Henry Fonda) sitting at a table in a ship's dining room to a group of rather unattractive women staring in his direction. Translated into words, the cut simply means: At that point a group of hopeful but ugly women gazed longingly at the handsome Charles Pike. In Charles Laughton's *The Night of the Hunter* (1955), there is a cut from Rachel (Lillian Gish) speaking of the innocence of children to the exterior of her house made quaint by falling snow. The cut is another way of saying that the children found warmth and security in the woman's home. In the opening sequence of *Serpico* (1973), Sidney Lumet repeats the same shot of the wounded Serpico (Al Pacino) lying on a stretcher, his eyes staring ahead and his cheeks splattered with blood. The first time Lumet cuts to Serpico on the stretcher, the meaning is evident: Frank Serpico lies wounded. The second time, the cut is making the same statement, only with greater urgency: Frank Serpico lies *wounded.* The third cut has the force of a distress signal: FRANK SERPICO LIES WOUNDED!

## The Contrast Cut

When two opposite shots are joined, they form a *contrast cut.* In *Medium Cool* (1969), for example, Haskell Wexler cuts from the lovemaking of a TV cameraman and a flashy nurse to a schoolteacher in her Chicago tenement. Dramatically, the cut is meaningful because the lives of the cameraman and the teacher will soon be intertwined. But the cut also contrasts the two women in the cameraman's life: a ravishing but vapid nurse and a plain but dedicated teacher.

## The Parallel Cut

*Parallel cutting,* also referred to as crosscutting, presents two actions occurring simultaneously. In *Saboteur* (1942), Alfred Hitchcock crosscuts an attempt to sabotage a battleship at a christening ceremony in the Brooklyn Navy Yard with the ceremony itself. In Laughton's *The Night of the Hunter,* at the very moment a widow is protesting that she does not want another husband, there is a cut to a speeding train that will bring her one. A very effective example of parallel cutting occurs in Joseph Losey's *King and Country* (1964). Losey crosscuts the trial of a deserter in a barracks with the mock trial of a rat the soldiers are staging outside in the rain, thereby equating the plight of the soldier with the plight of the rat. Both are victims—the deserter of a dubious military code, the rat of the soldiers' sadism that stems from their boredom.

## The Jump Cut

Sometimes when an action is not worth narrating in detail, a director breaks continuity with a *jump cut*. Jean-Luc Godard's *Breathless* (1959) contains a scene where Michel (Jean-Paul Belmondo) shoots a policeman in Marseilles, runs across a field, and emerges in Paris. Similarly, in John Schlesinger's *Darling* (1965), a shot of a couple about twenty yards from the entrance to a building is followed by a shot of them going through the door to the interior of the building. Obviously a director need not show everything in a particular sequence, but excessive jump cutting should be avoided. It has a disorienting effect on the audience and gives the film the continuity of a comic strip.

## TRANSITIONS

Film is rich in ways of moving from scene to scene. The chief transitional devices in film are the fade, the dissolve, the wipe, and the iris.

## The Fade

The *fade-out* is the equivalent of the end of a chapter, or more accurately, of the space between the end of one chapter and the beginning of another. Every novelist expects his or her readers to pause, however, briefly, between the episodes. Even those people who claim that they read novels all the way through at one sitting need at least a moment or two between chapters.

The fade-out is the simplest kind of transition: The light decreases and the screen goes dark. The opposite is the *fade-in*, where the light increases as the picture gradually appears on the screen. Most commonly, when the term "fade" is used, it refers to the fade-out.

Most fade-outs are no more profound than a blank screen. Yet some of them can bring an action to an artful close the way a gifted orator rounds out a sentence. An excellent example is the first fade-out in William Wyler's *Mrs. Miniver* (1942). The initial sequence covers a day in the lives of the Minivers. Each feels guilty for having purchased something the other might find frivolous:

3–1 *Cary Grant as the uninvited guest at Alicia's (Ingrid Bergman) party in* Notorious. *Hitchcock will fade out on the back of Grant's head and fade in on his face. Courtesy ABC Picture Holdings, Inc.*

Kay (Greer Garson) has bought a new hat, and Clem (Walter Pidgeon) a new car. At the close of the day the camera pans the bedroom, pausing at the hat smartly perched on the bedpost. The scene fades out with the hat in silhouette. Fading out on the hat brings the sequence full circle: It began with Kay's buying the hat and ends with her purchase artfully displayed. We smile at that fade because it provides the same pleasure of recognition we receive from a speech that begins and ends with the same image. But we also smile at its wisdom, for it represents one of those little domestic triumphs that seems more meaningful at the end of the day than at the beginning.

In the theater the curtain sometimes descends between the scenes of an act to mark the passage of time. In film the fade can act in the same fashion. The first fade in Hitchcock's *Notorious* (1946) occurs at a particularly dramatic moment. There is an unidentified guest at Alicia Huberman's party, sitting with his back to the camera. Curiously, he remains even after Alicia dismisses her guests, and although she addresses him, we do not see his face. The camera fades out on the back of the man and in on his face, which is none other than Cary Grant's. Hitchcock interrupted the party sequence with a fade to indicate a lapse of time; but the fade was also a clever way of introducing the male lead by linking two scenes in which he appears—one ending with his back to the camera, the other beginning with his face coming into view. The fade produces a much more natural rhythm than if Hitchcock had cut from the back of Grant's head to a close-up of his face.

A fade can also be commentative. In Vincent Sherman's *Mr. Skeffington* (1944), the aging Fanny Skeffington (Bette Davis) reassembles her former suitors, who are now either married or balding. The picture fades out as they enter the dining room and fades in on a gentleman's hat and gloves. A cut would have spoiled the mood, which was one of genteel hypocrisy. The hat and gloves belong to Edward (Jerome Cowan), an impoverished suitor, who has returned to court Fanny. The fade-out allows us to see a parallel between the two scenes. In the first Fanny has invited her suitors to dinner to reassure herself that she is still beautiful. However, Edward is not interested in her beauty, which is nonexistent, but only in her money, also nonexistent although he does not know it. One charade fades out and another fades in. A cut would have been too abrupt and would not have conveyed the idea of one farce rising out of another.

## The Dissolve

Instead of using a cut or a fade, a director may choose to merge one shot into another. The *dissolve* accomplishes this by the gradual replacement of one image by another. This kind of transition serves a variety of functions. Sometimes a dissolve simply has the force of "in the meantime" or "later." In *North by Northwest* (1959), Hitchcock dissolves a shot of Roger Thornhill bribing his mother to get a key from the desk clerk at the Hotel Plaza to a shot of the two of them walking down the corridor toward the room Thornhill was so anxious to enter.

A dissolve can mean "no sooner said than done." The Mother Superior in Henry King's *The Song of Bernadette* (1943) no sooner asks to see Bernadette than the shot dissolves into Bernadette's room. In *Caught* (1948), Max Ophuls dissolves a shot of Leonora (Barbara Bel Geddes) gazing at a picture of a woman in a mink coat into a shot of Leonora, now a model, wearing a mink.

When is a dissolve a transition and when is it more than a transition? This is rather like asking when is a word simply a conventional sign and when is a word a symbol. Water can simply be the wet "stuff" that quenches thirst or a sign of birth, rebirth, fertility, or a cause of death. When William Wordsworth writes in *The Prelude* (I, 385-6), "With trembling oars I turned,/And through the silent water stole my way," he is speaking of water in one of its most elementary meanings: a body of water, in this case, a river. In *The Waste Land*, T. S. Eliot uses "water" with a wide range of meanings, charging it with associations (renewal, baptism, death to the world/rebirth to a new life) that are religious, literary, and archetypal. It is the context that determines how a word is used; a poem about human and cultural sterility will explore the varied meanings of "water" to a much greater extent than a poem about the development of a poet.

It is the same with transitions. What a dissolve means—if, in fact, it means anything—is determined by the context. The dissolve in *North by Northwest* is Hitchcock's way of getting two characters from the lobby of the Hotel Plaza to one of the floors. Good directors vary their transitions as they vary their shots, preventing monotony and creating a diversified rhythm that approximates the ebb and flow of life.

### The Metaphorical Dissolve

When two images, on the surface innocuous and ordinary, blend in such a way that their union constitutes a symbolic equation, the film maker has created a *metaphorical dissolve*. The device is a visual form of synecdoche (or metonymy with which it is almost identical), a species of metaphor in which the part is substituted for the whole (roofs for houses, sail for ship) or a sign for the thing signified (green = Go, crown = royalty). We often use this figure of speech without knowing it: "Give us this day our daily *bread*" (bread = food); "All *hands* on deck!" (hands = crew); "He addressed his comments to the *chair*" (chair = chairperson).

Like synecdoche, metaphorical dissolves can be showpieces of ingenuity. In Peter Godfrey's *The Two Mrs. Carrolls* (1947), Geoffrey Carroll (Humphrey Bogart) is a wife poisoner. Early in the film, Sally (Barbara Stanwyck) discovers a letter he dropped, addressed to his wife. Because Sally is in love with Geoffrey, she questions him about his marriage. He replies that he is in the process of getting a divorce. The letter dissolves into a neatly wrapped package of poison Geoffrey has just purchased from a pharmacist. The merging of the two images, the letter and the package, results in the following equation: Mrs. Carroll + package = death. Dissolving an envelope bearing a woman's name into the means that will make her only a name is an ingenious touch.

The dissolves in George Stevens's films have an effect similar to the homogenization of cream and milk. In *Shane* (1953), when Starrett (Van Heflin) and Shane (Alan Ladd) succeed in uprooting a stubborn tree trunk, Stevens slowly merges their triumphant faces into the landscape, making the men one with nature. Later, when Starrett watches a homesteader's property go up in flames, Stevens dissolves his vengeful face into the burning house. The resulting equation—man + nature = natural man; face + burning house = consuming rage—do not advance the plot; their purpose is rather to illustrate one of the film's main themes: the pioneer's oneness with nature, which enables him to become part of everything he sees or does.

A dissolve can sometimes have the effect of dramatic foreshadowing if the film maker prepares the audience for subsequent events by hinting at their outcome earlier. In *King and Country* (1964), Joseph Losey dissolves a skull mired in mud into the face of a soldier playing a harmonica. The dissolve prefigures the fate of the soldier, who later dies in the mud, his voice silenced by a pistol shot in the mouth.

Just as they can foreshadow, so dissolves can recapitulate. At the end of Peter Bogdanovich's *The Last Picture Show* (1971), Sonny (Timothy Bottoms) returns to the house of Ruth Popper (Cloris Leachman), the coach's wife, with whom he had been having an affair. The movie house has closed its doors forever; Sam the Lion and Billy are dead; Duane is on his way to Korea. All that remain are Ruth and the dreary Texas town where the tumbleweed rolls down the main street. As Sonny and Ruth look at each other, their eyes forge the only bond that can unite them—loneliness. At that moment, Sonny and Ruth dissolve into the town and the vast Texas flatlands. There is no difference between a young man without prospects, a middle-aged woman without hope, and a town without a future: Their destinies have become one.

At the end of *Colorado Territory* (1949), Raoul Walsh's western remake of his earlier success *High Sierra* (1941), the hands of Wes (Joel McCrea) and Colorado (Virginia Mayo), touching in death, dissolve into a shot of a ringing bell. The dissolve does not so much connect two images as two events that the lovers' hands and the bell represent. Earlier in the film, Wes had hidden some stolen money in an abandoned church. After the death of Wes and Colorado, a priest discovers the money and uses it to restore the church bell, telling the villagers it was the gift of two lovers who passed by. It is an exquisite dissolve, and in the context of the movie, quite poignant.

### The Form Dissolve

A film maker can merge two images with the same shape or contours through a *form dissolve*. Often a form dissolve is merely easy on the eyes. For example, in Robert Stevenson's *Jane Eyre* (1944), the figure of a ballerina on top of a music box dissolves into a little girl dressed in the same costume. There is something undeniably charming about a figurine turning into a child; it affords the same kind of innocent pleasure we derive from a transformation of a cat into a lion in an animated cartoon or the vanishing of a magician in a magic show.

A form dissolve can also be directly related to the plot. An unusual one occurs in Hitchcock's *The Wrong Man* (1957), a factual account of a jazz musician who is falsely accused of a holdup. As the musician (Henry Fonda) prays in front of a picture of Jesus Christ, the scene seems on the verge of changing to one of a man walking down a dark street. Gradually the man's head merges with the musician's, which in turn becomes hollow enough to accommodate the other's face. The man whose head fitted into the musician's was the real criminal. The dissolve illustrates how easy it is to mistake the innocent for the guilty; it is just a matter of superimposing one face upon another.

## The Wipe

Some television news programs change news items flashed on the screen by means of a line traveling vertically across the screen. That traveling line s a *wipe*, and in the 1930s and the 1940s, this device was the most stylish of the transitions. Since the screen is rectangular, the wipe can move vertically, horizontally, or diagonally; it can create a theatrical effect by rising or falling like a drop curtain, as it did in a scene in Woody Van Dyke's *The Thin Man* (1934), where it moved from the bottom of the screen to the top, revealing a bevy of chorus girls; or it can split the screen so that both parties can be seen during a telephone conversation (Stanley Donen's *Indiscreet*, 1958). Often wipes were used to complement each other: One scene would end with a wipe traveling from left to right; the next would begin with a wipe moving from right to left. One of the best examples of complementary wipes can be found in the opening scenes of Henry Levin's *The Petty Girl* (1950).

More fluid than a cut and faster than a dissolve, the wipe is ideal for presenting a series of events in quick succession. Frank Capra, a frequent user of the wipe, employed it in the opening sequences of *It Happened One Night* (1934), *Mr. Deeds Goes to Town* (1936), and *Mr. Smith Goes to Washington* (1939). In the handwriting sequence in *Mr. Smith Goes to Washington,* for example, one expert after another testifies to the authenticity of Jeff Smith's signature. After each expert spoke, Capra simply "wiped" him off the screen, thereby showing the inanity of the investigation.

Rouben Mamoulian's excellent use of the wipe is apparent in *Dr. Jekyll and Mr. Hyde* (1932). After Jekyll (Fredric March) becomes Hyde, he goes off into the night, deserting Muriel Carew (Rose Hobart), his fiancée, who expects him at her dinner party. A wipe opens like a fan, dividing the screen diagonally: On the left is the departing Jekyll; on the right, the party in progress. When Jekyll leaves the Carew estate, Mamoulian wipes him out of the frame, which expands to disclose the dinner guests and the worried Muriel. At that point, the frame divides diagonally again: On the right is Ivy (Miriam Hopkins) sipping champagne, the woman Hyde will kill; on the left is Muriel, the woman Jekyll yearns to marry. The wipe acts as a parallel cut, informing us that while Muriel was at her party, Ivy was at home. But the split screen also represents the protagonist's ideal woman, who is similarly halved. It is only fitting that for a double man (Jekyll/Hyde) there should be a double woman (Ivy/Muriel).

When Muriel's father, furious at Jekyll's absence, cries, "Muriel, you will have nothing more to do with that man," a wipe begins to moves from the left of the screen to the center, revealing the "man" himself. However, it is not Jekyll but Hyde whom we see. The wipe is an ironic commentary on the father's outburst; clearly, he did not mean that Muriel should have nothing to do with Hyde (whom he cannot know) but with Jekyll. However, at this point Jekyll is Hyde.

Some writers compare the wipe to a windshield wiper. Hitchcock uses it as such in *Rebecca* (1940), when the second Mrs. de Winter sees Manderley for the first time through the windshield as the wipers clear away the rain. He repeats the technique in *Psycho* (1960): As Marion drives in the rain, the sign for the Bates Motel materializes on her windshield. In each film, the wipe introduces a new phase in the character's life by bringing the future before the character's eyes. In Mrs. de Winter's case, it was the house where she learned the truth about Rebecca, her husband's first wife; in Marion's, it was the motel where she met her death.

## The Iris

Mt. Rushmore as seen through a telescope in Hitchcock's *North by Northwest* appears inside a circle in the middle of the darkened screen. This is a *masking shot,* or to be more accurate, an *iris shot,* in which everything is blacked out except for what is to be

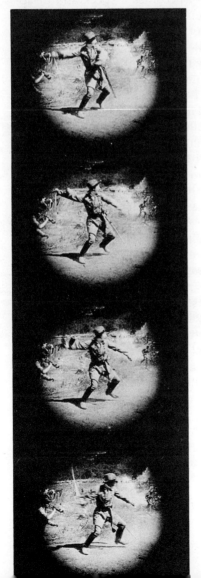

3–2    *A frame enlargement of an iris shot from D. W. Griffith's* The Birth of a Nation *(1915). In an iris shot, the image appears within a circle on an otherwise dark screen. Courtesy Museum of Modern Art/Film Stills Archive.*

seen telescopically. The frame* can also be altered to simulate other shapes (e.g., the view from a keyhole, a crack in a door, binoculars, a submarine periscope) depending upon the form in which the director wants the audience to see the image. In *The Birth of a Nation* (1915), Griffith represented the oval shape of Elsie Stoneman's picture through an iris shot.

In addition to the iris shot, there is what is known as irising in and irising out. *Irising in* consists of opening up the darkened frame with a circle of light that keeps expanding until the picture fills the frame. *Irising out* is the opposite; it is as if darkness is seeping into the frame from all sides, forcing the diminishing picture into some part of the frame until it becomes a speck and disappears.

A director can dolly in or out of a scene, or today, zoom in or out of one; but there is nothing quite like an iris to open the frame. Griffith used the iris breathtakingly in Sherman's March to the Sea in *The Birth of a Nation* (1915). The frame opens from the upper left-hand corner to reveal a mother and her children on a hill; at first we do not know why they are huddled in fear, but as the frame opens, we see Sherman's soldiers in the valley below. In *Intolerance* (1916), Griffith gradually disclosed the splendor of Babylon by expanding the frame, starting at the lower right-hand corner.

The iris is especially effective in death scenes. Lucy of *Broken Blossoms* (1919) and the Mountain Girl of *Intolerance* both die in iris. Irising out can suggest death because of the way in which darkness creeps into the frame, reducing the size of the image to a pinpoint and then annihilating it. Orson Welles chose the iris to symbolize both the death of Wilbur Minafer and the end of the horse and buggy era in *The Magnificent Ambersons* (1942). A horseless carriage moves in long shot across the snow. The passengers sing merrily, but their song is in sharp contrast to the landscape, which is dominated by a dead tree with wiry branches. As the motor buggy moves out of frame, Welles starts irising out until it disappears in the darkness that floods the screen. Welles irises out into a fade. One would have expected him to iris out of one scene and into another; but the shot that follows the fade is of a black wreath on

---

*The frame* is simply the rectangle within which the film appears. *A frame* is a single photograph on a strip of film. *To frame* is to compose pictorially a shot or a scene. Calling out "Frame!" during a movie means that the frame line, the dividing line between two frames, is visible and the projector must be adjusted.

the door of the Amberson house. The iris and the fade imply finality in different ways—the iris gradually and poetically, the fade irrevocably.

The principle of the iris unifies the flashbacks in George Stevens's *Penny Serenade* (1941). Julie (Irene Dunne) recalls incidents from her marriage by playing recordings of popular songs that had meaning for herself and her husband. Each flashback begins with a close-up of the center of the disc, which then opens up, irislike, to reveal the scene.

Because of their fondness for the movies of the past, both François Truffaut and Jean-Luc Godard use the iris more readily than their peers. Truffaut irises out repeatedly in *The Wild Child* (1969) to make the scenes resemble the stages of a scientific experiment conducted as dispassionately as possible. Godard uses the iris for sheer nostalgia in *Breathless* (1959). In one scene he irises out on Michel gazing idolatrously at a poster of Humphrey Bogart in his last film. One is tempted to say that Godard is irising out on the old Hollywood except that irising is still being practiced, although not as regularly as it was in Griffith's day or during the 1930s and the 1940s. However, we do find irising on certain television programs (an episode of *Mary Hartman, Mary Hartman* will often open and close with an iris) and in movies where techniques of the past function as period touches. When George Roy Hill irises out on the two con men at the close of *The Sting* (1973), it gives the ending a deliberately old-fashioned look. Similarly Peter Bogdanovich's use of irising in *Nickelodeon* (1976) lends an air of authenticity to the film, set in the early days of the movie industry. As directors become more interested in the films of the past, they may make greater use of their rich transitional devices. Karel Reisz in *Night Must Fall* (1964) and Martin Scorsese in *New York, New York* (1977) used an occasional wipe; evidently film history taught them that transitions relieve the monotony of straight cutting.

# 4
# Film Editing

Any student who has ever had a teacher rewrite his or her essay knows, at least in part, what editing is. Yet editing is more than rewriting; it is the act of selecting and assembling. The editor of a journal selects the articles for the next issue, arranging them in some kind of order (according to topic, author's reputation, last name, etc.). The editor of a book may have to transpose paragraphs and sometimes even chapters, excising material from one section and inserting it in another, before the manuscript is ready for publication. In film, *editing* consists of the selection and arrangement of shots based on their place within the narrative; their contribution to the mood of a particular scene or of the film as a whole; and their ability to enhance the film's rhythm, elucidate its symbolism, or simply help the film maker achieve his or her purpose, which can be anything from a desire to tell a story to a desire to reform the world.

When Alfred Hitchcock said that a film must be edited, he was echoing the belief of the Russian theorist and director, V. I. Pudovkin, who maintained that the basis of film art is editing. It makes no difference whether a director edits in camera as John Ford claimed to; whether he is a Hitchcock who arrives on the set the first day of shooting, knowing basically how the film will look in its final form; or whether he works so closely with his editor that they become a team like Arthur Penn and Dede Allen. In each case the film must be assembled.

The relationship between a director and an editor is a complex matter and not one that can be resolved in a chapter.[1] Some directors rely heavily upon an editor; other do not. Arthur Penn does; Billy Wilder does not. Yet at times an editor's judgment is crucial. John Schlesinger admits that the first two reels of *Midnight Cowboy* (1969) had been cut in so many different ways that they made no sense. Finally another editor was brought in, the reels were broken down into rushes (i.e., batches of the first prints made of the scenes), and the editing process began afresh.[2]

What exactly do editors do? Ideally, they are the directors' alter egos, carrying out what the latter would do if they had the time to be all things to the films they direct. Thus editors may select the shots or decide what portion of a shot is to be used; they can give an action scene its distinctive rhythm by alternating tempo and varying directional movement; and they can cut a scene of violence so rapidly that the movie will receive a PG instead of an R rating as was the case with Sam Peckinpah's *The Killer Elite* (1975).

Because all films require some form of editing, the importance of editors has often been exaggerated and their role equated with that of directors. Lee Bobker compares them with painters, working in isolation to create the movie's pace, mood, and rhythm. Yet despite his respect for the function of editors, Bobker is forced to admit it is a subservient one: "The editor should always enjoy a wide creative latitude, but he should never fall prey to the illusion that he is creating a new film from scratch. His primary purpose is to bring to completion an artistic work already in progress."[3]

In the first edition of *The Technique of Film Editing* Karel Reisz dubbed the editor "the interpreter of the small details rather than the prime creator of the continuity."[4] For the second edition Professor Thorold Dickinson provided an introduction to the second part of the book in which he stated: "The modern editor is the executant for the film-maker and no longer his equal on any self-respecting film."[5]

Aram Avakian, who edited Arthur Penn's *The Miracle Worker* (1962), is especially lucid on the role of the editor:

> Any director in his right mind will leave his editor alone until the first cut is finished. The notion that the director works continuously with the editor is a myth. It only happens that way when the director is

also a cutter. Usually, the director is there to screen the material after it has been cut in some form and when he's needed, that is, when something isn't going right. . . . When the director feels his intention in a specific sequence is not being served, or well enough, he will come into the cutting room and go over the footage with the editor cut by cut. But there are whole large portions of a film where the director will just say, "Go."[6]

Avakian went on to become a director himself, although as yet only a minor one (*End of the Road,* 1970; *Cops and Robbers,* 1973; *11 Harrowhouse,* 1974). As an editor turned director, Avakian can therefore say that directors only work closely with their editors if they had been editors once themselves. Consequently, director Robert Wise's comment during a television interview that the editor's role had not changed that much since he started in the industry should be understood in light of the fact that he began as an editor at RKO, where he cut Orson Welles's *Citizen Kane* (1941).

## EDITING AND MONTAGE

Film editing should be a relatively simple matter, yet it is the subject of more discussion than any other form of editing. One reason for so much theorizing is the similarity between editing and montage, a word of various meanings and interpretations.

The Russian theorist Pudovkin argued that editing involved simply the connecting of one shot with another; another Russian theorist and director, Sergei Eisenstein, advanced a different concept of editing called *montage.* He maintained that editing involved not a uniting of images but a collision of them that would shock an audience used to seeing one shot connect with the next. If a man postures like a peacock, cut from the man to the peacock; if he is figuratively a horse's ass, pair him with a real one. Similarly, if a scene requires people being killed like animals, cut from workers being massacred to an ox being slaughtered in an abbatoir. Or if the viewpoint a film maker wants to convey is that all wars waged in the name of God are immoral, arrange a series of shots starting with a baroque Christ and ending with an idol, thereby making militarism a form of regression.

Eisensteinian montage is based on contrast and conflict, which can exist both within the film as a whole and within a particular shot or scene. In the Odessa Steps massacre in Eisenstein's *Potemkin* (1925), a body lies diagonally across the steps; the

Cossacks cast shadows that fall menacingly at oblique angles to the steps; the steps form three contrasting planes, with the Cossacks at the top firing at a woman on a landing behind which lies a trail of bodies.

Eisenstein discovered how ideas could arise from the contrast and conflict of images. Without creating an actual series of cause and effect, Eisenstein opened *Potemkin* with a shot of breaking waves and followed this image of turbulence with shots of men sleeping in hammocks that formed a shroudlike tangle, mess tables swinging back and forth, meat crawling with maggots—each image jarring us, disquieting us, but ultimately preparing us for the sailors' revolt.

Eisenstein's influence was enormous, but not always beneficial. Instead of producing an artistic effect, sometimes the collision of images produced only pretentiousness. There is an embarrassing scene in Rouben Mamoulian's otherwise excellent *Dr. Jekyll and Mr. Hyde* (1932) when Jekyll, exulting over his impending marriage to Muriel, cries, "If music be the food of love, play on!" as he sits down at the organ and pounds away. Five shots appear in rapid succession commenting on his rapture: a lighted candelabra, an illuminated art object, a smiling statue, the butler's beaming countenance, and a blazing hearth. Such excess can hardly be justified. Lesser forms of montage exist today in consciousness-raising television commercials: The screen splits in two, showing an emaciated infant in one part and a mouth consuming an ice-cream sundae in the other. Conflict of images also appears in the way television commercials are worked into feature films. In the past the television viewer was prepared for the break: A segment of the movie would end, and there would be a graceful exit into the commercial. Today, the dying Beth of Mervyn LeRoy's *Little Women* (1949) no sooner tells her weeping sister that she will love her as much in heaven as she did on earth than someone appears extolling the joys of a new floor wax.

To Eisenstein, montage meant the visual conflict of images. On the continent, "montage" means editing: selecting and assembling the shots that will form the scenes and sequences of the film. In England, the same process is called "editing" or "cutting," but with a slight difference: "editing" means the step by step assembling of the shots in the cutting room while "montage" refers to the process considered as a whole. One further complication is that in the past, American directors used a technique that has since become known as *American montage*—a convenient way of collapsing time through a blend of dissolves, wipes, and superimposures (one shot appearing on top of the other). In a typical American montage sequence, newspapers would spin across the screen announcing a murder trial as one headline obliterates the other. The face of the judge would dissolve into the defendant's. Superimposed over the defendant's face would be his anguished wife's, and over hers, the face of the real murderer who was hiding out in a sleazy room above a bar. Although this form of montage is not in vogue today, in its time it was sometimes highly effective and was regarded as sufficiently important to warrant screen credit for the montage editor. Slavko Vorkapich was especially adept at montage (*Mr. Deeds Goes to Town, Mr. Smith Goes to Washington*, etc.); and director Don Siegel (*Invasion of the Body Snatchers*, 1956; *Dirty Harry*, 1971; *The Shootist*, 1976, etc.) began in montage at Warner Brothers.

## PRINCIPLES OF EDITING

In his book *Film as Art*, Rudolf Arnheim reduced montage to four principles, showing how editing can affect rhythm, time, space, and theme. His four principles can be outlined as follows:

I. *Principles of Cutting*
    A. Length of celluloid
        (1) long strips produce a quiet rhythm
        (2) short strips produce a rapid rhythm
    B. Length of scene
        (1) action can be sequential (played through to end)
        (2) action can be fragmented (broken up and crosscut)
        (3) long shots can alternate with close-ups

II. *Time Relations*
    A. Between events that are
        (1) successive
        (2) crosscut
        (3) inserted
    B. Between actions related not in time but through association (massacre of workers crosscut with slaughter of ox)

III. *Space Relations*
    A. Between the same place shown at different times

B. Between several places shown in successive or crosscut scenes

IV. *Relations of Subject Matter based on*
   A. Similarity of shape (round hill juxtaposed with round belly)
   B. Similarity of meaning (proud man/peacock)
   C. Contrast of shape (fat man/thin man)
   D. Contrast of meaning (mansion/hut)
   E. Combination of similarity and contrast (the shackled feet of a prisoner/the free feet of a dancer)

Although Arnheim's breakdown is valuable, it still does not explain how editing works in the film as a whole. The rhythms of a film are the rhythms of life; there is no single rhythm but many. Hence the greatest films have always varied the pace from one sequence to another.

## Editing for Pace

An excellent example of editing to achieve varied rhythms can be found in the first two sequences of Welles's *Citizen Kane* : "The Death of Kane" and "News on the March." The film begins with the camera ascending the gate of Xanadu, defying the No Trespassing sign. A series of dreamlike dissolves culminates in a shot of a lighted window that suddenly goes dark. A mouth utters "Rosebud!" through a veil of falling snow, and a glass paperweight with a snow-covered house inside it smashes without making a sound. A nurse enters a room and folds a dead man's arms on his breast. The mood of the first part of "The Death of Kane" is slow and languid. As the camera draws nearer to the window, the rhythm accelerates. Snow falls to the sound of crystal-pure music evoking Kane's Colorado boyhood. The paperweight breaks, and the nurse enters. Then the rhythm decelerates, and the mood becomes solemn as she places Kane's arms on his chest.

Without warning, a voice bellows "News on the march!" as a newsreel of Kane's life unfolds. In the second sequence the pace is frenetic; fifty years of a man's life are compressed into a few minutes. The pace builds inexorably until the "News on the March" is over and the camera sputters out, as if in exhaustion.

4–1  *Scenes from the Death of Kane in Orson Welles's* Citizen Kane *(1941).*

4–1  *Frame enlargement of the glass paperweight that falls from Kane's hand. The lighted window of Kane's bedroom goes dark. Suddenly snow begins to fall; it is the artificial snow in the glass paperweight that falls from Kane's hand as he utters his last word, "Rosebud!"*

4-1  *As the nurse enters Kane's room, her image is refracted through a piece of the shattered paperweight. Courtesy Janus Films. Photos courtesy Museum of Modern Art/Film Stills Archive.*

## Editing for the Total Effect

It is relatively easy to mistake good editing for technical variety—the alternation of long shots and close-ups, of fragmented and continuous presentation of the action. In fact, editing should be evaluated in terms of its effects: Does it achieve *rhythm* by varying tempo? *Balance* by alternating direction (an entrance from the left of the frame balanced by one from the right)? *Tone* by varying color? Francis Ford Coppola's *The Godfather, Part II* (1974) and

Robert Altman's *Nashville* (1975) are particularly good examples of editing to create a total effect.

## The Godfather, Part II

In the sequel to *The Godfather* Coppola was faced with the problem of integrating the lives of Vito Corleone and his son Michael. The purpose of the sequel was to depict Vito's pre-godfather phase and to contrast the immigrant world of Little Italy where he grew to manhood with the empire he bequeathed to his son. Since Vito is dead when the film opens, Coppola could not crosscut the lives of father and son. Instead, he told Vito's story in flashback.

The first time the film moves from the present to the past, from Michael (Al Pacino) to Vito (Robert de Niro), Michael is putting his son to bed. Michael's face is to the *left* of the frame. Slowly the scene dissolves to Vito, his face to the *right* of the frame, as he puts his son Fredo to bed. The transition from son to father, from present to past, is balanced by a movement from left to right. The transition also brings about a corresponding change of rhythm: As the action shifts from 1957 to the turn of the century, the frenetic pace of the present yields to Old World ease. The color also changes as Lake Tahoe dissolves into Little Italy. Michael's world has a dark mahogany look; everything about it is forbidding and austere. Vito's world is one of pastels; the colors are soft, delicate, warm. Coppola here contrasts not only father and son but also their respective eras: a sunlit past as opposed to a somber present.

The first flashback ends as it began—with a shot of Vito and his son—and suddenly we are in the late 1950s again with Michael en route to Miami. By ending with a cut instead of another dissolve, Coppola points up the difference between the feverish pace of Michael's life and the tranquillity Vito knew, at least in his early manhood.

The second flashback begins when Michael hears that his wife Kay has had a miscarriage, which is later revealed to be an abortion. The scene again dissolves to Little Italy, where Vito is hovering over his son who is ill with pneumonia. Again it is a child that effects the transition. Coppola ends the flashback by showing Vito with the young Michael on his lap; then he cuts to a car making its way along a wintry road and proceeding through the forbidding entrance to Michael's Lake Tahoe home. The cut propels us into a present that is so loveless that Kay does not even look up from her sewing to greet her husband.

Coppola could not use a child as a bridge three times in succession. Consequently, the third flashback in *Godfather II* does not spring from a particular image. Coppola merely dissolves a shot of Michael speaking with his mother into one of Vito buying fruit and ends the flashback with the formation of the Genco Importing Company. In the first two flashbacks it was a cut that restored the action to the present; in the third it is a dissolve. Just as Vito is about to enter the import business, Coppola dissolves to a congressional investigation at which Michael is being interrogated. By dissolving from the Genco Importing Company to the hearings, Coppola establishes a connection between them. The legitimacy of the Genco Importing Company, the foundation on which Vito built his empire, is now the subject of an investigation. Michael, who has inherited his father's empire along with its foundation, plays the honest businessman who refuses to take the Fifth Amendment, claiming that he has nothing to hide.

The final flashback begins after Kay tells Michael that her miscarriage was really an abortion. Coppola cuts to Vito's return to the Sicilian town of Corleone in order to avenge the murder of his parents, who were victims of Don Ciccio's vendetta. Here the link between present and past is something quite different from a child put to bed or the establishment of an import company: The link is death. An admission of abortion becomes the occasion for a flashback of a Mafioso's assassination. It is also death that returns the action to the present. As Vito leaves Sicily after killing Don Ciccio, Coppola dissolves to a casket containing the body of Michael's mother, Mama Corleone.

The editing in *Godfather II* not only interweaves past and present; it also contrasts them through variations of rhythm, balance, and color.

## Nashville

In *Nashville* Robert Altman interweaves the lives of twenty-four people, allowing their destinies to cross like threads in a medieval tapestry. The editing of such an intricate film cannot be uniform, any more than its rhythm can be. There are two worlds in *Nashville*: the political world represented by the unseen Hal Phillip Walker, a George Wallace-like presidential candidate who advocates abolishing the electoral college, taxing churches, and scrapping the national anthem; and the apolitical world of Grand Ole Opry that is satisfied with the status quo. Each world has its own rhythm, and each rhythm its own set of variations. The Opry is smooth on the surface, treacly underneath. Its rhythm alternates between the hard sell and the folksy drawl. The political world is sinuous, winding in and out of the Opry like a mountain stream that is always on the verge of contracting into a trickle until it gathers momentum from some hidden source and then gushes into life. Both worlds exist side by side in America, as the opening credits in red, white, and blue suggest.

At the beginning of the film we see the two worlds and hear their rhythms. *Nashville* opens with the Hal Phillip Walker campaign truck leaving a garage, a loudspeaker filling the silent streets with prerecorded platitudes about America. Altman then cuts to the studio where Opry star Haven Hamilton (Henry Gibson) is recording "200 Years," which contains almost as many platitudes as one of Walker's speeches. Hamilton is in a booth, isolated from the spectators. When he notices a BBC reporter (Geraldine Chaplin), he asks her to leave. The Opry distrusts strangers. Yet Hamilton is not the only singer recording in the studio; Altman then cuts from Hamilton to a black gospel group with its one white member, Linnea Reese (Lily Tomlin) as they record "Yes, I Do"— their free, handclapping vitality in sharp contrast to the forced solemnity of "200 Years."

A movie with twenty-four characters must be crosscut, the action broken up with one segment beginning before another is completed. Note what crosscutting accomplishes in the following sequence.

A bartender, looking for some unknown who would be willing to strip at a political smoker, hears Sueleen Gay (Gwen Welles) during an amateur night and knows he is in luck. Sueleen not only has an abominable voice; she also has no style or sense of pitch. However, the bartender is not interested in her voice, only in her body. As the bartender calls Del Reese (Ned Beatty), one of Nashville's leading attorneys, Altman interrupts Sueleen's song, but not her singing. We hear it the way it would sound over the telephone, the way Del Reese is hearing it. But by this time we are in the Reese home with Del's wife Linnea and their two children, who are both deaf. Linnea encourages her son to talk about his day in school. When her son does, there is applause—not for his triumph over his affliction but for the end of Sueleen's wretched song. The scene then shifts back to the bar, to allow Altman to introduce another character: Tom (Keith Carradine), the egocentric rock star, who is calling Linnea for a date.

The sequence serves several functions. First, it introduces the manipulation theme. The political machine will make Sueleen serve its ends by exploiting her desire to become an Opry star like her idol Barbara Jean (Ronee Blakley). Second, it prepares the audience for one of the most poignant scenes in the film, the scene at the smoker where Sueleen does her pathetic strip. Third, it portrays a relationship of expediency, one of many such relationships that exist in the film. Tom sleeps with Linnea because he is a stud and she is available. Linnea sleeps with Tom because her husband is so indifferent to their deaf children that he does not even bother to learn sign language; hence his apathy when he overhears Tom's phone call to his wife.

The manipulation theme carries over into another sequence during which Sueleen's performance at the smoker is crosscut with Tom's performance in a nightclub. As Tom sings "I'm Easy," other women in the audience think he is singing to them. Altman cuts to their knowing faces but all the time the camera is moving toward the corner table where Linnea is sitting, the person to whom the song should have been dedicated if Tom could limit himself to one woman. The rhythm of manipulation, slow and serpentine, comes through in the editing: The very moment a rock star is playing on the women's emotions, some unsavory politicians are playing on the desire of an untalented waitress to become a star. Even before Tom finishes his number, there is lusty handclapping—not for him but for Sueleen. But the sequence does not end with her strip. After she finishes, we hear "I'm Easy" again, this time from a tape deck in Tom's hotel; he is in bed with Linnea who apparently is no substitute for the sound of his own voice.

The structure of the sequence can be outlined as follows:

1. Tom's "I'm Easy" in the nightclub crosscut with Sueleen's "I Never Get Enough" at the smoker
2. End of "I'm Easy"/beginning of Sueleen's strip (*bridge:* applause)
3. "I'm Easy" on tape

One of the themes in *Nashville* is religion and its various forms, which range from Lady Pearl's (Barbara Baxley's) militant Catholicism that inspired her to campaign for the Kennedys, to Barbara Jean's ecstatic devotion to a Redeemer who is an extension of her own neurosis. Altman begins the religion theme with a shot of Tom lying on his bed, his long hair and messianic eyes giving him the appearance of a Christ. Altman then cuts from Tom to a stained-glass window of Christ as the Good Shepherd, contrasting the shepherd who exploits his flock with the shepherd who tends it.

However, the religion theme does not end with contrasting shots of two shepherd figures. What started as a simple shot of a rock star in bed grows into a four-part sequence portraying four different Sunday services as well as four different forms of worship. The camera tilts down the stained-glass window to the congregation. It is a Catholic service, formal and austere. Lady Pearl is there, as are Sueleen and Wade, the black man who looks after her. Next the scene shifts to a Baptist service, with Hamilton singing self-righteously in the choir, and then to a black Baptist church, where Linnea and her gospel group are singing with unfeigned enthusiasm. The mixed liturgy ends in a hospital chapel, where Barbara Jean, seated in a wheelchair, is pouring her heart out with pentecostal fervor. No sooner does she finish than Altman cuts to another part of Nashville, to the automobile graveyard through which Opal, the BBC reporter, wanders as she tries to find a suitable metaphor for the city.

The editing of *Nashville* links the destinies of twenty-four people over a five-day period; it connects related themes through image and sound; it creates ironic associations by juxtaposing images (rock star/Good Shepherd, neurotic Opry singer/wrecked automobiles); it produces the film's manifold rhythm. The rhythm of *Nashville* is the rhythm of manipulation, which can be soft or blatant, genteel or crass; it can be as deliberately slow as Sueleen's rendition of a suggestive song or as shockingly quick as the bullet that strikes Barbara Jean.

## NOTES

[1]For a clear but technical discussion of editing, see Kenneth H. Roberts and Win Sharples, Jr., *A Primer for Film-Making* (New York: Pegasus, 1971), pp. 193-250.

[2]Terence St. John Marner, ed., *Directing Motion Pictures* (New York: A. S. Barnes, 1972), p. 19.

[3]Lee R. Bobker, with Louise Marinis, *Making Movies: From Script to Screen* (New York: Harcourt Brace Jovanovich, 1973), p. 209.

[4]Karel Reisz and Gavin Miller, *The Technique of Film Editing*, 2nd ed. (New York: Focal Press, 1968), p. 84.

[5]Ibid., p. 277.

[6]Cited in Fred Baker, ed., *Movie People* (New York: Douglas, 1972), p. 137.

# 5
# Basic Narrative Devices:
## Print and Voice Over

Film makers have a variety of means at their disposal to bring a story to the screen. Those that are peculiar to film—cuts, fades, dissolves, wipes, and the iris—have already been discussed. Two narrative devices—print and voice-over—that film shares with other media are also of some importance.

## PRINT

### Titles

The silent film made great use of *titles* (sometimes called "intertitles"), printed inserts that were projected periodically on the screen. The title was one of the ways by which the silent film maker augmented the narrative or illuminated the action; it is also a reminder of film's early dependence on print.

D. W. Griffith's *Broken Blossoms* (1919) is a good example of the functions titles can perform. In that picture a title provides the poetic introduction: "It is a tale of temple bells, sounding at sunset before the image of Buddha." Some of its titles are moralistic: "In this scarlet house of sin, does he ever hear the temple bells?" Occasionally one of the titles is anticipatory: "THE TERRIBLE ACCIDENT" prefaces the scene where Lucy spills dinner on her father, who becomes so enraged that he tosses her out of the house. Finally, some of its titles play on the viewer's emotions: "Dying, she gives her last little smile to a world that has been so unkind."

Far from dying with the silent era, titles exist even today in the form of subtitles for foreign films and for American films such as Franklin Schaffner's *Patton* (1970) and Richard Fleischer's *Tora! Tora! Tora!* (1970), in which there are scenes requiring the characters to speak in a foreign language. For such scenes, which are generally few in number, contemporary film makers often prefer to have the actors use the characters' native tongue rather than simulate a foreign accent, and to translate the dialogue through subtitles. William Friedkin used this technique in *The French Connection* (1971), and, in *Godfather, Part II* (1974), Francis Ford Coppola employed subtitles whenever Sicilian, Italian, or Spanish was spoken. When French was spoken in Sydney Pollack's *Three Days of the Condor* (1975) and the Sioux dialect in Irwin Kershner's *The Return of a Man Called Horse* (1976), the subtitles provided a simultaneous translation.

## Headlines, Letters, Prologues, and Epilogues

There is usually a moment in World War II movies when a newspaper whips across the screen with its announcement, "PEARL HARBOR BOMBED!" On the right occasion a few words can be as powerful as an image. Alfred Hitchcock's *Topaz* (1969) closes with a newspaper headline, "CUBAN MISSILE CRISIS OVER," a fitting ending to a movie that portrayed the events leading up to it.

It is possible to formulate a general rule about the printed word in film: It should be used as a means of supplying factual information that can only be imparted in writing or that, within the context of the film, is best conveyed in print. Sometimes the plot demands print. In Alan J. Pakula's *All the President's Men* (1976) Woodward (Robert Redford), realizing that Bernstein's (Dustin Hoffman's) apartment is bugged, turns up the stereo and types: "Deep Throat says our lives may be in danger. SURVEILLANCE. BUGGING." In Michael Gordon's *An Act of Murder* (1948), a wife learns she is terminally ill from a letter her physician has written to her husband. The fact that we see the letter as well as the wife's face adds to the impact of the scene.

When a film deals with a little known historical event or with a topic that would be unfamiliar to most viewers, a prologue, like an author's note in a historical novel, is necessary to remind them that the film is based on fact. Robert Wise used a brief prologue in *Two Flags West* (1950) to state the essentials of Lincoln's proclamation of December 8, 1863, which guaranteed freedom to any Confederate soldier in a prison camp who would serve in the Union army. The prologue is necessary because the proclamation is the film's point of departure. And for those unfamiliar with the Mann Act, Mike Nichols explained it in the printed prologue to *The Fortune* (1975).

An epilogue in the form of a few succinct sentences can inform the audience of the characters' fate without breaking the mood. At the end of Hitchcock's *The Wrong Man* (1957), based on a true story, there is a printed epilogue stating that Rose Balestrero (Vera Miles), who became mentally unbalanced after her husband was falsely convicted of theft, was eventually cured and is now living in Florida. The text is a bald statement of fact and nothing more; when it appears on the screen, it has the effect of a case stamped "CLOSED." Had Hitchcock shown Rose basking in the Florida sun, he would have destroyed the film's fatalistic mood, gratifying only those few viewers who want storm clouds turned inside out to see the silver lining. The epilogue is neither a happy ending nor a successful resolution; it is simply a factual statement making it clear that Rose Balestrero did not remain a mental case for the rest of her life.

In Sidney Lumet's *Dog Day Afternoon* (1975), Sonny Wortzik (Al Pacino), a married Vietnam vet with two children, holds up a Brooklyn bank to finance a transsexual operation for his second wife—a man he married in a wedding ceremony complete with celebrant and bridesmaids. The film ends on a Kennedy Airport runway, a few feet from the jet Sonny had ordered to fly him to Algeria, the rebel's paradise. Then three titles appear on the screen without any fanfare, as if they were being typed by a secretary who was concerned only with the accuracy of her transcription, not with its implications: Sonny is serving twenty years in prison; his first wife Angie is on welfare; his second wife Leon is a woman and living in New York.

The prologue and epilogue to *Shock Corridor* (1963), Samuel Fuller's movie about an ambitious reporter who feigns madness to solve a murder, consist of the same quote from Euripides: "Whom the gods wish to destroy, they first make mad." When the same words reappear as the epilogue, we feel that shiver of irony that occurs when a statement that seemed so harmless turns out to be painfully prophetic: The reporter who feigned madness went mad himself.

## Dedications and Prefatory Remarks

Like an author, a film maker can dedicate a movie to someone as a mark of his esteem. John Ford dedicated *The Iron Horse* (1924) to the Scottish engineer George Stephenson; French director Jean Renoir dedicated the restored version of *The Rules of the Game* (1939) to the great French critic André Bazin. François Truffaut, another Frenchman, often uses dedications: *Stolen Kisses* (1968) was dedicated to Henri Langlois and the Cinémathèque Française, which Langlois co-founded; *The Wild Child* (1969) to Jean-Pierre Léaud; and *Day for Night* (1973) to Lillian and Dorothy Gish. Then there are less classic dedications, for example, Michael Curtiz's *Dive Bomber* (1941) to the flight surgeons of America and George Sidney's *The Harvey Girls* (1946) to the Harvey girls. A dedication may be the result of anything from a publicity gimmick to a studio head's patriotism; but Ford, Renoir, and Truffaut thought of themselves as authors and therefore used one of the oldest signs of authorship—the inscription.

More common than dedications are various prefatory remarks, which can be anything from a statement of fact ("This Is a True Story": Richard Fleischer's *Ten Rillington Place*, 1971) to an elaborate warning that "crime does not pay" (Mervyn LeRoy's *Little Caesar*, 1930).

There are also time-place introductions. Some give only the barest essentials: "ENGLAND 1851" appears at the beginning of Peter Godfrey's *The Woman in White* (1948). Some, however, omit nothing in their attempt to be accurate, as, for example, Hitchcock's introduction to *Psycho* (1960): "PHOENIX, ARIZONA. FRIDAY, DECEMBER ELEVENTH. TWO FORTY-THREE P.M."

Another type of prefatory remark is the literary epigraph. Albert Lewin's *The Picture of Dorian Gray* (1945) opens and closes with the same excerpt from the *Rubáiyát*. George Santayana's remark, "Those who do not remember the past are condemned to relive it," is the epigraph to Louis Malle's *Lacombe, Lucien* (1974), which shows how a French boy's indifference to humanity is used by the Nazis. Occasionally the epigraphs are fakes. Jacques Tourneur's *Cat People* (1942) opens with an excerpt from a book called *The Anatomy of Atavism* written by a Dr. Louis Judd. Psychologists might recognize the text as coming from Sigmund Freud, not from Dr. Judd, who is a character in the film. However, the epilogue to *Cat People* is accurate—a quote from one of John Donne's *Holy Sonnets*.

Sometimes prefatory remarks take the form of a "crawl" or "roll up," during which the text unfolds by moving either up or down the screen. William Wyler's *Mrs. Miniver* (1942) and Richard Brooks's *The Blackboard Jungle* (1955) both begin this way. The opening remarks of *Mrs. Miniver* are a tribute to the British who bore up so courageously during the Blitz of World War II, while those of *The Blackboard Jungle* provide MGM's justification for making a movie about juvenile delinquency.

Film makers continue to use printed material because certain movies require introductions that pure visuals cannot provide. Don Sharp's *Hennessy* (1975), which concerned an Irishman's attempt to blow up the Houses of Parliament on Guy Fawkes Day, incorporated some newsreel footage of the royal family at an actual state opening; at the beginning Sharp flashed the warning: "This motion picture incorporates extracts from a news film of the Queen at a State Opening of Parliament which, when photographed, was not intended for use in a fictional context. The Directors of Hennessy Film Productions, Ltd., would therefore like to make it clear that the Royal Family took no part in the making of this film." The text, although cumbersome to read on the screen, can be justified because the footage is so well integrated that viewers might mistake it for staged material. The text also functions as a legal disclaimer that protects the producers from a libel charge.

## VOICE-OVER

As movies learned to talk, film makers seized upon the voice as a narrative instrument, attempting to use it in the same way they had used titles. As often happens, the quest for novelty led to eccentricity. Frank Tashlin's *The First Time* (1952) was narrated by an unborn child; in Irving Reis's *Enchantment* (1948), the prologue was spoken by a house. On paper the talking fetus and the personified house may have seemed like good ideas: *The First Time* dramatized the disruptions that come with a first child, and *Enchantment* portrayed the two generations that lived in a London house. However, on the screen, baby talk can become monotonous, and a house that tells of itself and its inhabitants ("I miss my people; in me they live") is a fairy tale house, not an actual one.

Theoretically anyone or anything can narrate a movie. However, since *voice-over* (off-camera narration or commentary) is such a common narrative device, its appropriateness to a particular film deserves investigation. Is it a meaningful convention like a soliloquy in a play, or is it an emergency cord the film maker pulls when he or she cannot think of another way to begin a movie or deliver some important piece of information? There is no manual a film maker can consult to determine when to use voice-over and when to use print. Sometimes voice-over is preferable to print, and sometimes even voice-over requires some type of backup, such as sounds, a few chords, or a musical theme.

Jack Conway's 1935 adaptation of Charles Dickens's *A Tale of Two Cities* is a good illustration of the sensible use of print and voice-over. Conway wanted to retain the familiar opening of the novel ("It was the best of times, it was the worst of times") as well as the familiar closing ("It is a far, far better thing that I do, than I have ever done: it is a far, far better rest that I go to than I have ever known").

The opening appears as a title without voice-over. This is fitting because the words are those of Dickens, not one of his characters, and therefore, the text alone is sufficient. At the end of the film, however, voice-over is absolutely necessary. The audience must hear these noble sentiments because they are famous last thoughts, not famous last words. A title at the end would have been inappropriate because the thoughts are Sydney Carton's, not the author's.

Daphne du Maurier's novel *Rebecca* opens with the line, "Last night I went to Manderley again." In his film version of the novel, Hitchcock naturally chose voice-over for the opening of the film, in which we hear Mrs. de Winter (Joan Fontaine) speak the memorable line against a musical background.

The best film makers know intuitively when to use voice-over and when to use some kind of title; they also know that in some instances a combination can be justified. William Dieterle's *Love Letters* (1945) begins with a close-up of a letter a soldier is writing for a friend who does not have much facility with language. It is important for us to see the letter, since the handwriting is crucial to the plot. Although the audience has seen the letter, the "author" has not. Therefore, the soldier must read his friend what he has written. In *The Grapes of Wrath* (1940), John Ford gives us a glimpse of Tom Joad's funeral eulogy for his grandfather. Although we hear the eulogy, Ford shows us the part where Tom wrote "dyed" for "died." Tom Joad may be a poor speller, but he is an exemplary human being.

## The Narrating "I"

The most familiar form of voice-over is first-person narration, which is similar to "I narration" in fiction. Because of the similarity the same questions asked of the "I" of a novel can be asked of the "I" of a film: Why was the "I" chosen to tell the story? Has the "I" participated in the events it is recounting? Is the "I" reliable? How much does the "I" actually know?

There are as many voices of the "I" as there are "I's." As we have seen, anyone can tell a story; in Billy Wilder's *Sunset Boulevard* (1950) even a corpse has the opportunity. Narration by a dead man would pose severe problems of credibility in a work of fiction unless it were a tale of the supernatural. Yet it does work in *Sunset Boulevard*, which, for all its grittiness, is very much like a tale of the supernatural, in the way that most films about the old Hollywood are. In *Sunset Boulevard*, Norma Desmond (Gloria Swanson), an ex-silent star half-crazed by decaying memories, believes she can make a comeback in the role of Salome. The movie has all the gothic trappings: a mansion where the wind wheezes through the organ; a living room filled to surfeit with mementos of the past; a tennis court with faded markings and a sagging net; rats scampering about in an unused swimming pool; a pet monkey carried ceremoniously to its grave in a satin-lined coffin. *Sunset Boulevard* begins with the body of Joe Gillis (William Holden) floating in a pool; Gillis's voice then proceeds to tell the story of his fatal association with Norma Desmond. The narration is ironically fitting: A corpse is talking about the living dead.

Wilder is not tricking the audience: From the outset we know the body is that of Joe Gillis; we know too what is happening when the voice detaches itself from its body to observe how "he" liked swimming pools. Even at the end when the body has been fished out of the pool, the voice continues: "This is where you came in. Back at that pool again." And for those who like black humor the voice remarks that Gillis finally got the swimming pool he always wanted.

The ideal kind of narration occurs when the "I" has a specific connection with the story being told—the kind of connection actors have with their play as opposed to the kind dreamers have with their dreams. Billy Wilder achieved perfect "I narration" in *Double Indemnity* (1944), which opens as Walter Neff (Fred MacMurray) enters a Los Angeles building shortly before dawn. Neff describes himself as having "no visible scars"—that is, none that we can see *now*; actually, he has just been shot by his mistress, whom he then killed. Before the scars begin to show, he tells his story into a dictaphone: "Memorandum to Keyes. You want to know who killed Diedrichson? I killed Diedrichson." The film then becomes a flashback, and its credibility is due to a testimony we know is true because it is being recorded and dramatized at the same time.

Unlike many first-person films where the narrator's voice disappears after the first five minutes, Neff's narration bridges the scenes. It is really Neff's voice that unifies the film as the action shifts from present to past. Wilder often ends a flashback with a

*5–1    Walter Neff (Fred MacMurray) as the "Narrating I" of Billy Wilder's Double Indemnity (1944), one of the finest examples of first-person narration in film. Courtesy Billy Wilder and MCA Publishing.*

cue line, one that triggers the next line of dialogue, so that the action can return to the present without an awkward transition. When Neff and Phyllis Diedrichson (Barbara Stanwyck) are in a supermarket plotting the murder, she says, "Remember we're in it together." "Yes, I remember," Neff answers into the dictaphone.

Voice-over was also the ideal vehicle for Max Ophuls's *Letter from an Unknown Woman* (1948), which revolves entirely around a letter Lisa (Joan Fontaine) wrote to her former lover as she lay dying. Because it is such a personal document, Ophuls allows us to see only its powerful beginning ("By the time you read this letter I may be dead") and its unfinished ending. What the lover reads we hear in Lisa's own voice as she composes a deathbed autobiography for the man who never bothered to learn the name of the woman he seduced.

Sometimes the "I" tells his or her story, hoping to learn from it. Robert Bresson's *Une Femme Douce* (1969) opens with a suicide. Someone rushes to the veranda, a chair is overturned, a white shawl flutters through the air, and a woman's body crashes to the pavement. A man, later revealed to be the woman's husband, begins to speak of her. Bresson keeps returning to her body, which now lies on a bed, to remind us that her husband is narrating the film. The approach is psychologically valid, for the husband is not so much recalling his wife as he is trying to understand why she committed suicide. At the end he knows no more than he did at the beginning.

Why does a film maker choose the narrating "I"? Generally "I narration" has a distancing effect even when the "I" is an active participant in the story. It can create an objective type of movie in which the audience is expected to view the action dispassionately, the way a medical student might watch surgery in an operating theater. Terence Malick used first-person narration throughout *Badlands* (1973), a film whose characters are far from endearing. The heroine is a fifteen-year-old girl with cornflower eyes that look as if they have lost their physical and moral center; the hero, her boyfriend, can shoot a man in the back and then talk to him as if nothing had happened. Holly (Sissy Spacek), the heroine, narrates *Badlands* in a voice as flat as the country she and Kit (Martin Sheen) traverse. She is presumably telling the story to us, but it sounds as if she might be writing it for a pulp magazine. Some of the narration is grimly amusing, particularly when Holly tries to turn a phrase and instead produces a cliché ("Little did I realize that what began in the backways and alleys of this little town would end in the badlands of Montana"); or when she tries to be poetic and succeeds only in being puerile ("When the leaves rustled overhead, it was as if the spirits were whispering about all the little things that were bothering them"). Her boyfriend's inclinations cause Holly to remark: "Suddenly I was thrown into a state of shock: Kit was the most trigger-happy person I ever met." The banality of her voice merges with the banality of her style; and the apathy in her voice prevents our sympathizing with her.

An audience expects the voice of the "I" to be reliable—otherwise, why employ it?—but there are times when the voice can be at odds with the action because the voice is at odds with itself, thinking it is better than it actually is. In Robert Bresson's *Diary of a Country Priest* (1950), there is a discrepancy between what the priest writes about himself and what he really is. In Martin Scorsese's *Taxi Driver* (1976), the psychotic Travis writes in his diary: "I don't believe that one should devote his life to morbid self-attention." Yet this is precisely what Travis does when he goes into training to assassinate a presidential candidate. In such cases the audience will believe the deeds, not the words.

## The Disembodied Voice

### As Observer

In semi-documentaries* like Henry Hathaway's *The House on 92nd Street* (1945) and Jules Dassin's *The Naked City* (1948), the credits appear in typescript to give the movies a "case history" look. In both a solemn voice delivers the prologue, reminding the audience that the film sprang from today's headlines or from the FBI's files and that it was shot on location. Since the voice belongs to no character, it is completely disembodied; thus it can insinuate itself into the characters, noting their moods and idiosyncrasies. The voice in *The Naked City* speaks directly to the characters as if it were a combination of alter ego and confidant-conscience: "How are your feet holding out, Alan?" it asks: or, "Lieutenant Muldoon, what's your hurry?" It even speaks to the audience: "Ever try to catch a murderer?" Since the voice has the first word,

*A documentary is a nonfiction film; a semi-documentary, a type that was especially popular between 1945 and 1950 (e.g., Elia Kazan's *Boomerang*, 1947; Henry Hathaway's *Call Northside 777*, 1948), is a fiction film based on fact.

5–2  *This scene from Stanley Kubrick's* Barry Lyndon *(1975) between Barry (Ryan O'Neal) and his son (David Morley) was introduced by the off-camera narrator who said: "Barry had his faults, but no man could say of him that he was not a good and tender father. He loved his son passionately, perhaps with a blind partiality. He denied him nothing." Courtesy Warner Bros. Inc., copyright © 1975.*

it is only fitting that it have the last: "There are eight million stories in the naked city. This has been one of them."

Thackeray wrote his novel *Barry Lyndon* in the form of a memoir and hence used the first person. To give his film version the air of a Victorian novel set in the eighteenth century, Stanley Kubrick employed voice-over. But it is not Barry who tells his story; it is a suave, urbane voice (Michael Hordern's) that comments and muses, telling us about something before it happens or informing us of the outcome of an event without dramatizing it for us. Ordinarily we would resent this kind of voice for flaunting what it knows. But in Kubrick's *Barry Lyndon* (1975), the narrator's voice is in league with the camera, which, in turn, is under the control of the director. It is the director who delegates his omniscience to the camera, which then shares it with the narrator. Thus when Barry is about to die, the voice reads his obituary. The voice can speak with authority at this moment because it has been speaking with authority since the film began.

### As Deus ex Machina

Most of Euripides' plays ended with a *deus ex machina*, a god descending on a crane to resolve an action that had strayed beyond human control. Aristotle objected to the god from the machine, claiming it was inartistic, although Euripides may have been suggesting that some situations become so entangled that they require help from above. The modern equivalent of the *deus ex machina* is the chance ending, the eleventh-hour reprieve, or the last-minute rescue. If a great work of literature ends with a *deus ex machina*, we stress its greatness, not its conclusion. In fiction we overlook the endings of Charles Dickens's *Oliver Twist* (1838), Thomas Hardy's *Tess of the d'Urbervilles* (1891), and William Golding's *Lord of the Flies* (1954). In film we cheer when the cavalry arrives in time to save the fort, when someone finds the weapon to destroy the undying monster, when the police inspector breaks down the door in time to free a terrorized wife from her mad husband.

Although the *deus ex machina* can be tolerated, the *vox ex machina* ("voice from the machine") stretches credibility too far. At the end of George Sherman's *The Lady and the Monster* (1944), for example, a voice tells us that Patrick Cory (Richard Arlen) has been given a prison term for cooperating with the mad doctor in keeping a dead man's brain alive. The voice also reminds us that this is to be a film with a happy ending and that Cory will emerge from jail to find his beloved waiting for him. Since no voice was heard in the film until this point, we wonder whose it is. It must belong to a supernatural power who knows more about the script than the screenwriter.

Another bizarre example of voice-over appears in Jacques Tourneur's *I Walked with a Zombie* (1943), which, despite its title, is a superior horror film. Initially, the movie is narrated by the "I" of the title, a Canadian nurse who comes to the West Indies to tend a woman who turns out to be a zombie. At the end the zombie is killed by her brother-in-law, who then commits suicide. Suddenly a male voice asks God to pardon the unholy couple. The switch from the nurse's voice to the voice from outer space imparts a moralistic tone to a film that otherwise remains aloof from moral issues.

## The Epistolary Voice

Advancing the plot through letters is a device common to both fiction and film. The epistolary novel has a long tradition that reaches back to Samuel Richardson's *Pamela* and *Clarissa*, written in the mid–eighteenth century. Although there are few totally epistolary films *(Letter from an Unknown Woman* is the best), the letter is a familiar means of setting the plot in motion (William Wyler's *The Letter*, 1940; Joseph L. Mankiewicz's *A Letter to Three Wives*, 1948) or of bridging the years (Elia Kazan's *Sea of Grass*, 1947). When an exchange of letters is used to mark the passage of time, voice-over is quite sufficient. In *Sea of Grass* there is a sequence in which Brice Chamberlain (Melvyn Douglas) writes to Lutie (Katharine Hepburn) to tell her how her son Brock is growing up. Their correspondence is well motivated because Lutie has been prevented from seeing her son. Brice's voice supplies the information that Lutie and the audience require.

In *The Story of Adele H.* (1975), Truffaut puts the epistolary voice to a variety of uses. We hear Adele's voice as she writes to Lieutenant Pinson, whom she pursued to Halifax in an attempt to regain his affection. When she writes to her father, we hear his reply. In addition to her correspondence, Adele keeps a diary whose entries we also hear. When Pinson reads the love notes Adele has concealed in his pockets, her voice discloses their contents to us. After following Pinson to Barbados, she collapses in the street. A native woman brings Adele to her home; after learning her identity, the woman dictates a letter to Victor Hugo, informing him of his daughter's pitiful condition. Few film makers have utilized the potential of the human voice as creatively as Truffaut has done in *The Story of Adele H.*

In an era of film censorship the epistolary voice was one way of having a character acknowledge his or her sins by confessing off camera. Robert Anderson's play *Tea and Sympathy* (1953) was considered unfilmable because of its subject matter: Tom Lee, a prep school student thought to be homosexual because of his fondness for music and poetry, discovers his manhood with the aid of Laura Reynolds, the headmaster's understanding wife. The play is best remembered for the final scene when Laura comes to Tom's room and slowly begins to unbutton her blouse. Pressing his hand against her breast, she makes one request: "Years from now, when you talk about this, and you will, be kind." When MGM decided to film the play, the Johnston Office* felt that any woman who would offer her body to an adolescent should die.[1] After much wrangling, director Vincente Minnelli decided upon a storytelling device: The

*The Motion Picture Producers and Distributors of America, Hollywood's self-censorship organization, was called the Johnston Office when it was headed by Eric Johnston from 1945 to 1963.

movie would be a flashback occasioned by a class reunion, ending with Tom's discovering a letter that Laura had written to him. As Tom reads the letter, we hear Laura's repentant voice urging him to forget what they had done (which was "wrong") and to go out into the world and perform great deeds for humanity.

## The Voice in Transit

Voice-over is commonly used today to enable characters in transit to continue their conversation without being seen. When the characters are in a moving vehicle (e.g., a car, a funicular railway), we may see the vehicle but not the characters; yet we hear them speak. Or, when two characters are walking in the distance, we sometimes hear exactly what they are saying even though we cannot see their faces. This kind of voice-over minimizes cutting; otherwise, the director would have to cut from an aerial shot of the traffic to the characters in the car. Thus in *All the President's Men*, as Woodward and Bernstein are driving around Washington, we get an aerial view of their car, and voice-over provides us with the details of their conversation. The director may also want to establish a particular mood by having the characters off in the distance, a mood that would be broken if the camera zoomed in on them.

## The Repetitive Voice

A character, usually the heroine, tosses restlessly in bed while someone's voice reverberates in her unconscious, repeating key dialogue from an earlier scene in case she or the audience missed its significance. This kind of repetitive-voice technique is used by Hitchcock in *Rebecca* (1940), when some comments made about the late Mrs. de Winter give the future Mrs. de Winter a sleepless night; Jacques Tourneur uses the same technique, though less effectively, in a montage sequence in *Cat People* (1942), in which Irena (Simone Simon) keeps hearing her psychiatrist's warning about her need to unleash evil on the world while Halloween cats creep across the screen.

Unfortunately, the repetitive voice is so familiar it has become trite. Yet at times some kind of recapitulation is necessary, and the film maker must determine whether it is dialogue, a scene, or a shot that must be repeated. If a character's words alone are important, then all that is necessary is to hear what he or she has said. In this case the repetitive voice is ideal because it can easily disengage itself from the character. If what is seen is more important than what is said, then the shot or the scene must be repeated. For the resolution of *Murder on the Orient Express* (1974), Sidney Lumet repeats the crucial shots in which the passengers slipped up. Guilt is often a question not of what one says but of how one reacts. Lumet recalls for us the look on Greta Ohlsson's (Ingrid Bergman's) face when Hercule Poirot (Albert Finney) used the word "emolument" as he was questioning her. She understood its meaning, although as a dim-witted Swedish missionary she could not possibly have known what an "emolument" was.

## The Overlapping Voice

In *overlap*, sound or dialogue can either carry over from a previous scene or anticipate the next scene. In Sydney Pollack's *Three Days of the Condor* (1975), a CIA official in Washington is asking questions about an agent, who at that moment is hiding out in a Brooklyn Heights apartment. The official's voice carries into the next scene with the agent. The overlapping voice gives the impression that the CIA is everywhere, including Brooklyn Heights.

At the end of *Medium Cool* (1969), which is set in Chicago during the 1968 Democratic convention, director Haskell Wexler lets the audience hear of an event before it happens. As a TV cameraman and an Appalachian schoolteacher are driving away from a bloody confrontation between the police and the antiwar protesters, a newscaster's voice describes the smash-up of their car before it is actually shown. Like the film the untimely newscast is disturbing, for it is not merely a matter of overlap but of omniscience. It is as if the cool medium, as Marshall McLuhan referred to television, knows our destiny and therefore can compose our obituary before we die.

## The Subjective Voice

Movies abound in examples of the inner voice that literally speaks its mind because the audience requires access to the character's thoughts at a particular point. Pip (John Mills) of David Lean's *Great Expectations* (1947) wonders how Joe Gargery, the blacksmith, will greet him when he returns home dressed as a gentleman. In William Dieterle's *The Accused* (1948), we hear what a college professor who killed a student in self-defense is thinking when she realizes the consequences of her act. During Marion Crane's flight from Phoenix in Hitchcock's *Psycho*, she imagines what her employer will say on Monday morning when she fails to appear for work.

## The Subjective Camera Voice

When the *subjective camera* technique is used, the audience views the action from the character's point of view. This device is best restricted to individual scenes or sequences such as the drive into Hooverville in *The Grapes of Wrath* (1940), the scene in which John Ford puts us behind the wheel, making us see the poverty and squalor through the eyes of the Joads. Subjective camera should never dominate an entire film, as it did in Robert Montgomery's *Lady in the Lake* (1946), the textbook case of how not to make the audience a participant in the action. In this film oddity one character lights another's cigarette by thrusting the lighter into the lens of the camera; the effect is like the 3-D movies of the early 1950s when Indians scalped viewers, snakes bit them, and cowboys ran roughshod over them.

If a character speaks during a subjectively shot scene or sequence, the audience hears everything from his or her point of view in addition to seeing and feeling what he or she feels. The union of subjective camera and voice can only occur when the plot demands their coalescence, as it does in Delmer Daves's *Dark Passage* (1947). Unjustly convicted for his wife's murder, Vincent Parry (Humphrey Bogart) escapes from San Quentin to track down the real killer. Obviously he cannot solve the murder looking as he does since his picture is in every California newspaper. He must undergo plastic surgery. Daves, who also wrote the screenplay, had two options: He could use another actor in the early part of the film, and after the operation, introduce Bogart; or he could use Bogart's voice and never completely show Bogart for the first thirty minutes, and then shoot Bogart as usual for the remainder. Daves did the latter out of necessity: In 1947 Humphrey Bogart was too big a star to make his first appearance after the action was well under way.

Parry escapes by concealing himself in a barrel that has been loaded on a prison truck. The camera is totally subjective, jostling us as he maneuvers the barrel from the truck, and making us reel with dizziness as it rolls down a hill. When the barrel comes to rest, we peer out of it cautiously but get nothing more than a tunnellike view of the outside. Parry is now a Presence. When he hitches a ride, the driver speaks to the Presence, who answers like an unseen passenger. When the driver recognizes him, the Presence knocks him unconscious. The camera is the Presence as it parts bushes, scans the highway, and climbs into Irene Jansen's (Lauren Bacall's) waiting car.

When the Presence showers, a hand adjusts the shower head and a jet of water sprays the screen. Camera movements express the emotional states of the Presence. When the Presence is wary, the camera darts in the same direction as his apprehensive eyes. A telephone rings, and the camera swings around the way a tense person does at an unexpected sound. Gradually Daves begins to switch from subjective to objective camera, from Parry as a Presence to Parry as a character. The transition begins in a cab, with low-key lighting keeping Bogart's face in shadow. The sympathetic cabbie recommends plastic surgery and refers him to a reliable doctor. After the operation Bogart's voice returns to Bogart's body, and the camera becomes fully objective.

## The Stream-of-Consciousness Voice

*Stream of consciousness* has been applied to everything from inarticulate rambling to incoherent prose, yet it is really the unbroken flow of thoughts, memories, and associations in the waking mind. A good example of the stream-of-consciousness film is Alain Resnais's *Hiroshima Mon Amour* (1960). The film opens with a man and a woman making love. At first their skin looks charred like that of the Hiroshima victims; then it becomes dewy as if cleansed by the act of love. She is a French actress and he, a Japanese architect she met in Hiroshima while making a film. As their bodies move toward fulfillment, we hear their voices—his denying that she knows the significance of Hiroshima, hers claiming that she does. But these are not their actual voices; they sound distant, anesthetized. They speak in the rhythms of poetry, not prose. It is the character's interior that we hear, an interior expressing itself in the language of memory that is made up of both words and images. When the architect's voice says, "You know nothing of Hiroshima," her consciousness replies with pictures of the artifacts she has seen at the museum and in newsreels of the aftermath of the bombing. When the woman says "Who are you?" the camera answers with a shot of a Hiroshima street. The man is Hiroshima, the only name she will ever associate with him.

## The Voice of the Media

The media—radio, television, tapes, and so forth—can offer alternatives to the traditional means of storytelling, thus increasing the film maker's narrative options. Since film is one of the media, it can utilize the media's narrative potential more realistically than fiction can. In a novel a TV program is something we read about; in a movie it is something we see and hear. In film the media keep their nature intact as they become visible and aural channels of narrative. Records are made to be heard, photographs to be seen, tapes to be played; only in film, however, is it possible for the media to appear in their natural form and further the narrative at the same time. In Robert Altman's *Nashville* (1975), newscaster Howard K. Smith gives the details of a presidential candidate's background on the evening news. Harry Caul (Gene Hackman), the professional wiretapper of Francis Ford Coppola's *The Conversation* (1974), spends the entire film trying to determine the context of one sentence in a taped conversation between two seemingly ordinary young people. A confession on tape forms the denouement of Orson Welles's *Touch of Evil* (1958), and when Harry Devlin of Hitchcock's *Notorious* (1946) wishes to remind Alicia of her patriotism, he plays a recording of an argument she had with her father, in which she defended America against his fascist attacks.

Even a movie in which a radio program is central to the plot—Otto Preminger's *Laura* (1944), Michael Curtiz's *The Unsuspected* (1947)—is not necessarily dated although radio is no longer what it was in its heyday. Waldo Lydecker's (Clifton Webb's) effete broadcasts in *Laura* blend in perfectly with the shallow elegance of his world. Thus *Laura* is as engrossing now as it was in 1944. Waldo's radio show is a mirror image of himself and his social class, not merely a form of popular entertainment.

Finally, there is even a film that features a voiceless voice, one that the characters hear but the audience does not. In that film (William Wellman's *The Next Voice You Hear*, 1950), God usurps prime time on radio to tell the world to shape up—or else. The audience reconstructs the message of this voiceless voice through discussions the characters have with each other as well as through the anxious looks they exchange as they listen to the big but silent broadcast.

## NOTES

[1]Minnelli relates the complete story in his autobiography *I Remember It Well* (New York: Berkeley Medallion Books, 1974), pp. 310–313.

# 6

# Literary Devices:

## Dramatized Prologues, Flashbacks, Flashforwards, Point of View

Film shares some narrative devices with literature. When a film maker uses them, he or she becomes a storyteller in the literary sense. In this chapter the visual effect of these techniques concerns us less than their function in the film.

## THE DRAMATIZED PROLOGUE

A prologue, as we have seen, can appear as a printed text or an off-camera voice; it can also be dramatized, beginning before or during the credits. In the past a movie traditionally opened with the studio logo (*The Wizard of Oz*, 1939, with the MGM lion; *Double*

*Indemnity*, 1944, with Paramount's star-spangled mountain; *The Grapes of Wrath*, 1940, with Twentieth-Century-Fox's crisscrossing spotlights); title, cast, and credits then followed. Today, by contrast, *precredit prologues* (in which action begins before the credits) and *opening-credit prologues* (whose action begins with the credits) are commonplace. Robert Aldrich's *Hustle* (1975) begins cold, with a busload of children arriving for an afternoon at the shore, where they discover a girl's body washed up on the beach. Alan J. Pakula's *All the President's Men* (1976) has an elaborate prologue. First typewriter keys bang out a date—June 17, 1972; then a film clip shows Richard Nixon arriving on the lawn of the White House; finally the credits appear concurrently with the movie's first real scene—the Watergate break-in.

The dramatized prologue is a true prologue: an event occurring prior to the action and therefore set off from the film proper. On the stage there is usually some indication—a pause, a blackout, the lowering of the curtain—that the prologue is independent of the play. In a movie the intervening or accompanying credits perform that task.

The precredit sequence can be a great challenge to film makers because it defies them to make something creative out of a preface. Consider the prologue to Sam Peckinpah's *The Wild Bunch* (1969). What appears to be a detachment of cavalry troops rides into a small town. Some children are feeding a pair of scorpions to a horde of ants. The soldiers ride past the children and proceed up the main street toward the payroll office. On the rooftops of the buildings flanking the street is a band of armed men crouching behind the parapets. The soldiers dismount at the payroll office, enter it, flash their .45's, and pistol-whip the employees. The opening credits are interspersed with the prefatory action, but in a highly imaginative way. Periodically the frames freeze and turn brown as if they were old photographs in a family album; the credits are then stamped in the corner of the frame as if they too were being preserved for posterity.

By the time all the credits have appeared, the peaceful tenor of the town has been established and threatened. A film sequence has unfolded as a drama in miniature. We now know that the troops are bandits; the rooftop crowd, bounty hunters in the employ of the railroad; the townspeople and children, unsuspecting victims of the cross fire that will certainly erupt. Peckinpah has created an opening credit sequence that is also a true prologue.

# THE FLASHBACK

In ancient epic poems the flashback was a way of incorporating material into the narrative that could not be incorporated in any other fashion. For example, since the *Odyssey* begins twenty years after the Trojan War, the only way Homer could describe Odysseus' postwar exploits was by providing him with a situation—a banquet—where he could recount them. And in the *Aeneid* Virgil, imitating Homer, had Aeneas summarize his seven years abroad at a banquet also. A flashback has always been convenient for an author who is starting in the middle of the action (as Milton is in *Paradise Lost*) or who is working from the present back to the past, where the only explanation for the present resides (as is Thomas Pynchon in *V*).

In film a flashback can either be introduced by a slow fade-out/fade-in or by a quick cut. The flashback has three purposes: (1) to furnish information that is otherwise unavailable; (2) to dramatize a past event, even at the very moment it is being narrated, because words are inadequate for the situation (when Barry Lyndon hears the news of his son's death, Kubrick shows the actual incident of the boy falling from his horse); and (3) to connect past and present when none of the characters is knowledgeable enough to act as a narrator (*Godfather II*).

Films centering about the identity of a criminal (Michael Curtiz's *Mildred Pierce*, 1945) or an investigation into a man's life (Orson Welles's *Citizen Kane*, 1941) will often begin with the crime or the death and then backtrack. Regardless of the form a flashback takes (a remembrance, a confession, an inquest), it must be motivated. The memory flashback has always posed a credibility problem because it has been so misused by screenwriters who give amnesiacs total recall in the last reel or allow the heroine two minutes at the end to remember a girlhood trauma. In the best memory flashbacks, it is some object that provokes the reminiscence. In Jules Dassin's *Brute Force* (1947), the picture of a woman on a calendar causes four convicts to remember their own women; in George Stevens's *Penny Serenade* (1941), old phonograph records trigger Julie's memories of her marriage.

There is a unique flashback in John Ford's *The Searchers* (1956). As Laurie (Vera Miles) begins reading Martin's (Jeffrey Hunter's) letter, it seems as though Ford will be using an epistolary voice (see chapter 5) to summarize events that we will not see on the screen.

But this is not the case. Some of what Laurie reads we have already seen (e.g., the incident of the squaw who attached herself to Martin), but most of the letter is dramatized as she reads it. Because the sequence is so long, Ford obtains some variety by alternating between Martin's voice as he writes the letter and Laurie's as she reads it.

These flashbacks are personal, yet there are impersonal flashbacks that are not the result of a reminiscence or an inquest but merely pieces of the past worked into the film and narrated, not by the character or his or her unconscious, but by the camera. Such integration of past and present occurs in Francis Ford Coppola's *Godfather II* (1974), in which no one is recalling Vito Corleone's early life except the camera. Another example of the impersonal flashback is Stanley Donen's *Two for the Road* (1967), which crosscuts a European trip a couple is making with incidents from previous trips. Because of the ingenious way past and present intertwine, we accept *Two for the Road*, never asking if it is the wife or the husband who is remembering. Donen establishes at the outset that it is the camera—the same camera that apparently accompanied them on their former jaunts.

## THE FLASHFORWARD

A device that enjoyed popularity with film makers in the 1960s was the *flashforward*, in which some aspect of an event is shown before it occurs. The flashforward is a distant relative of the literary device called "dramatic foreshadowing," wherein one incident presages another or some indication is given that an event is going to happen before it actually does. But the true ancestor of the flashforward is a rhetorical device termed "prolepsis," in which a speaker anticipates and answers an objection before an opponent has even put it forth.

Sometimes what seems to be a flashforward isn't one. During the course of Sydney Pollack's *They Shoot Horses, Don't They?* (1969), the narrator (Michael Sarrazin) speaks directly to the camera—or is he speaking to someone we cannot see? We discover at the end that he is speaking to a judge, explaining why he shot Gloria (Jane Fonda) at her request. The reason why flashforwards succeed in *They Shoot Horses* is that from the audience's point of view they exist in the future, but from the narrator's they exist in the past. In retrospect, it becomes apparent that the entire film was a flashback told to a judge.

Because of their anticipatory force, proleptic devices can be dramatically effective. In George Stevens's *The Greatest Story Ever Told* (1965), after Pilate delivers Jesus to be crucified, an off-camera voice is heard saying, "And he suffered under Pontius Pilate." It is a compelling moment in the film, for it elevates a historical event to an article of faith without waiting for the Apostles' Creed to be written.

The way in which the credits appear on the screen often has a foreshadowing character. In Alfred Hitchcock's *Saboteur* (1942), during the credits the shadow of the saboteur moves from the right of the frame into the center. Billy Wilder used the same technique in *Double Indemnity* (1944); in that film the shadowy figure is on crutches, a prefiguration of Mr. Diedrichson's accident, which will make murdering him a bit more complicated.

Sometimes a shot has the impact of a flashforward although it is really a comment on an earlier incident. Well after the midpoint of *The Story of Adele H.* (1975), François Truffaut inserts a shot of Adele on the Isle of Guernsey, gloriously confident as she prepares to sail for Halifax to reclaim the affections of Lieutenant Pinson. Her voice is equally self-assured: "This incredible thing—that a young girl shall walk over the sea, from the Old into the New World, to join her lover—this, I shall accomplish." Obviously this is an Adele we have not seen before since the film begins with her arrival in Halifax. Truffaut inserts the shot where he does to mark the end of Adele's fruitless quest and the beginning of her descent into madness. If the shot had appeared at the opening, it would simply have been a prologue. Appearing where it does, it has the force of dramatic irony: Adele did make a journey from the Old World to the New, but it was also a journey from one form of neurotic behavior (obsession) to another (self-inflicted degradation). At the very end of the film, Truffaut repeats the shot, this time drained of its color and looking like a faded photograph. Adele's voyage is now just an item of memorabilia.

## POINT OF VIEW

Like a novel, a film can be narrated in the first or the third person. We have already seen examples of attempts at first-person narration through a voice that sometimes weaves in and out of the film and sometimes grows silent after a brief prologue. There is a difference between first-person narration in fiction and in film. Even if a film is being narrated in the first person, it is being dramatized in the third. The "I" of a movie will deliver a brief introduction, after which the dramatized action begins and the "I" becomes a "he" or "she." In a first-person novel one is always conscious of the narrator because he or she is always saying "I." In a film one is conscious of the "I" only at the beginning and the end of the narration because everything in between is usually dramatized.

If film can narrate in the first and third persons, the same points of view that exist in fiction (omniscient author, author's implied self, etc.) should also exist in film.[1]

## Omniscient Author

In fiction the *omniscient author* tells his or her story in the third person, moving from place to place, time to time, and character to character, disclosing or concealing details at will. In film "author" has a special meaning, particularly to those who hold that the director is the author (*auteur*) of a film, or, at least, that certain directors may lay claim to that title (see chapter 9). At this point, rather than argue over who the real author of a film is—the screenwriter who creates the script or the director who re-creates it—it is simpler to speak of the "omniscient camera."

There is always one more character in a film than is listed in the credits: the camera. When the camera is omniscient, it behaves very much like an omniscient author. The camera in Robert Altman's *Nashville* (1975) is omniscient. It can leave a freeway crack-up and move on to a hospital to look in on country singer Barbara Jean, who is recovering from one of her breakdowns. It can abandon the Reese home for a local tavern, a nightclub for a smoker, a church for an automobile graveyard.

Omniscient authors can be intrusive if they pass judgment on what is seen, unintrusive if they suspend it; similarly it is incorrect to assume that the camera is always impartial. In John Schlesinger's *The Day of the Locust* (1975), Homer Simpson (Donald Sutherland) is sitting in a wicker chair in the backyard of his Hollywood home. An orange drops from a bough with the sound of ripe fruit. In the yard above his, a woman looks down on this scene of otherworldly tranquillity. There is ripeness in her face, but it is the ripeness of fruit bursting with rot. The camera has said nothing, but by moving from Homer to the crone, it makes its own comment on Hollywood as the earthly paradise for those who embalm themselves in the glow of an endless summer and those who decompose in it.

Instead of traveling back and forth among their characters, authors can select one of them as a "center of consciousness," to use Henry James's phrase, or as a "reflector" through whose eyes readers will view the action. In film the reflector method works well when the script involves a character trapped by his or her fantasies or victimized by some neurosis. Don (Ray Milland) in Billy Wilder's *The Lost Weekend* (1945) is a genuine reflector. Without relying on bizarre camera angles or totally subjective camera techniques, Wilder draws us into the consciousness of an alcoholic. We share his experiences even when they are portrayed objectively, as they often are. Early in the film there is a scene in which Don is watching *La Traviata* and develops an uncontrollable urge to drink during the first-act "Drinking Song." Wilder cuts from Don to the stage where Violetta and Alfredo are toasting each other and back again to Don, who sees, superimposed against the stage, the checkroom where his raincoat is hanging, a bottle in one of the pockets. We clearly understand his craving.

## The Implied Author (Author's Second Self)

There is some fiction that is so impersonally written that it appears to be authorless. Hemingway's "The Killers" is often cited as the kind of story that seems to have been written by a vivisectionist rather than a novelist. In "The Killers" Hemingway obliterated his actual self and created a second self who mediates between Ernest Hemingway and the story that bears his name. Film makers can do likewise; they can suppress or mask their personal feelings so that they do not interfere with the film. This *implied author* method usually results in an impersonal movie that never achieves the gut level intensity of a *Serpico* because it does not encourage emotional involvement.

*Barry Lyndon* (1975) is such a film. First, it is Stanley Kubrick's *Barry Lyndon*, not William Makepeace Thackeray's; and it is Kubrick's film completely: He not only produced and directed it but he also wrote the screenplay. To say that Kubrick remains aloof from his characters is not the same as saying that he shuns them. The implied author approach is not emotional evasion; it is emotional noninvolvement. Kubrick was more interested in the characters as embodiments of their age than in the characters as human beings.

In adapting *Barry Lyndon* for the screen, Kubrick was dealing with a novel that was written in the nineteenth century but set in

6–1   *The famous* Barry Lyndon *candlelight. All the candlelight scenes were photographed with a special Zeiss lens and completely with natural light. Courtesy Warner Bros. Inc., copyright © 1975.*

the eighteenth century. Thus the tone had to be Victorian and the atmosphere neoclassical. Kubrick achieved an eighteenth-century air by framing scenes in the style of painters of that era—Watteau, Dayes, and Gainsborough—and by orchestrating them with selections from Bach, Handel, Vivaldi, and Mozart. He re-created Victorian detachment by using an off-camera narrator whose voice was fittingly snobbish.

Seeing *Barry Lyndon* is like viewing a painting. A great painting draws a viewer toward it; but once face to face with it, the viewer instinctively walks backward to see it from a distance. Kubrick uses the same technique. He begins with a close-up; he then gracefully withdraws until he is satisfied with the distance he has put between the audience and the image. *Barry Lyndon* is like a tour of the world's great museums. The glow of candlelight is not the smoky haze it usually is in most films; specially created lenses give the candlelight in *Barry Lyndon* the look of melting gold. Light floods a window, not in neat spotlighting cones but in a burst of silver. To achieve such beauty, Kubrick had to sacrifice a certain amount of emotion. However, when a novelist or a film maker discards his real self for a second self, there is bound to be some loss of feeling.

## The Narrator-Agent

As opposed to the mere observer, the *narrator-agent* participates in the events he or she is relating. In fiction the narrator-agent need not simply be an "I" like Nick Carraway in F. Scott Fitzgerald's *The Great Gatsby*; there are also third-person narrator-agents like Paul Morel in D. H. Lawrence's *Sons and Lovers*, who is so much a part of the action that we begin to think of him as an "I."

In film there are also first-person and third-person narrator-agents. A first-person narrator-agent can be a character recalling his or her youth, like Huw in John Ford's *How Green Was My Valley* (1941). The first-person narrator-agent method works well in films requiring several such narrators, who then become reflectors. In Joseph L. Mankiewicz's *All about Eve* (1950) and Vincente Minnelli's *The Bad and the Beautiful* (1952), various characters recall a person who played a vital role in their lives—a scheming actress and an unscrupulous film maker respectively—and who also appears in the movie. Thus we not only get the subjectivity of first-person narration but also the objectivity of multiple points of view.

There are also third-person narrator-agents in film. In King Vidor's *Stella Dallas* (1937), the heroine's actions shape the course of events to such an extent that the film becomes *her* story; in Billy Wilder's *The Big Carnival* (or *Ace in the Hole*, 1951), a reporter concocts a news story that alters the course of everyone's destiny including his own.

## The Self-Conscious Narrator

Self-conscious narrators are aware of themselves as storytellers or as artists and often remind the audience of the labors involved in being creative. Although self-awareness seems to be a first-person trait, self-conscious narrators need not speak in the first person. Just as there are third-person narrator-agents, there are also third-person self-conscious narrators. Federico Fellini's *8½* (1963) is an extremely personal film, but it is not a first-person narrative. Fellini is grappling with such questions as the extent to which directors put themselves and their lives into their work and the possibility that in film there is no distinction between illusion and reality, only varying degrees of illusion. The narrator of *8½* is Guido's (Marcello Mastroianni's) consciousness in the broadest sense: his complete inner life, including sense perceptions, memories, fantasies, conscious thoughts, and unconscious associations.

Throughout the film Fellini stays within Guido's consciousness, but there is a difference between Guido and his creator: Guido could not complete his film although Fellini completed $8\frac{1}{2}$.

Directors can be self-conscious narrators if they turn their films into commentaries on the complexities of their profession, as Fellini did in $8\frac{1}{2}$. The result is a film about film the way André Gide's The Counterfeiters (1926) is a novel about fiction. Directors can also be self-conscious narrators if they appear in their own films either as characters or as themselves. Some directors have directed themselves—Jean Renoir in The Rules of the Game (1939), Welles in Citizen Kane and others, Laurence Olivier in Henry V (1944) and Hamlet (1948)—but these particular films are not about film making and thus do not represent self-conscious narration. François Truffaut's Day for Night (1973) does, for the director plays a character in his own film, which is also about the making of a film. Truffaut appears as Ferrand, the director of an American-backed movie entitled Meet Pamela. Certain movies exude a warmth as if they were conceived by an act of love. This is precisely the case with Day for Night, a movie about movies—from the dedication to Lillian and Dorothy Gish to the scene where Ferrand dreams he is a child stealing stills from Citizen Kane. We forget Day for Night is Truffaut's creation; instead it becomes a tribute to the art of film made by a man who is deliriously in love with his profession.*

## Reliable and Unreliable Narrators

In The Rhetoric of Fiction Wayne C. Booth distinguishes between reliable and unreliable narrators in a way that has nothing to do with their veracity. A narrator is reliable "when he speaks for or acts in accordance with the norms of the work (which is to say, the implied author's norms), unreliable when he does not."[2] Again, this kind of narration is not limited to first-person accounts; a third-person reflector can also be a narrator, and his or her vision may mirror the norms of the film or obscure them.

As examples of third-person reliable and unreliable narrators, let us consider the ones we used of third-person narrator-agents. Stella Dallas is a reliable narrator because she reflects the cardinal

*Another example of a film about the making of a film is Contempt (1964), which Jean-Luc Godard directed and in which he appears as himself, playing the assistant director of a film version of Homer's Odyssey to be directed by Fritz Lang, who also plays himself.

virtue the film extols: a mother's selfless love for her daughter. In contrast, the reporter in Wilder's *The Big Carnival* is unreliable because he typifies the opportunism that the film condemns.

Thackeray's *Barry Lyndon* is a first-person novel, but Barry is hardly a reliable narrator. In fact, he is such an odious braggart that he is doubly unreliable: Not only does his narration inspire little confidence in the reader but his morals are neither those of the implied author nor of the actual author. Kubrick's *Barry Lyndon*, on the other hand, is a third-person film with an off-camera narrator who is quite reliable. His narration—tasteful, discreet, witty—is in keeping with the film's style.

Alex (Malcolm McDowell) of Kubrick's *A Clockwork Orange* (1971) is thoroughly unreliable. His pastimes (rape, mugging, murder, using Beethoven to feed his violent urges) are at odds with Kubrick's real and authorial selves; but more significantly, what Alex represents is not what the film is about. Alex is the incarnation of original sin; the film is the reincarnation of original sin with all the beauty and terror that Dante gave it in the *Inferno*. Alex only embodies one idea in the film: the impossibility of eradicating the human inclination toward evil. Kubrick dramatizes this inclination and even orchestrates it with music from Rossini, Beethoven, and Purcell in such a way that the violence assumes a bizarre kind of beauty like the transformations in Canto XXV of the *Inferno* where the thieves undergo a continual change from lizards to men. There is more in *A Clockwork Orange* than a thug like Alex can understand or appreciate. What Alex does not know, Kubrick does with a frightening clarity: free will is a paradox. It is indispensable to human beings, and any attempt to diminish it, even if it succeeds in conditioning the basest of human beings against violence, must be resisted. For a murderer conditioned against murder is no longer free and therefore no longer human.

"Film has nothing to do with literature," Ingmar Bergman claimed.[3] Bergman's argument—that film as a visual medium appeals directly to the imagination while literature as a verbal medium appeals to the intellect—can be refuted by the intellectual nature of Bergman's own work. Actually, the narrative film has much to do with literature. The various narrative forms (epic, drama, the short story, the novel, the opera libretto) share the same techniques: prologues, flashbacks, foreshadowing, authorial omniscience, point of view, and so forth. When a film maker uses these narrative devices, he is a storyteller drawing upon time-honored techniques to bring his story to the screen.

# NOTES

[1]The terms used throughout the rest of this chapter (author's implied self, self-conscious narrator, reliable narrator, etc.) come from Wayne C. Booth, *The Rhetoric of Fiction* (Chicago: University of Chicago Press, 1961).

[2]Ibid., pp. 158-59.

[3]Ingmar Bergman, "Film Has Nothing To Do with Literature," in *Film: A Montage of Theories*, ed. Richard Dyer MacCann (New York: E. P. Dutton & Co., 1966), p. 144.

# 7
# The Film Subtext

## PLOT (TEXT) AND SUBTEXT

Storytelling is an ancient art that many of us take for granted. Because almost every work of fiction tells a story, we often reply, when asked for the plot of a particular work, with a synopsis of the story line. However, as a critical term, plot is not a summary of the narrative. Plot has had many definitions but none better than Aristotle's in the *Poetics:* "Plot is the structure of the events." Note that he does not call it the story line, as many would, but the *shape* of the story line and the *form* it takes when it becomes a work of fiction.

To Aristotle the plot is the soul of the work—the source of its life. Remove the plot from a work of fiction and it ceases to be a work of fiction. Soul is structure; it is the harmony that exists when all the parts work together. Once plot is understood as the nucleus around which the incidents, the characters, the theme, and the setting gather, and the source from which they draw their life, it then can be perceived as the soul of the work and something quite distinct from the story line, which is a bodily part.

The total work consists of a text and a subtext. The *text* is the plot in the Aristotelian sense of the word, the order and arrangement of the incidents, their narrative structure, and the form that structure takes, which may be pyramidal if the events move forward and upward, or circular if they do not mount steadily toward a climax but merely repeat the same pattern. However, great literature is not one dimensional; there is also the *subtext*, the complex structure beneath the text comprising the various associations the text evokes in us.

An example of text and subtext should clarify the distinction. In Petronius' fragmentary novel, the *Satyricon*, there is the famous Milesian tale known as "The Widow of Ephesus." A woman is so shattered by her husband's death that none of the usual rites of mourning—breast beating or hair tearing—appeal to her. Instead, accompanied by her maid, she retires to the underground tomb where the body lies. A soldier, patrolling a crucifixion site nearby to prevent the bodies from being taken down from the crosses, notices her presence, gains access to the tomb, quotes Virgil to her, and finally wins her. When a corpse disappears from one of the crosses, the soldier fears his negligence will cost him his job. But after three consecutive nights of love-making, the widow of Ephesus offers him her husband's body as fair exchange.

Petronius created the text of the story by devising a situation (a widow in mourning), complicating it (the appearance of the soldier), and resolving it (the substitution of the husband's body for the criminal's). The subtext evokes certain feelings and associations in us. If we know that Petronius lived during the reign of Nero, we may place the story in the context of the decadence of imperial Rome. We may find "The Widow of Ephesus" a perverse joke, not an amusing vignette. The text is witty, but the subtext is cynical. The moral of the text is that love conquers all, but the subtext leaves the impression that love conquers lovers, reducing them to lunatics who apparently think nothing of sleeping three nights in a row next to a corpse.

A film also has a text and a subtext, an outer and an inner world. Whether or not we realize it, film has a dual nature: There is the film projected *on* the screen and the film projected *from* the screen. The first is the text—the collaboration between a director, a screenwriter, a cast, and a crew; the second is the subtext—the harmonization of the text and the associations it evokes in us. Since the text of any narrative is more readily understood than the subtext, this chapter will concentrate on the film subtext and the four main ways a film can bring the viewer into its inner world: through myths, visual associations, intellectual associations, and music.

## MYTHIC ASSOCIATIONS

### The Nature of Myth

To understand how myth is part of a film's subtext we must rid ourselves of the popular notion of myth as falsehood. Although myth is usually identified as falsehood in the popular mind, in film and literary criticism, it has another meaning altogether. William York Tindall defined myth as "a dreamlike narrative in which the individual's central concerns are united with society, time, and the universe."[1] Erich Fromm called myth "a message from ourselves to ourselves";[2] Parker Tyler regarded myth as "a free, unharnessed fiction, a basic prototypic pattern capable of many variations and distortions, even though it remains imaginative truth."[3]

Myths are ultimate truths about life and death, fate and nature, God and man. Thus myths can never be false; they endure long after the civilizations that produce them vanish because they crystallize in narrative form unchanging patterns of human behavior. Although the Greek deities no longer command belief, they have taken other forms. Wherever there are the sworn virgin and the youth who weakens her resistance, there are Diana and Endymion; whenever a society is polarized between reason and emotion, it is reenacting the eternal conflict between Apollo, who embodies the powers of reason and order, and Dionysus, who represents the life forces of creativity and anarchy.

Film is receptive to myth for two reasons. First, film and myth can speak the same language—picture language, not words; images, not arbitrary vocal symbols. Myth was originally a tale told, not read. Long before the advent of writing, myths were transmitted orally through epics and visually through artwork on walls, vases, bowls, and wine vessels. Thus from the very outset myth was oral and visual; and so was film, for even during the silent period there was generally some form of sound, as we have seen. Another reason why film and myth are so compatible is that both are intimately associated with the dream. The dream was the first form in which the myths made their appearance, and as Parker Tyler has noted, film is a kind of "daylight dream."[4] We dream individually, but we also dream collectively. The stuff of our dreams is the stuff of fairy tales, legends, and romances: quests, evil enchanters, enchanted princes and princesses, talking animals, transformations of men into beasts and ugly ducklings into golden girls. This dream material belongs to the human race, and thus our dreams make us one with humankind. Psychologist Carl Jung compared the dream to a screen on which the history of the race is projected. World literature and world cinema abound in works about heroes and villains, maidens and sorceresses, scapegoats and questers. When these figures appear in literature or in film, they strike a responsive chord in us: They are familiar because we have encountered them earlier—in our dreams.

Film has a dream level to which we respond the way we respond to myths—instinctively, never questioning their origins or even their existence. Making a mythic association involves remembering a pattern of experience that is universal. Sometimes we can determine the specific myth that is operating in the film; but often these unchanging truths are difficult to isolate except as archetypal themes (death/rebirth, the return of the hero, the descent to the underworld, etc.).

## Mythic Analysis of Shane

Every critic who has written about George Stevens's *Shane* (1953) has sensed a mythic subtext in the film. In *Shane* there appear to be at least three mythic levels.

### Shane as a Christ Figure

*Shane* begins with the credits, with Alan Ladd as Shane entering on horseback from the left to the "Shane theme," a melody suggesting cantering horses and deer drinking peacefully from a stream against a background of snow-decked mountains. Shane is descending into a valley; he is not moving horizontally across the frame like a gunfighter, although he will later change both speed and direction during his ride of vengeance. But for the moment he is moving *downward*—in symbolic terms, he might be said to be lowering himself—as he descends into the lives of the Starretts, a family of homesteaders.

Shane is a Christ figure. Just as Christ descended from heaven and humbled himself by assuming a human nature, Shane descends into the valley, temporarily putting aside his divinity to serve humanity. The resemblance of Shane to Christ has been noted by critic Donald Richie:

> Shane . . . came from nowhere and he is going nowhere—like the vagrant Jett Rink in *Giant,* like the hitchhiking George Eastman [in Stevens's *A Place in the Sun*], like Jesus Christ. . . . His difference from the romantic hero is that he—like Christ himself—rather than merely feeling that he ought to do something to express his inner values and to affect the world, actually does something about it.[5]

Shane's past is as enigmatic as Christ's. Before he began his public ministry at thirty, Christ's life was a mystery. And so is Shane's; Shane simply appears one day looking like a god in white buckskins. As part of his ritual incarnation, he sheds his divine trappings and dresses in the clothes of mortals—blue denim and dark trousers. But he will not retain that outfit forever. Before he avenges the death of Torrey (Elisha Cook, Jr.), he changes back to his buckskins, becoming a god once more.

Jesus Christ preached meekness: "If someone strike thee on the right cheek, turn to him the other also" (Matt. 5:40). Shane displays his meekness when Chris (Ben Johnson) challenges his manhood after Shane orders a bottle of soda pop for young Joey Starrett. Chris offers Shane a "man's drink" by spilling a jigger of whiskey on his shirt. At that moment Shane does not retaliate; but later when he returns to the saloon, he reciprocates by buying Chris a drink and disposing of its contents in the same way. In the ensuing brawl the abandon with which Shane swings his fists suggests a god of wrath, not unlike the Christ who overturned the tables of the moneychangers as he drove them out of the Temple of Jerusalem. Meekness and righteous anger are not incompatible in a Christ figure.

Shane's message is for the chosen: It is for the homesteaders, not for the cattlemen. Sometimes, as history has proved, the chosen people must take up arms. Thus Shane teaches young Joey how to shoot. When Marion Starrett (Jean Arthur) finds Shane teaching her son how to handle a gun, Shane's explanation is simple: "A gun is as good or bad as the man using it." Joey, who has a child's notion of manhood (men do not flinch when turpentine is applied to an open wound, and they settle disagreements with their fists), is given a rare opportunity to see his theory of manhood put to the test when he watches Shane kill Wilson (Jack Palance), the gunfighter. Shane leaves Joey with the

7-1    *Shane's farewell to Joey in George Stevens's* Shane *(1953). Shane (Alan Ladd) leaves Joey (Brandon de Wilde) with the command to grow up "strong and straight" as he departs, presumably to aid another family of homesteaders. Copyright © 1952 by Paramount Pictures Corporation. All rights reserved.*

command to grow up "strong and straight." Now Shane is no longer a man but a god delivering one of his commandments before he disappears from view.

### Shane as Apollo-Hercules

One writer has called Shane "the frontier Christ, coming down from a Western Olympus."[6] This description characterizes Shane as part Christ, part Greek deity.

In Greek mythology Zeus punished Apollo for killing one of his sons by forcing him to spend a year of servitude in the household of Admetus, the King of Thessaly. Admetus respected Apollo's godhead, and in gratitude Apollo allowed him the privilege of living beyond his allotted time, provided he could find someone to die for him. Unable to find a volunteer, Admetus turned to his wife Alcestis, who agreed. During the funeral Hercules stopped off at the palace on one of his labors, learned what had happened, wrestled with Death, and restored (or so the legend goes, although Euripides' *Alcestis* is intentionally vague on this point) Alcestis to her husband.

Although Shane's golden hair is a good metaphor for Apollo's radiance, Shane is as much of a Hercules as he is an Apollo. Shane's power of endurance is Herculean; in one scene a stubborn tree trunk is uprooted, a task that required Shane's perseverance as well as Starrett's brawn. Two themes are common to both *Shane* and the Greek myth: a god's bondage in a mortal's household in expiation for a crime and a god's saving a mortal's life. As we have seen, Shane's life is a mystery, yet from the way he draws when little Joey Starrett clicks the trigger of his unloaded rifle, he seems to be an ex-gunslinger. The fact that he humbles himself through voluntary servitude suggests that he is atoning for his past.

Just as Apollo served the family of Admetus, Shane serves the Starretts; just as Hercules restored Alcestis to her husband, Shane restores Starrett to his wife. Instead of allowing Starrett to kill Wilson (and lose his life in the bargain), Shane knocks him unconscious and goes in his place, thus augmenting Starrett's lifespan and saving him for Marion and Joey.

### Shane as Knight Errant

According to André Barzin the subtext also encourages us to think of Shane as a "knight errant in search of his grail," pursuing the ideals of courtly love in the American West.[7] While it is Starrett whom Shane aids, it is Marion whom he serves. But in the courtly love tradition the knight not only served the lady, but tried to emulate her gentleness and thus acquire some for himself to offset his rough ways. Physically, there is a great resemblance between Shane and Marion. Both have golden hair, blue eyes, and a diminutiveness that suggests a gentle heart, not a natural failing. It is significant that Shane chooses to wear blue, one of the lady's favorite colors. However, the medieval knight was a living ambiguity, for the lady he honored as the embodiment of natural perfection was frequently the unsatisfied married woman he took to his bed.

Here the analogies cease; the closest Shane comes to Marion is dancing the Varsouviana and shaking her hand in a farewell gesture. Yet *Shane* is a magnificently subtle film. When Marion is tucking Joey into bed, we hear his voice from behind the closed door: "Mother, I just love Shane." Goodnights are exchanged; Marion enters the bedroom where her husband is and Shane retires to the barn. "Goodnight, Shane," Joey calls , but there is no answer. A

7–2 *Chuck Tatum (Kirk Douglas) of Billy Wilder's* The Big Carnival (Ace in the Hole, *1951) unearthing his story. Tatum allows cave-in victim Leo Minosa (Richard Benedict) to remain entombed longer than necessary so he can win fame as a reporter. Courtesy Billy Wilder. Copyright © 1951 by Paramount Pictures Corporation. All rights reserved.*

declaration of love has taken place, shared by mother and son, but in different ways. Marion's graceful entrance into the bedroom is neither slinking nor erotic but willowy and feminine. She may be retiring to her husband's bed, but she is clearly thinking of Shane.

The subtext of *Shane* reveals a hero of many faces, only three of which have been explored here. His other faces manifest themselves as viewers superimpose the heroes and demigods of their own culture on him and discover that he can accommodate their features also. No single interpretation can exhaust the film, for myth is inexhaustible.

## The Genesis Myth in The Big Carnival

In Billy Wilder's *The Big Carnival* (or *Ace in the Hole*, 1951) an unscrupulous reporter deliberately allows the victim of a cave-in to remain entombed for a longer period of time than necessary so that he can cover the rescue operations. Chuck Tatum (Kirk Douglas) is en route to cover a rattlesnake hunt when the victim's wife (Jan Sterling) informs him of the cave-in. Sensing a story, he accompanies her to the site of the cave-in, where he strikes up a friendship with Leo, the entombed man, promising to immortalize him in print. Tatum never gets to the rattlesnake hunt, but in a perverse way the rattlesnakes come to him in the form of the pet rattler of the local sheriff, who carries it around in a cardboard box. Tatum convinces the sheriff that a dramatic rescue would insure his reelection. As the pact is ratified across a table where a snake moves restlessly in its box, it suddenly becomes clear what Wilder is doing: He is using as the film's subtext one of the oldest myths known to man—the lost paradise, the Eden infiltrated by the evil serpent. We are back in an archetypal garden, here a New Mexico desert community, where an innocent Adam lies transfixed in a cave, his Eve bites into an apple as if she were glorying in the taste of forbidden fruit (an unforgettable shot), and a serpent's coils vibrate against cardboard.

The film then becomes an inversion of the book of *Genesis*, complete with a parody of the six days of creation. Had the rescue operations taken place as planned, Leo would have been freed in sixteen hours. But he cannot last the week. A priest administers the last rites; a host is placed on the end of a long-handled device, which resembles a serpent creeping toward the dying communicant. Leo succumbs on the sixth day, his death bringing the grotesque parody of the creation myth to a close as the shadow of a snake passes across his resigned face. The desert is still; presumably the seventh day will be one of rest.

## VISUAL ASSOCIATIONS

### Typecasting

Proper casting is so important to a film that a different actor in a key role can create a different subtext. Consider the original choices for the following films: Judy Garland for the title role of George Sidney's *Annie Get Your Gun* (1950), which was finally played by Betty Hutton; Claudette Colbert as Margo Channing in Joseph L. Mankiewicz's *All about Eve* (1950); which revitalized Bette Davis's career; George Raft for Roy Earle in Raoul Walsh's *High Sierra* (1941), which went to Humphrey Bogart because Raft refused to appear in a film where he had to die.

George Raft could never have suggested that drive for freedom that propelled Earle to the summit from which he fell. *High Sierra* is a film about existential freedom—the freedom to which a human being is condemned, as Jean-Paul Sartre would say. That Bogart became the cult hero of the alienated 1960s was not surprising because he usually played an existential hero living

7–3 *The Actual and Intended Stars of Raoul Walsh's* High Sierra *(1941):*

7–3A *Humphrey Bogart, who played Roy Earle in* High Sierra. *Courtesy United Artists.*

7–3B *George Raft, who was slated for the part but refused to accept a role where he had to die. Courtesy United Artists.*

in the present, striving for freedom, and performing meaningful actions to achieve it—financing an operation for a girl with a club foot (*High Sierra*), helping a young husband win enough at roulette to buy visas for himself and his wife (Michael Curtiz's *Casablanca*, 1943), even putting a spiritually lost intellectual out of his misery with a bullet (Archie Mayo's *The Petrified Forest*, 1936). At the end of *High Sierra*, when Earle lies dead at the foot of the mountain, Marie (Ida Lupino) asks Healy (Jerome Cowan), "Mister, what does it mean when a man 'crashes out'?" "That's a funny question for you to ask, sister," Healy replies. "It means he's free." "Free," Marie says as she walks triumphantly into the frame, knowing that Earle has won his freedom—and his essence—through death.

7-4   *Al Pacino as Frank Serpico (Sidney Lumet's* Serpico, *1973), one of the few visually acceptable Christ figures in film. Copyright © 1973 by Produzioni De Laurentiis Inter. Ma. Co. S. p. A Rome. All rights reserved.*

The existential implications of "crashing out" would have eluded Raft; Bogart understood them and embodied them in his performance, thus giving the film its existential character. Even Bogart's face was extraordinary and fittingly existential. It was not a neighborhood face, nor was it especially handsome. It was a face that knew the mixed blessings of life; a face that did not slacken with age but grew tauter, the eyes retreating into their sockets until by the end of his career they had settled into omniscience.

### Al Pacino as Serpico

When Sidney Lumet's *Serpico* opened in 1973 several critics noted a resemblance between Al Pacino, who interpreted the title role magnificently, and the pop art pictures of Jesus Christ. Critic Vincent Canby of *The New York Times* also compared Pacino with St. Francis of Assisi. All sensed that there was more to Pacino's Serpico than just great acting; behind his Serpico they saw either a god-man doomed to suffer for his love of humanity or a saint who resisted the attempts of the religious establishment to interfere with his mission.

It was not merely Al Pacino's beard, his mesmeric eyes, or his uncontrollable rage at corruption that caused the critics to think of Jesus Christ. Certain details of Serpico's life also recalled similar details in Christ's; thus the text (Serpico) is coordinated with the

*7–5   Irena (Simone Simon) and her husband in name only (Kent Smith) in Jacques Tourneur's* Cat People *(1942). Note how sexually ambiguous Simone Simon appears. Courtesy Museum of Modern Art/Film Stills Archive and RKO.*

subtext (Christ), and both come together in the person of the star (Pacino). This coincidence does not occur with every movie-hero policeman or every actor. The identification of Christ with Serpico (a cop who found his apostolate on the streets and underwent the traditional scapegoat cycle of harassment, betrayal, and desertion) was visualized in Pacino's performance in a way in which it was not visualized in the performance of Stacy Keach in Richard Fleischer's *The New Centurions* (1972) or of Elliott Gould in Peter Hyams's *Busting* (1974)—both "hero cop" films with idealistic protagonists.

### Simone Simon in Cat People

The horror films Val Lewton produced at RKO in the 1940s are singled out today for serious consideration because they represent an exotic, and for their time advanced, kind of subtext.[8] In *Cat People* (1942) the casting of Simone Simon as the cat-obsessed Irena led to various interpretations of the film, each of which has some validity. The script tells of an Irena who is the ill-starred descendant of a Serbian cat cult. The visuals go much further; they tell of an Irena repelled by sex because she refuses to unleash the animal (or feline) part of her nature; an Irena who wants a man as a friend, not as a lover, and who registers disgust whenever her husband tries to touch her.

Because of Simon's performance, some critics also saw Irena as a repressed lesbian whose animal nature was roused to anger by the male, to passion by the female. While such an interpretation may seem unwarranted, it can be justified by the visuals, particularly the episodes where Irena stalks her rival through Central Park and follows her down the stairs to the swimming pool of a women's residence club. If *Cat People* were a novel, two such interpretations—repressed heterosexuality and repressed lesbianism—would imply that either the author could not make up his mind about his character or else that he fell victim to the fallacy that a nervous bride is a latent lesbian. But film, like myth, is similar to the dream where opposites are compatible: A beautiful face can dissolve into a skull, a prince into a wizard, a princess into a witch, or one gender into another.

Simone Simon had the appearance of a dream figure, and dream figures are never stable; they can be alternately sensuous and sexless. When she was cast in a film with ambiguous sexual overtones, she brought them to the surface, thereby activating the subtext, which in *Cat People* catalogued the various forms sexual repression could take (antipathy to men, tormenting of women, a self-administered penance in a scalding bath)—all rather daring for a movie of the 1940s.

## Jack Nicholson and Louise Fletcher in One Flew over the Cuckoo's Nest

The impression made by an actor's performance is based on many factors, including such seemingly irrelevant details as hairstyle and wardrobe. Yet it is through such details that film makers realize their intentions; it is also through such details that we see in characters what directors want us to see.

When Miloš Forman was about to direct *One Flew over the Cuckoo's Nest* (1975), he was faced with the task of making a movie out of a cult book of the 1960s. During the last few years of that decade, Ken Kesey's novel seemed a tragically accurate mirror of America. The animosity between Randle P. McMurphy and Big Nurse paralleled similar confrontations between the pacifist and

7–6A   Nurse Ratched (Louise Fletcher) and Randle McMurphy (Jack Nicholson) in Miloš Forman's One Flew over the Cuckoo's Nest (1976). Louise Fletcher's hairstyle is a throwback to the 1940s. Copyright Fantasy Films and United Artists Corp.

7–6B   Sheila Ryan in an authentic 1940s hairdo. Courtesy Twentieth-Century-Fox.

his draft board, the militant Students for a Democratic Society and the police, the student activists and the campus administration.

However, in 1975 Vietnam was a memory, the draft was in abeyance, and campuses were quiet. To make the film meaningful, Forman had to deemphasize all the political overtones the novel had acquired in the 1960s. The film's text emphasized the humanism and comedy of Kesey's novel; the subtext transformed the conflict between McMurphy (Jack Nicholson) and Nurse Ratched (Louise Fletcher) into a battle between man and woman. Forman capitalized on Nicholson's exposed and often vulnerable masculinity, but he also saw more in it than locker room bravado. There is an impishness about Nicholson; at times he seems to be putting us on, challenging us to make the hackneyed connection between a man's height (Nicholson is not tall) and a man's ego. Little details about Nicholson's portrayal of McMurphy suggest the imp: the cap pulled down over the ears, the hornlike tuft of hair that gives the impression of a satyr, the eyes that dart from one direction to another as if they too were free spirits.

Although the time of the film is the 1960s, Louise Fletcher's hairstyle came out of an entirely different era. Forman had her wear her hair the way career women did in the "lady executive" movies of the 1940s. If Nurse Ratched looks like an anachronism, that is what she is supposed to be: Boss Lady masking her contempt for men under the guise of professionalism, the way the heroines of movies like Mitchell Leisen's *Take a Letter, Darling* (1942) or Alexander Hall's *They All Kissed the Bride* (1942) did when they were the executives and men were their subordinates.

## The Associative Cut

It is not enough simply to shoot a film; there are images that stand behind the words, images that must interact if the movie is to be more than photographed theater. A film maker who understands picture language will allow the pictures behind the words to form a subtext that will deepen and enrich the text.

In Luis Buñuel's *Viridiana* (1961), a novice takes a leave of absence from a convent to visit her uncle, Don Jaime, whose sexual neuroses she is too naive to understand. Her life is haunted by reminders of Christ's crucifixion: a crown of thorns, a sponge, nails, and a hammer. When Don Jaime commits suicide, Viridiana's cloistered world is challenged by her cousin Renaldo, whose commitment is to the practical, not the speculative; to the natural, not the symbolic.

Buñuel is far too subtle a director for the anti-Catholic tag he has received; his is the Catholicism of reform and transformation, and thus his admission that he would have preferred to live in the Middle Ages was not said in jest. When Buñuel cuts from a crown of thorns to a cow's udder, from men surveying land to a dog dragged behind a wagon, *Viridiana* ceases being a polemic against Roman Catholicism and becomes a plea for communism in Roman Catholic countries. The text depicts a society too embroiled in its perversions to change; the subtext argues for change, encouraging the unconscious to replace symbols of degradation (a crown of thorns) with symbols of fulfillment (a cow's udder) and to see that private property (the estate) is acquired only through enslavement (the tied dog).

John Schlesinger's film of Nathanael West's novel, *The Day of the Locust,* also has a political subtext. West intended his novel as an anti-Hollywood tract, but it was also a subtle indictment of the political apathy that breeds moguls in the movie colony, dictators in the world at large. The 1975 film version followed a similar course. Nothing in the script's language implied there was a political dimension to the plot. Therefore, director John Schlesinger had to supply that dimension visually; he had to show a Hollywood where life is a soundstage and where reality becomes illusion and remains such even as the armies of Europe are preparing for World War II. Sometimes Schlesinger's cutting is so abrupt that it blurs the distinction between the real and the illusory. For example, he cuts from a father calling his daughter to passengers waving from a ship. At first this is puzzling until the ship is shown to be a soundstage prop whose passengers are movie extras.

The climax of the film is the brutal death of Homer Simpson (Donald Sutherland) on the night of a Hollywood premiere. Homer's death is a grim reminder of the price a nation pays when it turns inward upon its myths, where the dream is more glorious than the reality , and worships those who promise to make the dream come true. Schlesinger prepares us for the apocalypse earlier in the film with images of decay and perversity: a boy with platinum curls unsexed by his fame-hungry mother so he can look like Shirley Temple; a dead horse in a swimming pool; a death face peering into Homer's backyard; a bloody cockfight intercut with flashes of the gaudy dress Faye Greener (Karen Black) waves in front of Homer with a rhythm that matches, beat for beat, the quick jabs the roosters are giving each other.

Hollywood is an insular community that resents the intrusion of history and reality. Faye and her beaus leave a movie theater before the newsreel begins; having seen a film in which she had a bit part, Faye is uninterested in a newsreel about the rise of Hitler. On the night of the premiere a newspaper blows down Hollywood

Boulevard, its headlines announcing the advent of the Second World War. The master of ceremonies for the event is a Hitler look-alike, and the fans are the kind that would turn out for a premiere or a Nazi rally. Again Schlesinger crosscuts, this time between the premiere and the death of Homer. He is not crosscutting between illusion and reality but rather between two forms of madness as in the cockfight/swirling dress scene.

In the climax all the associations merge: political detachment, fascism, and the mob's need for a scapegoat. Adore, the androgynous child, strikes Homer in the head with a stone. In a rage Homer pursues him into a parking lot and stomps him to death. His reaction is our reaction: We want this junior hermaphrodite destroyed before it grows up into something worse. But the mob is so crazed by the sight of the gods and goddesses who sweep past them into Grauman's Chinese Theatre that it turns on Homer and tears him apart. As Tod the art designer watches in horror, he envisions the fans as zombies with death-mask faces, American grotesques mobilized to kill the destroyer of the dream.

By crosscutting between the premiere and Homer's ritual dismemberment, Schlesinger creates associations that are only implicit in the script. In the text the crowd destroys Homer because he kills Adore; in the subtext the crowd destroys Homer because he kills what Adore represents—the necessity of perverting one's nature to become a star. And if one must become dehumanized to be a star, one must do the same to worship the star; thus movie fans can be as grotesque as the objects of their worship, knocking down barricades to get a touch of mink or a piece of shirt. There is another motive for their behavior, a motive as old as the one that impelled the worshipers of Dionysus to kill the intruder who witnessed their sacred rites. Homer has wandered into a sacred ritual, the ritual of the Hollywood premiere; but Homer is also unclean from the blood of Adore. Thus the fans turn on him because he has polluted their rites and shed the blood of one of their own.

## INTELLECTUAL ASSOCIATIONS

When we make a mythic association, we are reminded of universal patterns true of all human beings at all times. When we make an intellectual association, we are reminded of something specific—of the film's relationship to its historical setting, to another work of art (e.g., a novel, a painting, a poem, or another film) or even to an earlier version of itself.

## The Film and Its Relation to History

The screwball comedy was a popular type of film in the 1930s. Screwball comedies thrived during the Depression, and their breeziness and improbably happy endings owe much to the era in which they were made. In Frank Capra's *It Happened One Night* (1934), an heiress who can never say yes to a man from her own class learns that class is no substitute for love after roughing it with a brash newspaper reporter. This kind of comedy, in which social barriers fall like the walls of Jericho, was ideal for the 1930s, when audiences delighted in seeing a socialite (Claudette Colbert) put in her place by a man who didn't even wear an undershirt (Clark Gable). *It Happened One Night* is pure fairy tale, a variation on "The Princess and the Commoner." Yet it is not a fairy tale set in legendary times, but in the early 1930s, the worst of times. The associations we bring to the film—breadlines, soup kitchens, former millionaire apple sellers—enable us to see it as a fable of the Great Depression.

Mitchell Leisen's *Easy Living* (1937) is another Depression fairy tale about the day a sable coat landed on the head of Mary Smith, an American working girl, as she was riding on the top deck of a double-decker bus. The text might be entitled "The Day Sable Fell from the Skies." The subtext reminds us that this day was not an ordinary day: It was a day in the mid-1930s in Depression America.

*Easy Living* is best remembered for the automat sequence when Mary (Jean Arthur), swathed in sable, is sitting by herself eating a beef pie, oblivious to the patrons who are fighting to get at the food that has suddenly become free. In the context of the film the scene is uproarious; in the context of Depression America it is disquieting. When the camera roams about the automat, observing the fur-clad Mary eating in the foreground while the masses are fighting in the background, it does more than record a comic free-for-all: It implies that there is a connection between a lucky lady and the luckless masses, between sable for the few and rags for the many. In a bizarre way it seems as if the presence of a woman in a sable coat precipitated the riot, an impossibility in terms of the text but not in terms of the subtext, which suggests in a way that is truly frightening what could happen if sable fell from the heavens during a depression.

## The Film and Its Relation to Other Films

Sometimes the subtext can be an x-ray of the film maker's mind. Bernardo Bertolucci's *Last Tango in Paris* (1972) is ostensibly about a woman caught between two men—one who debases her, the other who idealizes her. Bertolucci used this narrative structure to work out a theory of film that he illustrated with references to movies of the past. Thus when Pauline Kael reviewed *Last Tango*, she alluded to the film's constant "feedback"; she meant that much in the film—the performances as well as the imagery—recalled other films.

"Movies are a past we share, and, whether we recognize them or not, the copious associations are at work in the film and we feel

7-7    *Cinderella in sable (Jean Arthur) is exposed to the realities of the Great Depression in the famous automat sequence in Mitchell Leisen's* Easy Living *(1937). Courtesy MCA Publishing.*

7–8  *Jean-Pierre Léaud as Antoine Doinel in Truffaut's* The 400 Blows *(1959), perhaps the most famous of the New Wave films. Even when Léaud played Tom in Bertolucci's* Last Tango in Paris *(1973), he typified the casual, naturalistic form of acting the New Wave directors encouraged. Courtesy Janus Films. Photo courtesy Museum of Modern Art/Film Stills Archive.*

them," Kael observed.[9] As we have already seen, the way a movie is cast can create certain associations between the actor and his or her role. In *Last Tango* Marlon Brando plays Paul, an American in Paris, who meets Jeanne (Maria Schneider) when both of them show up to look at the same apartment; Jean-Pierre Léaud is Tom, the TV director and movie nut who is using Jeanne for a television film he is making. Brando and Léaud are not ordinary actors. Each epitomizes a style of acting and a type of film that revolutionized the cinema. Brando will always be synonymous with the Method, a system of acting that requires the performer to draw on his memory, utilizing past experiences and emotions to prepare for his role. Brando was the definitive Method actor of the 1950s—brooding, introspective, often even inarticulate. Léaud was the discovery of François Truffaut, who cast him as Antoine Doinel, the problem child of *The 400 Blows* (1959). Since that time, he and Truffaut have made other films: the "Antoine and Colette" episode in *Love at Twenty* (1962), *Stolen Kisses* (1968), *Bed and Board* (1970), and *Day for Night* (1973). Physically, Léaud has even begun to resemble the director. François Truffaut typifies the New Wave, that extraordinary burst of creativity that started in France at the end of the 1950s when directors such as Truffaut and Jean-Luc Godard rejected literary scripts for shooting scripts and improvisation, filmed in the streets rather than in studios, demanded naturalistic acting instead of old-fashioned emoting, and quoted liberally from the movies of the past.[10]

Just as Brando and Léaud represent two different eras of film making, the characters they portray represent two different ways of life. Paul isolates himself in the apartment where he works out his sexual aggression on Jeanne; Tom roams the streets of Paris, scouting for locations for his movie. Jeanne is trapped not just between two men but between their worlds: Paul's closed world of the apartment and Tom's open world of the city. Yet film makers are in the same predicament: Do they remain within the closed world of the studio set as their predecessors did, or do they venture outside where an entire city can be their soundstage?

What Kael calls "feedback" is not limited to the eras Brando and Léaud evoke. Bertolucci used *Last Tango* as a vehicle for his ideas on film in the same way Paul and Tom were using Jeanne for their respective purposes. Thus in the film Bertolucci invokes movies of the past that have some bearing on his own film. When Jeanne and Tom are on a barge, there is a life preserver with *L'Atalante* inscribed on it. *L'Atalante* is the title of Jean Vigo's classic film (1934), and the barge scene in *Last Tango* pays homage to Vigo's exquisite film in which a young bride leaves her barge captain-husband to experience the excitement of Paris, only to return to the secure world of the barge at the end. However, Bertolucci is also replying to Vigo's optimism: Vigo's bride can be reunited with her husband, but once Paul and Jeanne leave the apartment, no reunion is possible.

*Last Tango* is almost like a course in film history. The scene in which Paul looks out on the roofs of Paris before he dies recalls René Clair's *Sous les toits de Paris* (*Under the Roofs of Paris*, 1931), which the director made when he was thirty, the same age Bertolucci was when he made *Last Tango*. When Jeanne shoots Paul, the scene is a part not only of *Last Tango* but of all those Hollywood movies (e.g., William Wyler's *The Letter*, 1940; Michael Curtiz's *Mildred Pierce*, 1945; Irving Rapper's *Deception*, 1946, etc.) in which a woman whips out a revolver and pumps her lover full of bullets. The text of *Last Tango* may be about male-female relationships but the subtext is about the relationship between film makers and their art.

7–9A   *The trio of William Wyler's* These Three *(1936), the first film version of Lillian Hellman's* The Children's Hour: *Miriam Hopkins as Martha Dobie, Joel McCrea as Dr. Joseph Cardin, and Merle Oberon as Karen Wright. Courtesy Samuel Goldwyn Productions.*

7–9B   *The trio of Wyler's* The Children's Hour *(1962): Audrey Hepburn as Karen Wright, James Garner as Dr. Joseph Cardin, and Shirley MacLaine as Martha Dobie. The 1962 version, despite its fidelity to Lillian Hellman's play, is inferior to* These Three. *Courtesy United Artists.*

One should be careful not to associate all allusions with the film's subtext. In Robert Aldrich's *Hustle* (1975), a policeman is fascinated by the films of the 1930s as well as by John Huston's movie version of *Moby Dick* (1956), but these allusions do not make the policeman a Captain Ahab or a 1930s liberal; they merely define him as someone who is historically displaced. In Martin Scorsese's *Taxi Driver* (1976), Travis takes his date to see the hard-core flick *Sometime Sweet Susan,* which is a reflection of his taste, not a metaphor for the film.

## The Original and Its Relation to the Remake

William Wyler's *The Children's Hour* (1962) is three degrees removed from the original. First there was Lillian Hellman's 1934 play of the same name about a malicious child who accused her teachers of lesbianism. Then there was Wyler's 1936 film version, *These Three*. Since the Production Code forbade "sex perversion or any inference of it,"[11] the charge had to be changed: The girl accused the teachers of being in love not with each other, but with the same man.

If one knows Miss Hellman's play, it is possible to hear the original dialogue as it is being modified to fit the new situation. In the play when Martha confesses her love to Karen, she says, "I have loved you the way they said." In *These Three* the line becomes, "I have loved him the way they said." John Benson did much the same thing when he changed the pronouns in Shakespeare's "Sonnets to the Fair Youth" to give the impression they were written to a woman. Yet Wyler miraculously preserved the meaning of Miss Hellman's drama despite the strictures of the Code. Miriam Hopkins played Martha as if she were in love with Karen, thereby creating an antifilm within the film, a *Children's Hour* within *These Three*.

In the early sixties Wyler was able to film *The Children's Hour* as Lillian Hellman had written it; but the times had changed, and the entire venture was a mistake. Oddly enough, *These Three* was closer in tone to the original—a 1930s movie of a 1930s play—than the 1962 version, which followed the play closely but never captured its liberal spirit. Yet moviegoers who are watching *The Children's Hour* and who are also familiar with *These Three* are having an unusual experience: It is almost as if they were seeing the two films concurrently. If they know the original play, the experience is tripartite.

When we watch a movie that is a remake of one we already know, the original becomes part of the remake's subtext. Louisa May Alcott's *Little Women* was made twice—in 1933 by George Cukor and in 1949 by Mervyn LeRoy. When Jo (June Allyson) of the 1949 version jumps over the fence, we see both June Allyson and Katharine Hepburn, who played Jo in the original, hovering over her successor like a spectral presence or a TV ghost. "I've seen this before," we often say of a particular movie; quite possibly we have. Twentieth-Century-Fox was constantly remaking its musicals: To see Henry Koster's *Wabash Avenue* (1950) is to see Walter Lang's *Coney Island* (1943); Jean Negulesco's *How to Marry a Millionaire* (1953) was a remake of Bruce Humberstone's *Three Little Girls in Blue* (1946), which in turn derived from Walter Lang's *Moon over Miami* (1941). Often the time and place were changed and music added, but the situation remained the same: Raoul Walsh's

*Colorado Territory* (1949) is his *High Sierra* in a Western setting; Stuart Heisler's *I Died a Thousand Times* (1955) is *High Sierra* with Jack Palance in the Humphrey Bogart role; Charles Walters's *High Society* (1956) is George Cukor's *The Philadelphia Story* (1940) with a Cole Porter score.

There is nothing quite like watching a remake. It is like viewing both versions—one subliminally, the other directly—on a split screen.

## MUSICAL ASSOCIATIONS

Music can be part of a film's text or subtext.[12] When it belongs to the text, it is a narrative device that advances the plot. Sometimes music provides the explanation for a character's behavior. In Mitchell Leisen's *Lady in the Dark* (1944), a childhood song the heroine tries to remember is the key to her neurosis. Many a Twentieth-Century-Fox musical included the tender ballad the heroine was belting out until the hero taught her how to sing it properly ("Cuddle Up a Little Closer" in *Coney Island*; "Baby, Won't You Say You Love Me?" in the remake *Wabash Avenue*). There are also songs that drift in and out of the characters' lives, becoming *their* song and played at appropriately dramatic moments: "I Can't Begin to Tell You" in Irving Cummings's *The Dolly Sisters* (1945); "As Time Goes By" in *Casablanca*. Some movies have a classical score, usually a ballet or an opera, that catapults an unknown into stardom (Michael Powell's *The Red Shoes*, 1948) or notoriety (the synthetic opera *Salammbô* in Orson Welles's *Citizen Kane*, 1941). And sometimes a piece of music forms the film's climax, achieving an effect that words cannot: "Remember My Forgotten Man" in Mervyn LeRoy's *Gold Diggers of 1933*, George Gershwin's Concerto in F in Irving Rapper's *Rhapsody in Blue* (1945), the title ballet in Vincente Minnelli's *An American in Paris* (1951).

Music has even more functions in the subtext. It can be used as adjunct to the action or as leitmotif, for irony or characterization, as a means of identifying races and nationalities or as the basis for the film's structure.

### Music as an Adjunct to the Action

During the golden age of radio and film, audiences were often exposed to classical music without their even knowing it. On radio Rossini's *William Tell* Overture ushered in "The Lone Ranger";

Sibelius' "Valse Triste" introduced "I Love a Mystery," and Prokofiev's March from *Love for Three Oranges* was the theme of "The FBI in Peace and War." Before many moviegoers even knew what Rachmaninoff's Second Piano Concerto was, they had heard it as background music in David Lean's *Brief Encounter* (1946). In fact, for people who know the film, Rachmaninoff's music has such indelible associations that it never fails to evoke a dingy railroad station where two married people say good-by, never to meet again.

The Rachmaninoff concerto also figured in another vehicle of extramarital love, William Dieterle's *September Affair* (1950). Admittedly, neither *Brief Encounter* nor *September Affair* is great art, although the former has superb performances by Trevor Howard and Celia Johnson. What redeemed *Brief Encounter* was Rachmaninoff's music with its surging recklessness that speaks of romance. The music of the concerto also suggests yearning and unfulfillment; thus it was ideal for a movie about an affair that never went beyond the encounter stage. The music elevates two ordinary people to the stature of star-crossed lovers so that the audience thinks of them not as a doctor and a housewife but as the tragic Tristan and Isolde.

## Music as Leitmotif

A *leitmotif* is a recurrent musical phrase associated with a character or a concept. Since a leitmotif identifies a character, it may be considered the character's signature. The true leitmotif is inseparable from the individual with whom it is associated or the concept which it underscores; it also enjoys a kind of autonomy. A leitmotif can confirm a declaration of love, but it can also recur when the lovers are quarreling or parting, now mocking what it had approved earlier. As part of the character a leitmotif can remind the audience of what the character is feeling at a particular moment. In Hitchcock's *I Confess* (1952), when Ruth (Anne Baxter) tells her husband she does not love him, we hear the motif associated with the man she really loves.

The leitmotif can function independently of the text because it is something heard beneath the text. In the classic film scores of Erich Korngold, Max Steiner, Miklos Rosza, and other composers, the music was always played *beneath* the pitch of the actor's voice as if it were speaking in counterpoint with him. The leitmotif expresses aspects of the character that lie beyond the capability of language and below the visual level. The nursery tune that opens *Cat People* is the first indication that the movie is not an ordinary horror film. It is fitting that such a singsong motif should be Irena's signature, for she is sexually and emotionally a child.

The leitmotif also concretizes abstract themes. "Power" is an abstraction, yet Bernard Herrmann, who composed the music for *Citizen Kane*, called one of the leitmotifs in the film "Power." As a musical phrase "power" is no longer abstract because we hear it. The Power motif is heard for the first time as the camera ascends the gate of Xanadu, taking us into the pleasure dome and then to Kane's deathbed. But it is a *synesthetic* experience: We see, feel, and hear Power. We watch its calculatingly slow rise, feel the isolation it brings, and hear the grim consequences it holds for those who seek it.

There are all kinds of motifs—love motifs, death motifs, and even love-death, or *Liebestod*, motifs. At the end of King Vidor's *Duel in the Sun* (1947), which must have one of the steamiest scores ever composed,* Pearl Chavez (Jennifer Jones) crawls over sun-baked rocks to die in her lover's arms. As their blood mingles, the love motif heard when they first met seems to surge out of some chasm in the great Southwest to become their *Liebestod*.

For *The Private Life of Sherlock Holmes* (1970), Billy Wilder fashioned a love motif out of a few measures of Miklos Rosza's Concerto for Violin and Orchestra. It is a bittersweet but dignified theme expressing a yearning never to be satisfied—in this case, Holmes's love for Ilse von Hofmannstahl. When Holmes receives the news of Ilse's death, the same theme is heard, no longer an expression of unfulfilled love but of love irretrievably lost.

## Ironic Music

Like verbal irony, musical irony can be subtle or obvious. In Liliana Cavani's *The Night Porter* (1974), two inmates in a Nazi concentration camp commit sodomy to the music of Mozart's *The Magic Flute*. The impact may be emotionally devastating, but ultimately it is cheap. The idea of juxtaposing Mozart and sodomy in a death camp seems promising, but it is the kind of idea a film maker should consider briefly and then reject. For pure musical irony there is the scene in Ingmar Bergman's *Through a Glass Darkly*

---

*The film was alternately dubbed "Lust in the Dust" and a "Wagnerian Horse Opera."

*7–10   Karin (Harriet Andersson) in Ingmar Bergman's* Through a Glass Darkly *(1961) as she discovers her father is using her schizophrenia for his novel. At that moment we hear the haunting opening of* Bach's Suite No. 2 in D Minor *for violoncello. Courtesy Janus Films. Photo courtesy Museum of Modern Art/Film Stills Archive.*

(1961) when the schizophrenic daughter discovers that her father is using her sickness as material for a novel. The cello, the noblest of instruments, replies to the ignoblest of intentions.

## Music for Characterization

Music is ideal for illuminating the darker aspects of a character that even elude the visuals. In Jules Dassin's *Brute Force* (1947), Munsey (Hume Cronyn), a prison captain, tortures an inmate to the Venusberg music from Wagner's *Tannhäuser*. An unusually small man, Munsey performs a ritual before the torture: Shirtless, he struts around with his chest sucked in behind a skin-tight undershirt. That the captain is a homoerotic sadist is evident, but Wagner's music, with its historical and erotic associations, characterizes him even further.

There has always been a connection between Wagner and the German Third Reich. Wagner was Hitler's favorite composer; in fact, Hitler identified with Wagner's Siegfried and maintained that anyone wishing to understand "national socialism "as his brand of fascism was termed must first understand Wagner. To Hollywood of the 1940s Wagner was the composer of the Third Reich; it is difficult to recall a movie where Nazism was not orchestrated with a Wagnerian motif. In *Brute Force* there is no escaping the fact that Munsey is a Nazi type right down to his affinity for Wagner. But more important, the music selected from *Tannhäuser* is among the most erotic Wagner ever composed. The captain uses Wagner as torture music because orchestrated torture gives him the only sexual pleasure he gets. The captain is impotent; his sexuality goes no further than his tight undershirt. Music unites his lust for power and his need for sex, neither of which he can achieve except through the degradation of others. Music does not always soothe the savage beast; it can make certain beasts more bestial.

## Music and Ethnic and National Associations

In the pre–civil rights days blacks were stereotyped both dramatically and musically. Whenever they appeared in a scene, the original musical score usually ceased and a spiritual was heard in the background, presumably because it was a fitting motif. Even in such a brilliant film as William Wyler's *The Little Foxes* (1941), the black domestics were given this kind of musical treatment, which not only identified them with their spirituals but also perpetuated the image of the Southern black as passive darkie. Music, whether it wishes to or not, equates, and a moviegoer's earliest associations are equations: "Deep River" = blacks; Rachmaninoff's Second Piano Concerto = unconsummated love. A few gongs link a character with the mysterious East, "The Volga Boatman" with Mother Russia, *"Deutschland über Alles"* with Nazi Germany. Although only the slightest references were made to the fact that the title character of Vincent Sherman's *Mr. Skeffington* (1944) was Jewish, a Semitic leitmotif said it all.

During World War II, movie music programed its audiences to patriotism. People not only saw flag wavers, they also heard Old Glory hymned on the sound track. Planes would stream across the sky to the accompaniment of "Anchors Aweigh" (Henry Hathaway's *Wing and a Prayer*, 1944) or men would march off to death to the brisk measures of "Wild Blue Yonder" (Lewis Milestone's *The Purple Heart*, 1944).

## Music as the Basis for Structure

The music in Stanley Kubrick's *A Clockwork Orange* (1971) is more than merely associative. What happens to music in Kubrick's film is what has happened to society. In *A Clockwork Orange* the social order gives way as thugs and disenchanted youths, leather boys and loafers become the citizens of the future. There is a corresponding degeneration of music; it becomes estranged from art, perverted, capable of producing effects that its composers never intended.

One of the most innocent songs ever written is "Singin' in the Rain," which conjures up the sight of Gene Kelly sloshing around without missing a tap in the 1952 musical of the same name. It is hardly the kind of song we would associate with violence, yet Alex does a soft shoe to this innocuous ditty while he brutalizes a writer and his wife.

Rape was once considered so heinous that the camera would retreat in horror as the rapist backed his victim against a wall. If there was background music at all, it was stark and chilling. However, Kubrick uses Rossini's *Thieving Magpie* Overture to accompany a rape scene. It is a giddy piece of music; on the surface it seems totally unsuited to sexual violence because it makes something gross into something ludicrous. But this is Kubrick's thesis: Rape has become ludicrous because, like everything else in an inverted world, it has become surreal.

Rimsky-Korsakov's *Scheherazade* is an exotic piece of music, lush and sensuous, the kind we might associate with a veiled seductress on a chaise longue upholstered in leopard skin. Yet this is the music we hear when Alex imagines himself as a Roman centurion lashing Christ on his way to Calvary. *Scheherazade* is one of the most pleasurable compositions ever written, and Alex would be the first to admit it. But the pleasure we receive from it is clearly not the same as he does.

Alex is also a lover of Beethoven's Ninth Symphony with its ringing affirmation of humanity in the last movement. Alex knows that such sublime music can only be the result of intense suffering. While he listens to it, on one occasion masturbating to it, Kubrick cuts to various shots of Christ, as Alex associates Christ with suffering and suffering with music. Therefore, the sublimity of music inspires us to make our fellow man suffer. "Preposterous!" we say; or, if this is so, how can the love of music be the mark of a cultivated person? It would be better to raze the concert halls and ban recordings. But in a world where good and evil have lost their meaning as moral terms, music also has no value except the value one puts on it. In such a society, it makes no difference if one rapes to the music of Rossini or masturbates to Beethoven. Yet Alex is not alone in misusing the classics; his elders have discovered an equally perverted use for the Beethoven Ninth. During his rehabilitation, Alex is forced to watch Nazi films while the last movement is played electronically.

Kubrick is one of the few directors who has been able to integrate music and screenplay so that they become inseparable. "All art constantly aspires towards the condition of music," Walter Pater wrote. If music is the most universal of the arts, it should be applicable to any situation, as Kubrick continues to show in his films.

## SUMMARY

A film has an outer and an inner world, a text and a subtext. Beneath the text that human creativity and modern technology have fashioned is the subtext with its network of associations and implications that often exist independently of the text and that, when understood, deepen our knowledge of the film.

Because what lies beneath the surface is always more intriguing than what lies above it, there is a temptation to investigate the subtext before mastering the text. However, it is important to understand the film's structure before proceeding to its substructure; we must comprehend the plot before we can go beyond it. Once this is done, we are free to seek out associations—mythic and archetypal, literary and musical—that can enhance our appreciation of the film.

## NOTES

[1]W. Y. Tindall, *James Joyce* (New York: Grove Press, 1960), p. 102.

[2]As quoted in W. Y. Tindall, *A Reader's Guide to James Joyce* (New York: Noonday Press, 1959), p. 129.

[3]Parker Tyler, *Magic and Myth of the Movies* (New York: Simon & Schuster, 1970), p. xviii.

[4]Parker Tyler, *The Hollywood Hallucination* (New York: Simon & Schuster, 1970), p. 230.

[5]Donald Richie, *George Stevens: An American Romantic* (New York: Museum of Modern Art, 1970), p. 62.

[6]Michael T. Marsden, "Savior in the Saddle: The Sagebrush Testament," in *Focus on the Western,* ed. Jack Nachbar (Englewood Cliffs, N.J.: Prentice-Hall, 1974), p. 97.

[7]André Bazin, "The Evolution of the Western," in *What Is Cinema?,* Vol. 2, trans. Hugh Gray (Berkeley: University of California Press, 1971), p. 152.

[8]For an excellent study of Lewton, see Joel E. Siegel, *Val Lewton: The Reality of Terror* (New York: Viking, 1973).

[9]Pauline Kael, "Introduction," *Bernardo Bertolucci's Last Tango in Paris: The Screenplay* (New York: Dell, 1973), p. 17.

[10]On the New Wave, see Peter Graham, ed., *The New Wave* (London: Secker and Warburg, 1968); and James Monaco, *The New Wave: Truffaut, Godard, Chabrol, Rohmer, Rivette* (New York: Oxford University Press, 1976).

[11]For the various prohibitions with which the film maker had to contend, see Benjamin B. Hampton, *History of the American Film Industry* (New York: Dover, 1970), pp. 300–302.

[12]On movie music, see James L. Limbacher, *Film Music: From Violins to Video* (Metuchen, N.J.: Scarecrow Press, 1974); and Thomas Maremaa, "The Sound of Movie Music, " *New York Times Magazine* (March 28, 1976), pp. 40, 45–50.

# 8
# Total Film

To the question "What is the essence of great film?" most of us would answer by citing our favorite movie, scene, or shot. One might claim, for example, that nothing expresses the potential of film better than the ending of Sir Carol Reed's *The Third Man* (1950), in which Anna (Alida Valli) gives Holly Martins (Joseph Cotten) the second greatest snub in history, the first being the cold shoulder Dido gave Aeneas when they met in Hades. Anna walks down a Vienna road through a drift of leaves, her face immobile, her eyes fixed on a never-ending present. Martins leans against a cart and lights a cigarette, waiting to be recognized. As the autumn leaves fall in a silent shower, Anna moves out of the frame—and out of Martins's life—without even a glance in his direction. Martins grows progressively smaller until he is nothing but a tiny figure by the side of a road, ready to disappear like the smoke from his cigarette. The ending achieves what only film can: eloquence without words. Not one line of dialogue is spoken; the zither alone speaks as it plays the famous *"Third Man* Theme" with restrained sadness, its strings quivering with loss but too proud to snap from heartbreak.

8–1 *The penultimate snub: The ending of Sir Carol Reed's* The Third Man *(1950), in which Anna (Alida Valli) walks past Martins (Joseph Cotten) without even a nod in his direction. Courtesy EMI Film Distributors Ltd.*

Someone else, of course, might argue that the ultimate in film is Isak Borg's final vision in Ingmar Bergman's *Wild Strawberries* (1957), in which Sara, his boyhood love, leads him through a meadow to a bay. Across the bay Isak sees his mother knitting while his father fishes, apparently with some success, for the rod is beginning to curve over the water. They wave at their son, and he smiles back at them. There is a sacred tranquillity about the place, the kind Homer must have had in mind when he wrote his famous description of the Isles of the Blessed (*Odyssey* IV, 565-568):

> *Where men lead a life of perfect ease.*
> *Snow does not fall there, nor does rain or sleet.*
> *There is only the clear-blowing breeze of the West Wind*
> *That Ocean sends to refresh mankind.*

Isak's vision of his parents has the texture of an impressionist painting. Not only is the shot perfectly composed but it also captures the essence of its subject; the shot objectifies eternity as a state into which we do not freeze like figures in a mural but rather melt imperceptibly, the way spring softens into summer or summer ripens into autumn.

Great film is the ending of *The Third Man*, Isak's vision in *Wild Strawberries*, the penitents flagellating themselves in Bergman's *The Seventh Seal* (1957), Tamura of Kon Ichikawa's *Fires on the Plain* (1959) walking with his arms raised high while enemy bullets ignore his gesture of surrender, Antoine Doinel's once vital face frozen into an ID-card photograph at the close of François Truffaut's *The 400 Blows* (1959), the climactic shoot-out in the hall of mirrors in Orson Welles's *The Lady from Shanghai* (1948)—to cite some favorites.

It is natural to have a favorite scene; yet scenes are parts of a whole, a fact we tend to forget when we single them out for special consideration. When we praise the ending of *The Third Man* or the last vision of *Wild Strawberries*, we are praising the scene's visual, not its verbal, artistry. In film the images are generally more memorable than the dialogue; in fact, in screenplay form a movie usually seems ordinary and undistinguished. Take, for example, a screenplay about one person's assuming another's identity. The subject is hardly original. In literature it was treated by, among others, Plautus, Terence, Boccaccio, Shakespeare, Molière, Jean Anouilh, Jean Genêt, and Eugene O'Neill. In film assumed identity was the basis of Frank Capra's *Lady for a Day* (1934), Billy Wilder's *The Major and the Minor* (1942), Mitchell Leisen's *No Man of Her Own* (1950), Wilder's *Some Like It Hot* (1959), Paul Henreid's *Dead Ringer* (1964)—to give a partial list. And yet impersonation is the subject, if not the theme, of a major film, Michelangelo Antonioni's *The Passenger* (1975).

# THE PASSENGER

## The Assumed Identity Theme

On the surface *The Passenger* is an assumed identity film. This kind of movie works according to a formula that admits of some variation depending on whether the act of deception is a comic masquerade (*The Major and the Minor, Some Like It Hot*), a means of saving face (*Lady for a Day*), or a matter of survival (*Dead Ringer*). In its more serious form the assumed identity film has the following features: (1) The masquerade ends in failure, often in death; (2) the pretender becomes a fugitive from society, forsaking even family and friends; (3) if the identity assumed is of someone with underworld connections, the pretender runs afoul of the syndicate because he is unable to deliver what is expected of him; (4) the pretender then becomes a man on the run, and his odyssey turns the film, for the moment, into a road movie with its own conventions including the traveling companion with whom the fugitive has a short-lived but blissful affair, and the chance event (e.g., car trouble) that brings the journey to a close; (5) the key figures in the deception assemble in the same place for the film's resolution.

What distinguishes *The Passenger* from other films of this type is Antonioni's approach. "The business of the poet is not to find new emotions," T. S. Eliot wrote in "Tradition and the Individual Talent" (1917). There are no new emotions, nor, for that matter, new themes; there are only old ones waiting to be reborn. Antonioni takes the conventions of the assumed identity film and pushes them to their logical conclusions. Any serious film or work of literature that centers upon masquerade, deception, or the discrepancy between illusion and reality (Cervantes' *Don Quixote*, Pirandello's *Six Characters in Search of an Author*, Anouilh's *Traveller without Luggage*, Genêt's *The Balcony*) is, at least implicitly, epistemological; that is, it is concerned with man's ability to know reality. It asks the same question that Pontius Pilate posed to Jesus Christ: "What is truth?" (John 18:38).

It is fascinating to see how a movie about one man's assuming another's identity becomes a movie about the limitations of knowledge. Antonioni starts this process of transformation with a very simple, uncluttered script. The film opens in an unspecified part of Africa (probably North Africa) where British-born, American-educated journalist David Locke (Jack Nicholson) is attempting to make contact with some guerrilla leaders whom he hopes to interview for a television documentary. Unable to locate them, he returns to his hotel, where he discovers that Robertson, the businessman in the next room, has died of a heart attack. Noting a physical resemblance between them, he assumes Robertson's identity and itinerary, as yet unaware that his look-alike was a gunrunner for Third World revolutionaries. Locke flies to London, then to Munich, where he is paid handsomely by two men from the United Liberation Front; and finally to Barcelona, where he meets a nameless girl (Maria Schneider) who becomes his traveling companion. In the meantime Mrs. Locke receives her "dead" husband's belongings, including his passport with Robertson's picture (the resemblance is by no means perfect) and a tape of a conversation between himself and Robertson. Mrs. Locke turns sleuth, the police are contacted, and the manhunt is on. Urged by The Girl to keep an appointment that Robertson had made in Osuna, Locke proceeds to the place of the rendezvous, the Hotel de la Gloria. However, it is an appointment with death.

The screenplay as described sounds conventional enough. However, Antonioni's working out of the text and subtext raises the material from a banal to an affecting screen experience.

## The Text of The Passenger

The first time we see Locke he is asking directions; the world-famous reporter and interviewer is now a tourist, speaking haltingly as all tourists do. Locke is a passenger, or rather, he is Everypassenger. "Do you speak English?" he asks the boy riding with him in his Land Rover. He repeats the question, this time in French. The boy appears to understand neither language, but things are rarely what they seem in Antonioni. "Stop!" the boy cries, darting out of the vehicle. Locke drinks some water from his canteen and then notices an Arab approaching on a camel. Perhaps this is his contact. The Arab is also a traveler, but with a destination; like the Levite in the Parable of the Good Samaritan, he ignores Locke out of apathy or lethargy and continues on his way. Suddenly a contact materializes; he is about to bring Locke to the rebels' camp when the sight of some soldiers frightens him and he flees. Locke returns to his Land Rover and tries to start it, but the wheels sink into the sand and churn up a fine powdery spray. Locke lets out a primal scream, lowering his head in the sand. In frustration he strikes the vehicle with a shovel; the camera responds by panning the mute desert.

Locke walks back to his hotel. The heat has even affected the cockroaches, which have trouble climbing the wall. He checks on Robertson in the room next to his. When there is no answer, Locke enters the room. Robertson is lying on the bed, apparently the victim of a heart attack. There is no thundering chord from the sound track, no close-up of a shocked face. The dispassionate Locke turns the body over and sits down on the side of the bed. He pages through Robertson's appointments book, noticing that the dead man has a date coming up with someone called Daisy at the Hotel de la Gloria in Osuna, Spain. Although the other entries in the book look promising, it is the rendezvous at the Hotel de la Gloria to which Antonioni keeps returning.

Locke studies Robertson's face; then he examines Robertson's passport and airline ticket, the latter bearing the number of a locker in the Munich airport. Finally he notices Robertson's revolver. Casually, he lights a cigarette and then looks up at the ceiling fan, its blades cutting the air in an unchanging pattern. The sight of an object doomed to follow the same predictable course is all the encouragement Locke needs to become Robertson. Suddenly he finds himself wearing Robertson's blue shirt, which he had just picked up. He dresses Robertson in his checkered shirt. All that remains for him to do is to switch passport photos.

Next there is a knock at the door, and we hear Locke talking to Robertson. Since Robertson is dead, the scene appears to be some sort of flashback, but clearly not the traditional kind where the present dissolves smoothly into the past. The camera focuses on a tape recorder, a possible clue to the scene's meaning, since in an Antonioni movie objects have considerably more significance than they do in most other films. The camera moves to the window where the two men are conversing on the veranda. They are speaking personally; the usually reticent Locke is unburdening himself to Robertson as if some fraternal bond existed between them. He admits he cannot reach the black leaders he is interviewing for his documentary. Robertson replies that he has no trouble "reaching" them; Locke deals in language, but Robertson deals in merchandise, the nature of which will soon be revealed. At the end of their conversation, the camera moves in again for a close-up of the tape recorder: The flashback was a dramatization of the tape. Locke is a true reporter; he records everything, even conversations with fellow travelers.

David Locke becomes David Robertson, achieving what many middle-aged men secretly desire—the ultimate trade-in. Sporting an artificial moustache and sunglasses, Locke flies to London. A television program on his death is in progress as he walks through his old neighborhood, where the streets literally echo with tributes to him. He sees a girl sitting on a bench, reading. It is a typical Antonioni shot that can mean nothing or everything: In London, it means nothing; in Barcelona, everything. Since he has adopted Robertson's itinerary, his next stop is Munich to determine the contents of locker #58. The black zipper bag he finds there contains requisitions for guns and grenades. Two men approach him in the airport; one is white, the other black. Their English is accented. When the black man thanks Locke for the arms, we realize that Robertson was a gunrunner. To Robertson, Third World revolutionaries were a source of income; to Locke they are material for a documentary.

Throughout the first half of *The Passenger*, Antonioni incorporates excerpts from the documentary that Mrs. Locke and the producer are watching. Although Locke has the interviewer's knack of asking the right questions, he receives answers that are so politically cautious that they mean nothing. In one case a witch doctor, annoyed by Locke's question about the disparity between the man's education and his profession, terminates the interview and walks off camera. Sometimes Antonioni crosscuts the documentary with other scenes; at one point Locke is speaking to a garrulous Spaniard in Barcelona when there is a violent cut to the execution of a rebel.

The documentary is very much like the old Locke; by its very nature it is an impersonal form, leaving its maker little room for creativity. Since the documentary was part of Locke's past, it appears with the force of a flashback, for it represents the career he is abandoning. Locke wants not only to change lives but also to change films; as David Locke he was the creator of documentaries; as David Robertson he can be the star of a road flick or a cloak-and-dagger movie.

We know nothing about David Locke's earlier life except that he was born in London, educated in America, is married, and has an adopted child. Yet it is unimportant for us to know anything more about him. Since he is abandoning his past, there is little reason for us to see it. All we must do is look at his wife, played with glacial indifference by Jenny Runacre, to know why he is exchanging a life of dull routine for one of glorious unpredictability. Rachel Locke is an extension of her husband's profession. There is an abrupt flashback that not only crystallizes the differences between Mr. and Mrs. Locke but also explains his decision to lead the rest of his life without her. In Munich Locke enters a magnificently ornate church where a wedding is in progress. Antonioni cuts to the backyard of the Lockes' London home where Locke is burning leaves, behaving the way children do around a bonfire. His wife looks at him incredulously and asks if he's mad. He replies joyfully in the affirmative. Antonioni cuts back to the church where Locke is stepping on the petals that have fallen from the wedding bouquets. Locke has terminated his marriage to both Rachel and his former life, which are as dead as the petals that clutter the aisle. But his new life is already present in the church; the men from the United Liberation Front have followed him. They thank him for the ammunition, pay him handsomely, and remind him that their next meeting will be in Barcelona.

In Barcelona he encounters The Girl again. She is a drifter like himself with no past, only a present. She readily becomes Locke's traveling companion. Meanwhile, Rachel Locke becomes suspicious after she receives her "dead" husband's belongings, which include the Robertson tape and Robertson's photo in his passport. She and Martin Knight, the television producer, take off for Barcelona to check on Robertson while Locke and The Girl head south.

"What are you running away from?" The Girl asks as they drive along a tree-lined road in a white convertible. "Turn your back to the front seat" is his reply. She obeys and with childlike elation watches the road recede into the distance. This stunning tracking shot is typical of the film's rich ambiguity. The shot is ambiguous because the past is ambiguous. Subjectively, the past is no more permanent than the roads a person travels. Objectively, the past, like the road, exists whether an individual is aware of it or not. One road may be abandoned for another or a person may opt for a fresh present over a dead past; but neither can be willed out of existence. The road taken seems to lie in the distance; actually, it connects the passenger's past with his present, bringing him closer to his destination—and his destiny. Robertson's destiny is now Locke's because Robertson's present is Locke's present.

Locke's present, however, will be short lived. When he learns from The Girl that his wife is in Barcelona to warn "Robertson" that he may be in danger, he replies naively, "In danger of what?" The answer comes not from The Girl but in the form of a cut to a wayside cross. Death has replied to Locke's question.

Plagued by car trouble and pursued by the police, Locke and The Girl reach a town in southern Spain where the streets are sun-blanched and the chalk-white buildings look as if they would crumble in a powdery residue if anyone leaned against them. An adventure that began in the dry heat of Africa ends in the white heat of Spain. Antonioni, who has been using some of the oldest plot devices in movie history (look-alikes, snooping wives, dragnets), has Locke send The Girl off to Tangier with the promise that he will meet her there in three days if all goes well. But she knows that Robertson had an appointment in Osuna at the Hotel de la Gloria and begs Locke to keep it. He agrees and proceeds to the ironically named hotel, only to discover that she has checked in before him. One cannot help recalling all those Hollywood heroines who boarded a Greyhound after a spat with their lovers; as the bus pulled out, the boy would walk away in dejection and then turn around for one last look, only to see True Love standing on the platform with her suitcase.

Locke is not surprised to see her, nor does he even ask how she got there. She will not stay long, for she knows he must keep the appointment by himself. Their leave-taking is as unemotional as their first meeting. After she leaves, Locke opens a window and looks out through the grille at the white, dusty square. Then he lights a cigarette and lies down. Somehow we are more concerned with what might happen in the square than with what might happen to Locke, who is about to take a nap. Yet there is something about the present hotel room that recalls the African fleabag: a surface wire running down the wall. In the African hotel the camera followed the curve of the wire until a knock at the door interrupted its ascent; as if reprimanded, the camera moved over to the door where its presence was required. One is intrigued by the similarity of the rooms, which suggests some kind of repetition—another death, perhaps. But our immediate concern is to get out of the room and into the square where something seems about to happen.

What happens at this point almost defies description. A small white car pulls up; there is a sign on its roof advertising something, but it is difficult to make out the words because the camera refuses to leave the room. The Girl moves into the square; an old man is there, a boy, and a dog. Suddenly we notice that the camera has moved closer to the window grille. Another car, a much larger one, pulls into the square. The two men from the United Liberation Front step out; one stays outside and approaches The Girl; the other, the black man, enters the hotel. He is obviously going to see Locke. A door opens; then there are some ambiguous sounds. The camera, which could show us what is happening in the room between Locke and the revolutionary, has made more progress in its attempt to reach the window. The grille still faces us, imprisoning us and the camera with its bars. But then they begin to disappear until only two bars remain, which separate like sliding panels, revealing the square.

The camera is free, and we are also. But free for what purpose? To speculate on what is happening (or has happened) in the hotel room? Ironically, the frustration of not being out in the square has changed to the frustration of being in the square when we would

*8–2   David Lockel Robertson (Jack Nicholson) and The Girl (Maria Schneider) looking through the window grille of the Hotel de la Gloria. From the MGM release* The Passenger © *1975 by Metro-Goldwyn-Mayer Inc.*

rather be back in the room. A police car arrives with two po-licemen, one of whom tells the driver of the white car to move out of the square; another police car arrives with Rachel Locke and Martin Knight, who enter the hotel. But the camera does not follow them inside. Once liberated, it will not enter the Hotel de la Gloria again, although it should, to answer the many questions the action has given rise to: Did the black man murder Locke for not being able to deliver the anti-aircraft guns? Did he discover that Locke was not Robertson? And who is Daisy, the girl referred to in Robertson's appointments book? Like an eavesdropper, the camera hovers at the window, peeking at Mrs. Locke, Knight, the manager and The Girl as they stare at the figure on the bed. The manager asks Mrs. Locke if she recognizes the man lying there. "I never knew him," she replies; it is a fitting answer, for she only knew David Locke. The manager asks the same question of The Girl. She answers in the affirmative, for she knew David Locke/Robertson.

The sun sets in Osuna, and a guitar plays a soothing melody. The Hotel de la Gloria assumes the colors of evening; the man whom we saw in the square ambles up the dirt road, and the dog follows him. It is a soundstage tranquillity, and the setting, once so gritty right down to the powdery dust, now resembles something from a Latin musical like Minnelli's *Yolanda and the Thief* (1945) or *The Pirate* (1948): a quaint hotel caught in a pink and blue sunset. The music is so mellow that it almost defies us to leave the theater in anything but a state of serenity. The sky laughs too, daring us to see crimson in those shards of pink or darkness in that blue expanse. Finally the credits pass across the screen as the house lights slowly come up.

## The Subtext of The Passenger

To understand the subtext, it is necessary to go from the exterior to the interior of the film. Certain conclusions, which do not contradict the text but rather supplement it, seem plausible. They involve a recognition that the film is not at heart an exploration of mistaken identity but is rather an existential examination of life, a mythic interpretation of it, and a statement about the nature of knowledge, specifically the knowledge available to the world through film.

### The Mistaken Identity Theme

In an effort to force the viewer to go deeper into the film, Antonioni used the device of mistaken identity, but an exploration of that theme is not his real purpose. Indeed, Antonioni makes it impossible to take the film solely on this level because there is only the slightest physical resemblance between Locke and Robertson. In films about identical twins—Robert Siodmak's *The Dark Mirror* (1946), Curtis Bernhardt's *A Stolen Life* (1946)—or look-alikes—Peter Godfrey's *The Woman in White* (1948), Robert Hamer's *The Scapegoat* (1959)—it is customary for the same actor to play both roles. In *The Passenger* Jack Nicholson plays Locke, and Chuck Mulvehill, Robertson. When a director deviates from this tradition, it should only be because the film cannot accommodate the star in a dual role, for such casting would be at variance with the plot. In Alfred Hitchcock's *The Wrong Man* (1957), Henry Fonda could not play both the innocent musician and the criminal because the whole point of the film—an innocent man's being confused with a guilty look-alike—would have been lost. However, the plot of *The Passenger* would have allowed Antonioni to cast Nicholson in a dual role. Nicholson could easily have played both parts since Locke has only one scene with Robertson. Yet Antonioni chose another actor to play Robertson, an actor who was not a dead ringer for Nicholson.

Antonioni apparently intended *The Passenger* to be something more than another variation on an old theme. By making mistaken identity his point of departure, Antonioni was free to explore a related idea: the impossibility of absolute certitude. "Can one know anything for certain?" Antonioni asks in the subtext. The closer a person gets to truth, the more elusive and the more ambiguous it becomes. A smile in long shot may be a smirk in close-up. A fly on the wall is a black speck; under the microscope it is so multifaceted that one does not know at which facet to look first. Life conceals its secrets even from the scrutiny of the camera. Just as the camera was about to clarify what was happening in the square, something began to happen in the hotel room. But the camera had gone too far to turn back; if it did, it would be returning to the past, thus undoing everything Antonioni had set out to accomplish.

**Existential Implications**

Almost inevitably an exploration of the consequences of exchanging one life or one mode of being for another involves a move into the realm of the existential. Why would one man switch places with another unless his own life were purposeless, unless he wanted to *become* something and not merely *be*?

The existential individual is trapped in a world that is senseless, a world that gives rise to anxiety when one realizes there is only existence and nothing else. A person must exist in the here and now; but the here and now is precisely the source of anxiety. Jean-Paul Sartre compares existence to a viscous substance that sticks to men like glue. Existence is sticky filth, a sweetish sliminess that induces nausea; it is so overwhelming a concept that it can immobilize a person, causing a loss of freedom and self-deception, preventing that individual from investing his or her actions with meaning. The only way a human being can escape from this viscous mass is to assert that there was nothing before him and to work toward achieving an essence by the performance of meaningful actions. In short, individuals must make themselves *something*, not merely *be*.

Antonioni expresses visually what Sartre expresses verbally: the state of being trapped in the glue of existence. When fluidity has congealed, when freedom has ossified, there can be no movement. David Locke is a man whose freedom has ossified. He has no being-for-others, only being-for-itself which is mere nothingness. He will remain in that state until he frees himself of David Locke and becomes David Robertson, who, despite his profession, was at least committed to something.

The first time we see Locke he is in the desert, the perfect metaphor for his existence. Nothing ever changes in the desert except the color of the sand, which alternates between a reddish brown and an iridescent beige. The desert objectifies his life, which is equally static; married to a woman he does not love, frustrated by a profession that requires him to track down wars in obscure parts of the globe and to interview men who speak equivocally when they speak at all, he inhabits a world as depersonalized and uncommunicative as the one he finds in Africa.

The desert is not only static but silent as well. Men stare at Locke with empty eyes or bum cigarettes from him, not by asking for them but by raising two fingers to their lips. The desert is also incongruous: An African in a white headwrap pours himself a cup of hot tea in the midday sun; a boy who does not appear to understand English cries "Stop!" Silence, sterility, and incongruity: the three faces of the desert and the three faces of David Locke.

Existential man must be committed (in Sartre's terminology, *engagé*); Locke becomes committed when he keeps Robertson's appointment at the Hotel de la Gloria. He has no idea what the appointment is for except that it is with a contact known as "Daisy." It is not just a sense of fatalism that drives him to keep it, but the realization that keeping an appointment, even one he does not understand, is a form of commitment; or phrasing it existentially, commitment (*engagement*) can be nothing more than keeping another's appointment. One may be reminded of Vladimir's eloquent admission in Samuel Beckett's *Waiting for Godot*: "We have kept our appointment and that's an end to that. We are not saints, but we have kept our appointment. How many people can boast as much?"

## Mythic Elements

While they are in the Hotel de la Gloria, Locke asks The Girl to look out the window and tell him what she sees. Her reply is insignificant because the passing show is insignificant. "Wouldn't it be terrible to be blind?" she muses. Locke replies with a parable about a blind man whose vision was restored. At first the man was elated, but gradually he became aware of life's ugliness. Finally, he withdrew into his room and after three years of sight committed suicide.

Locke's parable recalls the tragedy of Oedipus who renounced his sight after he "saw" the truth about himself. Like Oedipus, Locke has certain characteristics of a tragic figure. He too learns something about existence: To be committed, one must keep his appointments regardless of the consequences. Commitment, even if it ends in death, is preferable to a life of detachment and bad faith. Oedipus investigated a murder that brought about his downfall; Locke kept an appointment that took his life. But at least both of them acted instead of being acted upon; both Oedipus and Locke exercised their freedom. Like Oedipus, Locke is caught between the poles of light and darkness, between living in the light as David Robertson and living in the darkness as David Locke. In choosing the light, Locke chose death; in choosing to see, Oedipus chose darkness.

The Oedipus myth is not the only one operating in *The Passenger*. The film is also reminiscent of the mythic descent to the underworld that the hero makes under the guidance of a seer or a shade. Locke is accompanied by The Girl on his journey, just as Aeneas was accompanied by the Sibyl through Hades or Dante was led by Virgil through the circles of hell. The Girl is Locke's companion and conscience, urging him on as the Sibyl urged on Aeneas when he became fainthearted or as Virgil buoyed up Dante's spirits when they flagged. When Locke is about to abandon Robertson's itinerary and renege on the meeting in Osuna, The Girl insists that he keep the appointment because Robertson had made it; if he is Robertson, he must do what Robertson would have done. All we know of The Girl is that she is a student of architecture, but she gives Locke's odyssey direction and form.

### The Nature of Film

Antonioni adds still another dimension to the film in the last seven minutes by articulating a theory of film through the movement of the camera alone. This sequence is his answer to the question that continually plagues the artist: Can one ever record what is seen or experienced with total accuracy? It would seem that although this may not be possible with words, which can be fuzzy and inexact, the camera may have the ability to record reality with clarity and precision. Yet Antonioni would deny this premise, for film is also limited. Reality even eludes the camera whose vision is often more reliable than our own. In our folly we think that the closer we get to an object, the better we can discern its nature; but in fact the closer we get to the object, the more ambiguous it becomes. The closer one gets to the *Mona Lisa*, for example, the more puzzling her smile appears. Is she smiling benignly or smirking? Is it the smile of contentment or the smile of complacency? Or is there a smile at all?

The final sequence of *The Passenger* states with wonderful economy Antonioni's position on the human capacity to know. Earlier the camera caught sight of a little white car with an undecipherable sign on the roof. At the end of the film, the car returns, this time with the sign more legible: We can make out the word "Andalusia." That we are in the south of Spain should come as no surprise after all those whitewashed dwellings and sepulchral villages. Recall also that the last shot of the film is of a man walking up a road followed by a dog, an Andalusian dog.

Luis Buñuel's first film was *Un Chien Andalou (An Andalusian Dog,* 1928); it was totally plotless, consisting of a series of dreamlike images, the most unforgettable being the slicing of a woman's eye with a razor. Summarizing what happens in the seventeen minutes of *Un Chien Andalou* would be like summarizing the contents of a dream. We can try to describe in words what happened in pictures but we would be giving our dream a form it never had. Antonioni's incredibly subtle bow to Buñuel in the final sequence is his explosion of the myth of objectivity. Truth is like *An Andalusian Dog,* a film that neither takes place in Andalusia nor has anything to do with a dog.

*The Passenger* can truly be classified as a total film experience because it fulfills all of the qualifications of great art in that medium. It is first a film whose ideas could not be realized in any other medium. Film was the only medium for *The Passenger* because Antonioni's purpose was to make us *see* the limitations of both human and cinematic knowledge.

It is also a film whose greatness does not depend upon the screenplay but upon its visualization. (Great literature is rarely successful on the screen because it has achieved its greatness in another form.) Antonioni's scripts are deliberately non- or even antiliterary; they are so sparsely written that the dialogue may sound flat and prosaic:

THE GIRL: People disappear every day.
LOCKE: Whenever they leave the room.

Antonioni wants a script that will allow him to make up visually for what is lacking verbally.

A total film experience is one whose text leads naturally to the subtext. The text of *The Passenger* concerns the consequences of assumed identity; the subtext locates the origin of the text in the human desire to know reality, a desire that throughout history people have expressed mythically and philosophically, in their private thoughts and in their public acts.

Finally, *The Passenger* qualifies as total film because it has the density of great art. Its meanings multiply and interlock. No single interpretation can do it justice, for there is always another veil to strip away.

# 9
# Film
# Authorship

If film is a collaborative effort, it would seem illogical to credit a movie to any one person. Thus, instead of referring to "Alfred Hitchcock's *Family Plot* (1976)," it might be more reasonable to say "the Alfred Hitchcock–Barbara Harris & Bruce Dern & Karen Black & William Devane (stars)–Ernest Lehman (screenplay)–Leonard J. South (photography) *Family Plot* (Universal, 1976)." Still, such designations, although accurate, are cumbersome, and the practice of attaching only the director's name to a film has now become common. To understand this practice, it is necessary to explore the theory of film criticism known as *auteurism*.

## THE BEGINNINGS OF AUTEURISM

During the German occupation of France in World War II the French were denied American movies, but after the war was over, they began to rediscover the greatness of the American cinema. The movies Americans often took for granted the French took seriously. André Bazin wrote appreciatively of William Wyler and Orson Welles; Jean-Luc Godard saw more in the B movies of

Monogram studios than the kids did who saw them as the second half of double bills at their neighborhood theaters.* The rediscovery of American films by the French led to a reconsideration of the director as artist. What impressed the French was the fact that a Hollywood director could be—and frequently was—handed a screenplay, a cast, and a crew (none of which he had personally selected) and still manage to leave the stamp of his personality on the film.

In 1951 André Bazin and Jacques Doniol-Valcroze began publication of *Cahiers du Cinéma*, a journal that was to film what the *Kenyon Review* was to literature: a critical forum for young film enthusiasts (Jean-Luc Godard, François Truffaut, Eric Rohmer, Claude Chabrol, and others) who expressed themselves in its pages and later went on to become directors. Like each of its writers, *Cahiers du Cinéma* had a reputation as a maverick; it was often pretentious and erratic in its preference of one director over another. Still, whatever one may think of the journal and the eccentric taste of its writers (e.g., Luc Moullet who found in films such as Edgar G. Ulmer's *Bluebeard* (1944) the theme of the loneliness of man without God), it did move the director from the background to the foreground, establishing him as a creator instead of a studio orderly.

For the first three years of its existence *Cahiers du Cinéma* had no real editorial policy; in 1954 Truffaut provided it with one in his famous essay, "Une certaine tendance du cinéma français," which attacked classic French cinema for preferring literary scripts to shooting scripts, adaptations to original screenplays, studio sets to actual locations, and a team of specialists to a single *auteur*. Truffaut argued for "a cinema of auteurs"; and so it was that *auteur*, the French word for "author," entered the critical vocabulary of film.

*Cahiers du Cinéma* now had a policy: *la politique des auteurs*, "the policy of authors," which has had various interpretations, the most common one being that the journal was partial to certain directors (e.g., Orson Welles, Alfred Hitchcock, Jean Renoir) but indifferent to others (e.g., John Huston, René Clair, René Clément). Another misconception of the meaning of "the policy of authors" was the

*Monogram made low-budget movies and "series pictures" (The Bowery Boys, Charlie Chan, Bomba the Jungle Boy, the Cisco Kid, etc.). The Monogram product was undistinguished except for an occasional melodrama like Frank Tuttle's *Suspense* (1946) or Gordon Wiles's *The Gangster* (1947).

notion that *Cahiers's* directors were infallible and incapable of making bad films. This impression was corrected by Bazin in 1957, when he pointed out what should be obvious—that a great director can make a dud and a mediocre director can occasionally make a classic.

Essentially, Bazin endorsed the policy of ranking directors, although he was often disturbed by the indiscriminate taste of some of his writers. Bazin, who had the characteristically French gift of clarity, summed up his position in the equation: author + subject = work. He asked of a critic only slightly less than what Alexander Pope required in *An Essay on Criticism:*

> *You then whose judgment the right course would steer,*
> *Know well each ancient's proper character;*
> *His fable, subject, scope in every page;*
> *Religion, country, genius of his age:*
> *Without all these at once before your eyes,*
> *Cavil you may, but never criticise.*—I, 118–23.

*Auteurism* entered America through Andrew Sarris. In his essay "Notes on the Auteur Theory in 1962,"[1] Sarris defended the ranking of directors as an extension of a critical policy that has always prevailed in the other arts: We rank William Shakespeare over Ben Jonson, Beethoven's symphonies over Mozart's, Mozart's opera *Don Giovanni* over Beethoven's *Fidelio.* It was inevitable that Sarris would establish a ranking order of his own. In *The American Cinema* he divided American directors into eleven categories including the "Pantheon" (Charles Chaplin, John Ford, D. W. Griffith, Howard Hawks, Alfred Hitchcock, Orson Welles, etc.); "The Far Side of Paradise" (Robert Aldrich, Frank Capra, Samuel Fuller, Vincente Minnelli, etc.); "Expressive Esoterica" (Tay Garnett, Arthur Penn, Edgar G. Ulmer, etc.); and "Less Than Meets the Eye" (John Huston, Elia Kazan, William Wyler). Despite the historical importance of *The American Cinema,* it is the kind of book that requires periodic revision. The current critical estimate of William Wyler and the American Film Institute's tribute to him in 1976 have not borne out Sarris's thesis that there is less to Wyler than meets the eye. Similarly, in 1968 there might have been a reason for including Sidney Lumet in the "Strained Seriousness" group; but after *Serpico* (1973), *Murder on the Orient Express* (1974), *Dog Day Afternoon* (1975), *Network* (1976), and *Equus* (1977), Lumet merits a reevaluation.

Sarris reduced the essence of the *auteur* theory, which is how *la politique des auteurs* came to be known in America, to three principles:

1. An *auteur* is technically competent.
2. An *auteur* has a personality that manifests itself in recurring stylistic traits that become his or her signature.
3. An *auteur*'s films have an interior meaning that arises from the tension between the director's personality and his or her material. Thus there will always be some ambiguity in an *auteur*'s films because who the *auteur* is, including those aspects of the *auteur*'s personality that no one will ever see, will filter into his or her work and become invisible, or at least not readily discernible.

# THE DEBATE OVER AUTEURISM

## Arguments Against Auteurism

Not everyone accepts *auteurism* and what it implies about the nature of film making. The major arguments against the theory may be summarized as follows:

1. If James Cagney's theories carry any weight (or more weight than those of Andrew Sarris), *auteurism* is nonsense. In his autobiography *Cagney by Cagney*, he characterizes directors as "pedestrian workmen, mechanics," some of whom "couldn't direct you to a cheap delicatessen."[2]

2. Some films are the result of a producer's conception rather than a director's. Thus the disaster films *The Poseidon Adventure* (1972) and *The Towering Inferno* (1975) are usually associated with Irwin Allen the producer, not Ronald Neame or John Guillermin, the directors, respectively, of those films. Moreover, although Val Lewton never directed a single film, he left his mark on everything he produced at RKO (*Cat People, I Walked with a Zombie, The Curse of the Cat People*, etc.). Thus we think of *Cat People* primarily as a Val Lewton film and only secondarily as Jacques Tourneur's.

3. During the 1930s and the 1940s, each studio had its own production style, which caused its films to have a distinctive quality. A Twentieth-Century-Fox musical was not an MGM musical; it was brassier, tougher, less restrained. An MGM musical was warm, friendly, often naïve; one has only to see *That's Entertainment* (1974) or *That's Entertainment, II* (1976) to understand what the phrase "an MGM musical" means. Therefore, those who reject

*auteurism* would argue that the musicals Vincente Minnelli directed at MGM—*Meet Me in St. Louis* (1944), *Yolanda and the Thief* (1945), *The Pirate* (1948), *An American in Paris* (1951), and *The Bandwagon* (1953) among others—reflect MGM's style, not the director's.

4. Since film is the result of teamwork, it is important to know the contributions made by the various members of the team. The shot that most moviegoers remember from William Wellman's *Public Enemy* (1931) is the one in which Tommy Powers (James Cagney) pushes a grapefruit in his mistress's face. However, the idea for that shot originated not with Wellman but with Darryl F. Zanuck, at the time head of production at Warner Bros.[3] In recognizing only the director's contribution, *auteurism* may be too restrictive.

## A Justification for Auteurism

Although the *auteur* theory has limitations, forms of *auteurism* are recognized in other performing arts. Thus one theatergoer may say to another, "Have you seen the new Bob Fosse musical?" Fosse is a director who is equally at home on the Broadway stage (*Sweet Charity, Cabaret, Pippin, Chicago*) and in films (*Cabaret* 1972, *Lenny* 1974). His musicals are so individualistic that discerning theatergoers look forward to the next one regardless of cast, composer, or lyricist; for them it is enough that it will have the Fosse touch.

Other similar examples abound. Lovers of ballet will often speak of Natalia Makarova's *Swan Lake,* as opposed to another ballerina's, not "Tchaikovsky's *Swan Lake.*" In doing this, they recognize the primary importance of the interpreter's contribution. Similarly, lovers of Shakespeare will compare Richard Burton's Hamlet with Nicol Williamson's or Richard Chamberlain's, and operagoers will speak of Leontyne Price's Aida, not Verdi's. If interpretation is so important to the other arts that the originator takes second billing, it may be equally as important in film.

A symphony orchestra provides an even better analogy with film. The conductor of a symphony orchestra, like the director of a film, knows what it is like to cope with the two most unpredictable objects in the world: human beings and instruments. If the brass section is mediocre, if the woodwinds fail to come in on time, if the horns sound gaseous, the conductor must assume the blame. The critics have always operated on this principle. We are constantly reading about the conductor who "led a sluggish performance of the Schubert Ninth" or the conductor who "failed to get any thing more than a reedy sound from the orchestra." When Leonard Bernstein conducts Gustav Mahler's First Symphony, it is no longer Mahler's symphony but his. At that moment Leonard Bernstein is standing in for Gustav Mahler as he is about, one hopes, to realize the composer's intentions. If he succeeds, he is praised; if he fails, he is censured. No one will criticize Mahler; but they will criticize his interpreter.

Therefore, when a music critic speaks of "Bernstein's Mahler," he means several things: Bernstein's conception of the Mahler work, his ability to communicate that conception to the orchestra, and his success in eliciting a performance from the orchestra that matches his conception. *Auteurists* mean the same when they speak of "Alfred Hitchcock's *Family Plot.*" They are not slighting the cast without whom there would be no movie, nor are they slighting the screenwriter without whom the cast would have nothing to do. They are merely saying that the director molds the cast and script to fit his or her vision of the film. If the director's integration succeeds, the film succeeds; if the director cannot get everything to mesh, the film appears disjointed, and the critics will note the faulty direction.

Here the analogy between the conductor and the director ends. Although both are surrogate authors, the conductor is dealing with something he cannot change. Leonard Bernstein cannot add a single note to the Mahler First, but directors can alter scripts while they are filming. If an actor has a worthwhile suggestion, a director can always incorporate it into the film. Robert Altman always works this way. In *Nashville* (1975), some of the actors not only wrote their own songs but also improvised some of their scenes. Ronee Blakely wrote her own dialogue for Barbara Jean's breakdown scene; Lady Pearl's moving reflections on the Kennedys were written by Barbara Baxley.

## TYPES OF AUTEURS

There is no question that directors such as Orson Welles, William Wyler, Billy Wilder, and Ingmar Bergman are *auteurs,* authors in the fullest sense of the word. Their films can be studied for thematic repetition and recurrent imagery in the same way the works of a creative writer are studied in English courses. It is easier to give the title of *auteur* to Bergman, who almost always writes his own scripts, than to a director like Sidney Lumet, who never does. Yet Lumet's films can also be approached thematically. Since Lumet began directing in 1956 he has shown an interest in scripts about loners, freaks, and outcasts: the teen-age boy accused of killing his father in *Twelve Angry Men* (1956), the vagabond and the unfulfilled wife of the *The Fugitive Kind* (1959), the incestuous longshoreman of *A View from the Bridge* (1962), the haunted Tyrones of *Long Day's Journey into Night* (1962), the emotionally calcified death camp survivor of *The Pawnbroker* (1965), the policeman who becomes a pariah in *Serpico* (1973), the trainload of misfits in *Murder on the Orient Express* (1974), the bisexual bank robber of *Dog Day Afternoon* (1975), the television humanoids of *Network* (1976), the boy who blinds a stable of horses in *Equus* (1977).

There have also been *auteurs* who worked within the studio system and still made films that were their own. William Wyler made some of his best movies for Samuel Goldwyn (e.g., *Dead End*, 1937; *Wuthering Heights*, 1939). Shortly before Pearl Harbor he was hired by MGM to direct *Mrs. Miniver* (1942), which dramatized the impact of World War II on a typical British family. In one sense *Mrs. Miniver* was an MGM film; it was made for a specific studio because its vice-president, Louis B. Mayer, believed in the family film. However, it was directed by a man who was not an MGM regular but who was able to make an MGM film as well as a William Wyler film. Many of Wyler's techniques are evident in *Mrs. Miniver*. Wyler always tried to encompass as much as he could in a single shot, thus minimizing cutting. *Mrs. Miniver* is filled with such shots—Kay Miniver sitting on the bed while her husband is off in the dressing room; the Minivers seated at the dinner table while their son is seen talking on the telephone in the alcove; Kay standing on the bridge with the station master below her and the water behind him.

## CHARACTERISTICS OF THE AUTEUR

Whether they are writers, interpreters, or studio regulars, all *auteurs* have certain characteristics in common. All of them (1) collaborate with others, (2) seek variety in their work, (3) repeat motifs, (4) allude to their earlier works, and (5) borrow from the past to enrich their films.

# Collaboration

The true *auteurs* have always practiced some type of collaboration. But in film, collaboration can take many forms. The most common types of collaborations are as follows:

1. *Collaboration between a director and screenwriter*: Sometimes a director will have the same screenwriter for several movies; undoubtedly, those movies will have certain features in common. Joan Harrison worked on the scripts for Hitchcock's *Rebecca* (1940), *Foreign Correspondent* (1940), *Suspicion* (1941), and *Saboteur* (1942), in all of which the wrong man was under suspicion. Billy Wilder and Charles Brackett coauthored the scripts for three Mitchell Leisen films: *Midnight* (1939); *Arise, My Love* (1940); and *Hold Back the Dawn* (1941). All three entail some form of deception.

2. *Collaboration between a director and cinematographer*: Some of the more creative director-cinematographer collaborations have been between Eric von Stroheim and William Daniels (*Blind Husbands*, 1918; *Foolish Wives*, 1921; *Greed*, 1924; *The Merry Widow*, 1925); Josef von Sternberg and Lee Garmes (*Morocco*, 1930; *Dishonored*, 1931; *Shanghai Express*, 1932); Ingmar Bergman and Gunnard Fischer (*Smiles of a Summer Night*, 1955; *The Seventh Seal*, 1957; *Wild Strawberries*, 1957).

3. *Collaboration between a director and composer*: Examples of this type include John Ford and Alfred Newman (*Arrowsmith*, 1931; *The Hurricane*, 1937; *The Grapes of Wrath*, 1940; *How Green Was My Valley*, 1941); Federico Fellini and Nino Rota (*La Strada*, 1954; *La Dolce Vita*, 1960; *8 1/2*, 1963; *Juliet of the Spirits*, 1965); and Hitchcock and Bernard Herrmann (*The Wrong Man*, 1957; *Vertigo*, 1958; *Psycho*, 1960; *Marnie*, 1964).

4. *Collaboration between a director and actor(s)*: Notable here are John Huston and Humphrey Bogart (*The Maltese Falcon*, 1941; *Across the Pacific*, 1942; *Treasure of the Sierra Madre*, 1948; *Key Largo*, 1948; *The African Queen*, 1951); von Sternberg and Marlene Dietrich (*The Blue Angel*, 1930; *Morocco*, 1930; *Dishonored*, 1931; *Shanghai Express*, 1932; *Blonde Venus*, 1932); Truffaut and Jean-Pierre Léaud (*The 400 Blows*, 1959; *Stolen Kisses*, 1968; *Bed and Board*, 1970; *Day for Night*, 1973); Bergman and Liv Ullmann (*Persona*, 1966; *Hour of the Wolf*, 1968; *The Shame*, 1968; *A Passion of Anna*, 1969; *Scenes from a Marriage*, 1973; *Face to Face*, 1976); Billy Wilder and Jack Lemmon (*Some Like It Hot*, 1959; *The Apartment*, 1960; *Irma la Douce*, 1963; *The*

*Fortune Cookie*, 1966; *Avanti!*, 1972; *The Front Page*, 1974); John Ford's stock company (Ward Bond, Victor McLaglen, John Wayne, Maureen O'Hara, Ben Johnson); and Robert Altman's stock company (Keith Carradine, Shelley Duvall, Bert Remsen, David Arkin).

5. *Collaboration between a director and editor:* The most evident is that between Arthur Penn and Dede Allen *(Bonnie and Clyde,* 1967; *Alice's Restaurant,* 1969; *Little Big Man,* 1970; *Night Moves,* 1975; *The Missouri Breaks,* 1976).

6. *Collaboration between a director and producer:* The best examples of this are Wyler and Samuel Goldwyn *(Dead End,* 1937; *Wuthering Heights,* 1939; *The Westerner,* 1940; *The Little Foxes,* 1941); Jacques Tourneur, Robert Wise, and Mark Robson, who directed the films Val Lewton produced for RKO; and William Dieterle and Hal B. Wallis at Paramount *(The Searching Wind,* 1946; *The Accused,* 1948; *Rope of Sand,* 1949; *Paid in Full,* 1950; *Dark City,* 1950; *Red Mountain,* 1951).*

7. *Collaboration between a director and studio:* Frank Capra and Columbia, Ernst Lubitsch and Paramount, Preston Sturges and Paramount, Raoul Walsh and Warner Bros., Vincente Minnelli and MGM all collaborated in film efforts. Paramount was synonymous with sophisticated comedy during the 1930s and 1940s, and it was directors such as Lubitsch, Sturges, and, to a lesser extent, Leisen who gave Paramount that reputation. Lubitsch could do more with the closing of a bedroom door than most directors could if they kept it open.

## Variety

The great *auteurs* have a varied body of work that reflects a limited number of themes. Billy Wilder's films, for example, center about two major themes: deception and its various forms (disguise, fraud, masquerade); and the impact of one order on another (capi-

*The relationship between producer and director can be as creative or destructive as the parties make it. On the one hand there is Dino de Laurentiis who reedited Robert Altman's *Buffalo Bill and the Indians* (1976) so drastically that Altman said—hyperbolically, perhaps—that the film was no longer his. On the other hand, there is Robert Evans, coproducer of John Schlesinger's *Marathon Man* (1976), about whom Schlesinger said: "I need a producer because I get too close to the film, and I need an objective eye. . . . If two people agree about everything, one is unnecessary. I want a genuine collaboration, and for that you need a strong and creative producer like Evans" (*New York Times*, Sec. 2, August 15, 1976, p. 13).

talism/communism, rich/poor, youth/age). Even the scripts that he and Charles Brackett wrote prior to his directorial debut reflect these themes: the female commissar of Lubitsch's *Ninotchka* (1939) who comes in contact with capitalism and falls under its spell; the chorus girl of Leisen's *Midnight* (1939) who impersonates a countess; the lady reporter of Leisen's *Arise, My Love* (1940) who rescues a man from prison by pretending to be his wife; the gigolo of Leisen's *Hold Back the Dawn* (1941) who feigns love to become an American citizen; the college professors of Howard Hawks's *Ball of Fire* (1941) who find themselves learning slang from a stripper.

Then there are the films that Wilder directed himself:

*The Major and the Minor* (1942): A woman disguises herself as a twelve-year-old to purchase a train ticket at half fare.

*Five Graves to Cairo* (1943): A British officer impersonates a lame servant in a desert hotel.

*Double Indemnity* (1944): An insurance agent tricks a man into signing a policy with a double-indemnity clause; the agent and the client's wife conspire to kill her husband to collect on the policy; the agent briefly poses as her husband on board a train.

*The Lost Weekend* (1945): An alcoholic is continually devising ways of concealing his bottle.

*The Emperor Waltz* (1948): An Austrian countess meets an American phonograph salesman (a "two orders" film).

*A Foreign Affair* (1948): An army captain in postwar Berlin tries to conceal his relationship with a nightclub singer from a visiting congresswoman.

*Sunset Boulevard* (1950): An aging silent star deludes herself into thinking she can make a comeback as Salome; her kept man conceals his status from his girlfriend.

*The Big Carnival* (*Ace in the Hole*, 1951): A reporter deceives the victim of a cave-in into believing he is the victim's friend.

*Stalag 17* (1953): An informer infiltrates a POW camp.

*Sabrina* (1954): A rich boy courts a chauffeur's daughter (a "two orders" film).

*The Seven Year Itch* (1955): A summer bachelor plays at being Don Juan.

*The Spirit of St. Louis* (1957): This is an atypical Wilder film, which depicts Lindbergh's flight across the Atlantic.

*Love in the Afternoon* (1957): A May–December romance develops between an older man and a young girl whose father is a detective.

*Witness for the Prosecution* (1957): A woman tricks a noted barrister into thinking she is a cockney.

*Some Like It Hot* (1959): Two musicians dress up as women; a millionaire (male) falls in love with one of the disguised men.
*The Apartment* (1960): A girl with a checkered past masquerades as a virgin.
*One, Two, Three* (1961): An American Coca-Cola executive and a radical East Berliner clash ideologically.
*Irma la Douce* (1963): To keep a prostitute from sharing her favors with others, her lover resorts to disguise.
*Kiss Me, Stupid* (1964): A barmaid impersonates a married woman; a wife allows her songwriter-husband to think his song succeeded on its own merits although it became a hit because she spent the night with a famous pop singer.
*The Fortune Cookie* (1966): A TV cameraman is persuaded by his brother-in-law to sue for nonexistent injuries.
*The Private Life of Sherlock Holmes* (1970): Deception is implicit in any treatment of Holmes.
*Avanti!* (1972): A married man and the daughter of his late father's mistress arrange to have a yearly rendezvous in Italy, repeating the deception their parents (his father, her mother) had practiced until their death.
*The Front Page* (1974): An editor will do anything to get his star reporter back, even resorting to a lie that also happens to be one of the most famous curtain lines in the American theater: "The son of a bitch stole my watch."

Variety in an *auteur's* work is not thematic, but generic. While deception/disguise is a recurring theme in Wilder's films, it is a theme that manifests itself in a variety of genres: farce (*The Major and the Minor, Some Like It Hot, Irma la Douce*), romantic comedy (*Sabrina, Love in the Afternoon, Avanti!*), political comedy (*A Foreign Affair; One, Two, Three*), social comedy (*The Apartment, The Fortune Cookie*), social realism (*The Lost Weekend, The Big Carnival*), espionage and wartime melodrama (*Five Graves to Cairo, Stalag 17*), courtroom melodrama (*Witness for the Prosecution*), gothic melodrama (*Sunset Boulevard*), period pieces (*The Emperor Waltz, The Private Life of Sherlock Holmes*), film noir (*Double Indemnity*).

The films themselves derive from several sources: novels (*The Lost Weekend, Love in the Afternoon*), plays that are either adaptations (*Stalag 17, Sabrina, The Seven Year Itch, Avanti!*) or almost total rewrites with little of the original left intact (*One, Two, Three; Irma la Douce; Kiss Me, Stupid*), stories (*Double Indemnity*), and original scripts (*The Emperor Waltz, Sunset Boulevard, The Big Carnival, The Apartment, The Fortune Cookie, The Private Life of Sherlock Holmes*).

## Repetition of Motifs

Repetition does not bother an *auteur*. A true *auteur* will repeat his or her basic themes not only in various genres but also as motifs within those genres. Thus, the theme of deception/disguise recurs as various motifs in Wilder's films:

1. adultery (*Double Indemnity, The Seven Year Itch, Love in the Afternoon, The Apartment, Kiss Me, Stupid, Avanti!*)
2. insurance fraud (*Double Indemnity, The Fortune Cookie*)
3. women physically altering their appearance (*The Major and the Minor, Witness for the Prosecution*)
4. men physically altering their appearance (*Some Like It Hot, Irma la Douce*)
5. a woman deceiving the man she loves (*The Major and the Minor; The Apartment, Kiss Me, Stupid, The Private Life of Sherlock Holmes*)
6. a man deceiving the woman he loves (*The Seven Year Itch, Some Like It Hot, Irma la Douce*)
7. men deceiving each other (*Five Graves to Cairo, Double Indemnity, The Lost Weekend, The Big Carnival, The Fortune Cookie*)

Similarly in the "two orders" films the following motifs can be found:

1. distinctions of class (countess/commoner in *The Emperor Waltz;* common girl/privileged boy in *Sabrina*)
2. distinctions of age (young girl/older man in *Sabrina, Love in the Afternoon, The Apartment,* and *Avanti!;* young man/older woman in *A Foreign Affair* and *Sunset Boulevard*)
3. distinctions based on war (allies/enemy in *Five Graves to Cairo* and *Stalag 17;* victor/vanquished in *A Foreign Affair*)
4. distinctions of ideology (capitalism vs. communism in *One, Two, Three;* freedom vs. fascism in *A Foreign Affair*)

## Quotations

Saying that *auteurs* repeat themselves is not the same as saying they continually make the same film. Hitchcock often quotes himself, but his quotes are rarely verbatim. Rowley's (Edmund Gwenn's) fall from the cathedral tower in *Foreign Correspondent* (1940) prefigures similar falls, but in totally different contexts, in *Saboteur* (1942), *Vertigo* (1958), and *North by Northwest* (1959). The airplane wing that becomes a life raft when a plane crashes in the

9–1    *A Director Quotes Himself*

9–1A    *Marlene Dietrich as Erika, a cabaret singer in post–World War II Berlin, and John Lund as her lover Captain John Pringle in Wilder's* A Foreign Affair *(1948). Courtesy Billy Wilder and MCA Publishing.*

9–1B    *Marlene Dietrich as Christine, who meets her future husband Leonard Vole (Tyrone Power) in a Hamburg nightclub at the end of World War II in Wilder's* Witness for the Prosecution *(1957). Wilder added the nightclub scene, which does not appear in the Agatha Christie play, to show how the Voles met. He was clearly repeating a plot device from* A Foreign Affair—*the smoke-filled basement nightclub where Pringle came to hear Erika sing. Courtesy Museum of Modern Art/Film Stills Archive and United Artists.*

Atlantic in *Foreign Correspondent* yields to the real thing in *Lifeboat* (1944), a completely different film that uses a more conventional form of survival at sea.

In *Family Plot* when Blanche (Barbara Harris) and her boyfriend are driving along in a car whose brakes give way, she grabs hold of his necktie, almost strangling him with it. Her action recalls the necktie murders in *Frenzy* (1972). Similarly, when the pair are on a deserted stretch of highway, we almost expect the crop duster from *North by Northwest* to materialize and spray them with bullets. And at one point the boyfriend is in a jewel thief's home; to avoid detection, he takes the same precautions Marnie took in Hitchcock's film of that name: He removes his shoes and tiptoes past the kitchen. In fact, we wait for him to drop a shoe, just as we thought Marnie might. These are old tricks, but they are appearing in a new setting.

In *Witness for the Prosecution*, Billy Wilder added a flashback to show how Leonard Vole (Tyrone Power) met his wife Christine (Marlene Dietrich) in a Hamburg nightclub at the end of World War II. Dietrich had the same profession in Wilder's *A Foreign Affair*. Wilder must have had his earlier film in mind when he decided to open up the Agatha Christie play a bit by putting in the flashback. Yet *Witness for the Prosecution* is not a *A Foreign Affair* any more than *Family Plot* is *Frenzy* or *North by Northwest*.

## Borrowings

*Auteurs* are generally not troubled by the question of originality because they see themselves as part of a tradition. Although they respect the past, they neither worship it blindly nor lean on it as if it were a crutch; instead, they view it as a legacy on which they can draw. When they borrow from the past, they are paying it homage, not practicing plagiarism. The Odessa Steps massacre in Sergei Eisenstein's *Potemkin* (1925) left its mark on many film makers, including Busby Berkeley, who paid it a curious tribute in the "Lullaby of Broadway" sequence in *Gold Diggers of 1935*. Hitchcock did the same in *Foreign Correspondent*, in which an assassination was staged on the steps of a conference hall in Amsterdam.

Wilder regarded Ernst Lubitsch as the unrivaled master of subtlety. Whenever someone in a Lubitsch film closed a door, drew the curtains, or shut the blinds, one always wondered, "Did they or didn't they?" In *Double Indemnity*, the camera dollies back from Phyllis and Neff as they sit snugly on the sofa in his apart-

9–2   *The Odessa Steps sequence in Eisenstein's* Potemkin *(1925) has influenced many film makers. This is Alfred Hitchcock's homage to the Odessa Steps in* Foreign Correspondent *(1940). Courtesy Learning Corporation of America and Audio Brandon.*

ment. "We just sat there," Neff's voice is heard saying. We no more believe him than we believe the Lubitsch heroine who closes the door of her lover's bedroom and in the next shot awakens in her own.

## AN INTERVIEW WITH BILLY WILDER

Billy Wilder is an ideal director for study. Along with Hitchcock and Joseph L. Mankiewicz, he is one of the few major directors to survive the switch from the studio system to the conglomerates. Raoul Walsh made his last film in 1964; William Wyler in 1969; Howard Hawks in 1970. Yet Wilder is still directing. He is also a true *auteur,* for he coauthors the script of every film he directs. Since *The Big Carnival,* he has produced his own films with a few minor exceptions. Wilder has been the subject of retrospec-

9-3   Walter Neff (Fred MacMurray) and Phyllis Diedrichson (Barbara Stanwyck) about to weave a web of deception in Billy Wilder's Double Indemnity (1944). Courtesy Billy Wilder and MCA Publishing.

9-4   Billy Wilder today. Courtesy Universal.

tives at the Museum of Modern Art in New York, in Berlin, Cork, and even Kuala Lumpur. He is a six-time Academy Award winner: twice for direction (*The Lost Weekend, The Apartment*); three times for best screenplay (*The Lost Weekend, Sunset Boulevard,* * *The Apartment*); once for best picture (*The Apartment*).

D. H. Lawrence said, "Trust the tale, not the teller." Yet the teller can have much to tell, especially one who writes, directs, and produces his own tales. Billy Wilder is a practical film maker; although he knows film theory, he is only interested in its connection with an actual movie. To Wilder, *Auteurism* is an abstraction, a critical term; since he is an *auteur*, he does not theorize about being one.

Billy Wilder's office is on the lot of Universal City Studios. From the large trestle table and the ample supply of pencils, yellow paper, and felt-tip pens, one knows it is a working office, not a showroom. But it is also the office of a film director: his six Oscars line the top of his bookshelf; there are autographed photos of stars he has directed, contact sheets of Marilyn Monroe, and a metal figure of Marilyn on his bulletin board in that classic pose from *The Seven Year Itch* with her dress billowing.

It was within this setting that the following interview took place on June 11, 1976:

DICK: The critics who like to minimize the director's role will say that all a director did during the Studio Years was carry out his studio's policy. They would not speak of "Billy Wilder's films" but of "Billy Wilder's Paramount period [1942–1954]." When you were at Paramount, were you conscious of turning out a Paramount product?

WILDER: Never, not even in the early days when I did not have script approval and the right of final cut. If this were true, then Lubitsch's pictures, Sturges's pictures, Mitchell Leisen's pictures, my pictures—in fact, all the pictures made during those interesting days at Paramount—would have been the same. They were not. Once Paramount and I agreed on the subject of the movie, the cast, and the budget, and once they realized I would not have censorship problems (and in those days we had to smuggle things past the censors)—once all of this was settled—I was on my own. I wrote the film the way I wanted to, I cut it the way I wanted to. Of

*The *Sunset Boulevard* Oscar was technically for story and screenplay.

course, I may have to give a little when a picture is sold to television and make a cut here or a cut there. But even when I was beginning and did not have the ultimate control I have now, never for a moment did I think of myself as a foreman on the Paramount lot.

You see, the *auteur* theory, in emphasizing the director who takes over someone else's script, has little to say about a director like myself who writes, directs, and produces his own. Although I do not belong to the producers' guild ( I do, of course, belong to the screenwriters' and directors'), I think I can evaluate the *auteur* theory better than most critics. Being the writer, director, and producer of a picture, naturally I am the *auteur*.

DICK: Then you do not accept the *auteur* theory?

WILDER: I accept it only up to a point. The *auteur* theory does not emphasize the script. I deeply believe in the script and in the director's getting the maximum out of it. A mediocre director with a great script will still come out on top, but a brilliant director with a poor script will inevitably fail.

DICK: Is it easier to become a director now than it was when you began in the industry?

WILDER: It is much easier now because television provides you with a training ground. In the past there was no training ground except shorts and a series like MGM's "Crime Does Not Pay" where Fred Zinnemann got his chance. Otherwise, unless you worked on Broadway or had important connections, or unless powerful stars requested you, it was extraordinarily difficult to get a break. You might think that by becoming an assistant director you would stand a good chance of becoming a director. Yet the assistant director had the least chance of ever becoming a director. The dialogue coach, the cameraman, the actor, the actor's relatives stood a better chance of becoming directors.

Of course, all that has changed with television. With the enormous demands it makes on one's time, you can learn by being on the set long enough. And with highly trained crews at his disposal, a director can't make a total ass of himself.

Directing is not Chinese glass blowing or the art of making Inca gold statuettes. It can be learned and it can be learned quickly if you have a flair and a style for it. It is also an exhausting profession and one that has a finality about it. In the theater, you can rewrite a play during its tryout; in my profession you can't say, "Let's reshoot the film" if you don't like it. The sets are down, the actors are in Yugoslavia, and plans have already been made for the picture's distribution.

DICK: Do you have an image in your mind of what the film will look like in its final form?

WILDER: Even though you lose yourself in the picture while you're making it, ultimately it is back to what it was when you did the script, which is proof that the script was good and that the choice of material was good. If a film doesn't work—and often it doesn't—it was because I was telling the wrong story or an uninteresting story; I was telling a story that didn't have a chance no matter how brilliantly I might do it. Maybe I chose the right story at the time but it turned out to be the wrong time for the picture. If I write an article for a magazine, it will be published a few weeks later. The mood of the public has not changed, and there is still interest in the subject. But my picture will not see the light of day for two years when the mood of the public may be entirely different.

DICK: Are your scripts complete when you begin shooting?

WILDER: They are complete in the sense that I know how the film will end; but I want to see how the first two acts will play before I go on to the third. They are not complete in the sense that every line has been written down. I am always open to suggestions. If a scene does not play well in rehearsal, I will change it. If an actor has a good idea or even an electrician, I can add it. But you must first have something to add it to.

DICK: Is there any truth to the story that Shirley MacLaine and Jack Lemmon were handed their dialogue for the final scene of *The Apartment* on the last day of shooting?

WILDER: Could be. But we knew very well how it would end: the boy would get what he wanted, give it up, and get the girl. Maybe the actual words were typed the night before. But we did not improvise; I never depend upon improvisation.

DICK: Your films evidence an incredible range—romantic comedy, farce, social drama, *film noir*, melodrama, biography. Did you aim for such diversity?

WILDER: I know a man who always wears a dark blue suit when he goes out in the evening. It's rather boring, you know. Why not a striped suit once in a while? Sometimes I wonder if I did the wrong thing by experimenting so much. Hitchcock, whom I greatly admire, stayed with one kind of picture. When people go to a Hitchcock movie, they know what to expect. Certain directors develop a style, refine it, and never give it up; they never leave their own neighborhood. I ventured out and tested myself. But whatever kind of film I make, there is always one quality I aim for: a complete simplicity of style, a total lack of pretentiousness; there is not one phony setup in a Billy Wilder picture.

Also making films is a matter of mood. Now I am in the mood for something a bit serious, so I will do *Fedora,** which may remind some of *Sunset Boulevard* at least in texture, but it will be quite different.

DICK: It's well known that you write your scripts with a collaborator, but do you ever look upon your editor as a collaborator? I ask because Doane Harrison edited several of your early films.

WILDER: Doane Harrison was an old-time cutter, going back to the time when George Stevens was a cameraman for Hal Roach. He was very close to me when I made *The Major and the Minor*; he taught me a great deal because until then I had spent my life behind the typewriter, not behind the camera.*

DICK: How did you get behind the camera?

WILDER: How I became a director is very interesting. When I was writing scripts with Charles Brackett, we were never allowed on the set when the film was being shot. First of all, directors didn't want writers on the set; and second, we were off writing another picture. I decided to assert myself because I wanted some control over my scripts. So I started to raise hell, and Paramount finally let me direct a picture. Actually it was no big deal because at that time Paramount was turning out fifty pictures a year. They said, "Let Wilder make a picture and then he'll go back to writing." Everyone expected me to make something "fancy-schmancy." Yet I made something commercial. I brought back the most salable hunk of celluloid I could—*The Major and the Minor*.

You see, unless you control your film, you are also at the mercy of actors. It's easy for an actor to argue with a director who is weak or who isn't convinced about the script. I remember Mr. Brackett and I were working on the script for *Hold Back the Dawn*, which Mitchell Leisen was directing. We had written a very fine scene for Charles Boyer, who was playing an immigrant waiting for his visa to come through. Unkempt and unshaven, Boyer waits in a cheap Mexican hotel. Well, to show the kind of hotel it was

*Fedora*, the first novella in Thomas Tryon's *Crowned Heads* (1976), is about a movie star who does not seem to age.

*Wilder began his career as a reporter in his native Vienna. It was in Berlin in the late 1920s that he turned to screenwriting.

and to suggest something about the character Boyer was playing, we included a scene where Boyer makes some cynical remarks to a cockroach climbing up the wall. I assumed the scene would be shot as we had written it. A short time later, I ran into Boyer and asked him how he liked the scene with the cockroach. He said, "We cut that scene." I was shocked. "Why was it cut?" I asked. "How can I talk to a cockroach when the cockroach can't answer?" was Boyer's reply. I was so angry I told Brackett, "If that son of a bitch ain't talking to a cockroach, he ain't talking to anybody." We hadn't finished the script yet, so we pared Boyer's remaining scenes down to the bare minimum.

DICK: Is it important for a director to be able to write?

WILDER: It is more important for a director to be able to read. Many directors do not understand the script and they don't have the nerve to say so. But they go ahead and shoot it, regardless.

DICK: There is a great deal of confusion today about the role of the editor. Did an editor ever change the form of any of your films?

WILDER: No. I learned to shoot with utmost economy so there is not much an editor can do. I cut the film in the camera. I do not protect myself by shooting a scene eighteen different ways; it exhausts the actors, and the words begin to lose their meaning. I will go over the rushes with the editor and we will discuss them. I may say to him, "I need an additional shot here," but that is the extent of it. The worst that can ever happen is that I must alter my film or add to it.

DICK: Yet some directors rely very heavily on their editors. Dede Allen has become a legend in her own lifetime. Some critics have even said that she bails out Arthur Penn time and time again with her editing.

WILDER: I would not say she "bailed" him out; it was more like the way Maxwell E. Perkins helped Thomas Wolfe reorganize his novels for publication. If an editor bails a director out, it is because he shot crap. Dede Allen fully deserves the billing she gets because she makes the picture better. It is the same with Verna Fields who cut *Jaws*. She has the knack of knowing which frames to cut and how fast to cut them.

DICK: You edited *The Front Page* in four days, yet Terence Malick supposedly spent a year editing *Badlands*.

WILDER: That is because he shot a great deal of film; I don't. I also work with very expensive actors, so I do not have the time. In the case of *Badlands*, you have a crew of very talented beginners who do everything themselves, including moving the camera from place to place. They can go out and shoot where they like; and by the time the sheriff comes around to ask if they have permission, they've gone. I must apply for permission and wait until I get it. If I pick up a chair on the set, I have the unions to contend with. Our approaches are totally different; it's like commedia dell'arte as opposed to the legitimate theater.

DICK: Did you go into producing because you wanted more control over your pictures?

WILDER: Yes, and also because there were so few creative producers. Look at this ad in *The Hollywood Reporter*:

### Silver Streak
A MARTIN RANSOHOFF-FRANK YABLANS PRODUCTION
AN ARTHUR HILLER FILM
A MILLER-MILKIS-COLIN HIGGINS PICTURE

This is insane. What happens is that somebody buys a property or two people buy it, so their names must appear. If the star becomes involved in the production, then his name appears. The director says it must read "A Bill Friedkin Film" or "Bill Friedkin's Film." Then the schleppers and the hangers-on get into the act. The vanity game is enormous. Even in the theater, it's "a such-and-such production in conjunction with so-and-so." Ultimately, when it's all over, it's Josh Logan's *South Pacific*.

The true producers like Thalberg, Selznick, and Goldwyn would add to a picture and enrich it; they were there when you needed them for important decisions. When the picture was finished, they got the maximum exposure for it and arranged for it to be shown in the best theaters.

DICK: Since *Ace in the Hole*, you produced all of your films except for *The Spirit of St. Louis* which Leland Hayward produced and *Witness for the Prosecution* which Arthur Hornblow, Jr., produced. Was there any reason for your not producing these yourself?

WILDER: Leland Hayward was my agent when I first came to Hollywood, so there was no real problem with his producing my film. Arthur Hornblow produced my very first film, *The Major and the Minor*. He was also a friend of Marlene Dietrich who wanted the part in *Witness for the Prosecution* and asked me to direct so she would be sure to get it.

DICK: How do you feel about directors like Peter Bogdanovich who pay homage to the work of other directors?

WILDER: You know what we call Bogdanovich? "The Frank Gorshin of directors." He is so steeped in film history that it is difficult for him to find a style of his own.

DICK: Have you ever paid homage to other directors?

WILDER: If I did, it was unconscious.

DICK: What about Lubitsch? There is a Lubitsch quality about *The Emperor Waltz* and *The Private Life of Sherlock Holmes*.

WILDER: I advise everyone to stay away from Lubitsch; he cannot be imitated. I did not set out to make a Lubitsch film in either case. And incidentally, you picked two of my failures. *Holmes* didn't make a ripple. I even had to cut two episodes out of it.

DICK: It is a film that is gaining in popularity. It was recently revived as part of a Sherlock Holmes Film Festival in New York and those who have never seen it before were quite taken with it.

WILDER: It was, I think, the lushest of the Holmesiana and truest to the period.

DICK: Most of your films employ some form of disguise or deception. Would you agree?

WILDER: Some, but not all. Not in *Double Indemnity*.

DICK: It does appear in the way Neff gets Diedrichson to sign the insurance policy.

WILDER: Yes, I see what you mean. Well, there is a lot of that in *Fedora*, I assure you.

DICK: You said before that you were not conscious of any Lubitsch influence. Were you aware of the fact that in both *Five Graves to Cairo* and *The Private Life of Sherlock Holmes* you used a parasol as part of the plot and as a symbol of femininity. In *Five Graves*, Bramble places it on Mouche's grave; in *Holmes*, Ilse uses her parasol to send messages as well as to say good-by to Holmes.

WILDER: No, I was not conscious of *Five Graves to Cairo* when I was making *Holmes*. In *Five Graves to Cairo* the parasol was a sentimental touch; there are no flowers in Tobruk so he brings her a parasol. In *Holmes* Ilse used it for Morse code. And a parasol is so photographable, you know. There is something exquisite about it, especially when it is opened out against the sun. I am very fond of the proper use of props and I like to make them part of the script. In *The Apartment* I used a broken compact mirror as the means of identifying Shirley MacLaine as the girl Fred MacMurray had been bringing to Jack Lemmon's apartment.

DICK: Were you influenced by the book of *Genesis* when you were writing *Ace in the Hole*? I am thinking of the continual emphasis on serpents, the desert as a kind of Eden that turns into a carnival, the rescue operations that take six days.

WILDER: That is a very interesting theory. You see, personally my mind doesn't go that way. And if it did, I couldn't admit it.

DICK: Several years ago you made this statement: "We're just like the guys in Detroit, putting out cars, no matter what anyone thinks we are." This is rather strange coming from a man who is the subject of retrospectives, books, articles, and Ph.D. dissertations. Do you still believe it?

WILDER: I did not mean what people think. How do you interpret it?

DICK: That directors are assembly-line workers.

WILDER: What I meant was that it takes tremendous artistry to put something into an assembly-line product so it will not have that mass-produced look. If someone is writing a poem or composing a symphony, he is doing it himself and on his own time. In our business we are playing for enormous chips supplied by other people. They give me the chips to gamble with, and I in turn am responsible to them. In this kind of situation it takes more artistry to produce something of value—sometimes to sneak in something of value—than it does when you are given as much money as you want, with no strings attached, and told to go to Salzburg and bring back a two-hour film. If I get behind schedule or exceed my budget, or if I indulge myself, after a couple of such pictures I would be flat on my ass. I would not get a chance to work again. I must do something that is hopefully superior, hopefully innovative, and at the same time it must be profitable. I personally believe that anything worthwhile ultimately finds some kind of audience. If somebody says. "This is the goddamnedest greatest picture ever made but no one went to see it," then it is not the goddamnedest greatest picture ever made.

I assure you, I have as many sleepless nights and as many ulcers as the truest of artists. But I have an added burden. If a painter buys a canvas for a couple of dollars and does not like what he has painted on it, he can throw it away. My canvas costs $4 million; if I don't like it, it can't be thrown in the fire. It's going to be shown, reviewed, maybe even play to empty houses. In the theater the producers can decide to close a show on the road and not bring it to Broadway. I can't. I've always said that the trouble with making pictures is that we can't try out in New Haven. If a picture is bad, it will come back to haunt you on the late late show. Its stench will endure forever.

## NOTES

[1]The article appeared in *Film Culture* (Winter 1962–63); it is reprinted in Gerald Mast and Marshall Cohen, eds. *Film Theory and Criticism: Introductory Readings* (New York: Oxford University Press, 1974), pp. 500–515.

[2]James Cagney, *Cagney by Cagney* (New York: Pocket Books, 1977), p. 169.

[3]Mel Gussow, *Don't Say Yes Until I Finish Talking: A Biography of Darryl F. Zanuck* (New York: Pocket Books, 1972), p. 46.

# 10
# Film Criticism:
## Theory and Practice

## CRITICISM AS THEORY

Most criticism from Aristotle to John Dryden is really theory of literature. Students reading Aristotle's *Poetics* for the first time may be disappointed if they expect a detailed analysis of a Greek tragedy. In the *Poetics* Aristotle was practicing legislative criticism: He was setting forth certain principles (art as imitation, plot as soul, the tragic hero as midway between perfect goodness and utter depravity) and establishing various categories and distinctions (the simple versus the complex plot, the kinds of recognition). But he was not explicating a text or exploring its levels of meaning.

In *On the Sublime,* Longinus analyzed one of Sappho's poems, but the bulk of his treatise as it has come down to us is also legislative: how to achieve the sublime, how not to achieve it, what elements of the sublime can be learned, what elements are innate. Horace's *Ars Poetica* also ignores practical criticism, as does Sir Philip Sidney's *An Apology for Poetry,* which by its very title is a defense of an art rather than an interpretation of it.

*Descriptive criticism,* which is based on the analysis of a literary work, is relatively new; it began in 1688 with Dryden's *An Essay of Dramatic Poesy*, and not very successfully at that. Dryden was superb when he championed the cause of English drama, but deficient when he tried to analyze a particular English play, Ben Jonson's *The Silent Woman*. The kind of criticism to which most of us are accustomed—where a text is examined line by line, image by image—started with the New Critics (John Crowe Ransom, Cleanth Brooks, Robert Penn Warren, and others), who focused almost exclusively on the work, ignoring the historical milieu out of which it came as well as the author's biography.

Early film criticism was also theoretical and reflected the basic premises of literary criticism, namely, that criticizing a medium requires a knowledge of what the medium can and cannot do, and that this knowledge is obtained by learning the theory behind the medium. Theory always precedes practice; therefore, before one can be a film critic, one must first be a film theorist.

## THE HISTORY OF FILM CRITICISM

### The Russians

Film criticism really began in Russia with the Revolution of 1917. It is true that before that time newspapers had reviewers, that in 1915 Vachel Lindsay published *The Art of the Moving Picture*, and that in 1916 Hugo Munsterberg's *The Photoplay: A Psychological Study* appeared. But no film maker attempted to explain the nature of his craft until Lev Kuleshov started writing in 1917. In the famous Kuleshov Workshop at the State Film School in Moscow, which included such famous pupils as V. I. Pudovkin and briefly Sergei Eisenstein, Kuleshov performed various experiments in montage, which he defined alternately as "the joining of shots into a predetermined order," "the alternation of shots," and "the organization of cinematic material." To show how editing can alter the face of objective reality, Kuleshov intercut a close-up of an actor's neutral face with three different shots: (1) a bowl of soup, (2) a woman in a coffin, and (3) a little girl with a toy bear. Audiences marveled at the actor's "versatility" in expressing (1) hunger, (2) sorrow at his mother's death, and (3) joy at the sight of his daughter.

Pudovkin continued in his teacher's footsteps. He idolized Kuleshov and made the extravagant claim that while others made films, Kuleshov made cinematography. Kuleshov was not infallible; although much of his theory still has value, some of it is either erroneous or misleading. His belief that the shot is the equivalent of the word has led to a misunderstanding of what the shot can say and what it cannot; his comparison between a sentence and a sequence limits the sequence to imparting only the information of which a sentence is capable; his view that the way a film is put together is more important than what it means is equivalent to the fallacy that form is more significant than content.

To his credit Kuleshov was critical of the way Russian directors shot scenes. A great admirer of American films, he contrasted American "fast montage" with Russian "slow montage." He envisioned a suicide scene where a despondent man would sit down at his desk, remove a pistol from the drawer, press it to his forehead, and pull the trigger. The American director would fragment the scene by breaking it up into its components: a close-up of the man's agonized face, a shot of his hand reaching into the drawer, an extreme close-up of the man's eyes, and finally the firing of the pistol. The Russian director would simply film the scene as if it were taking place on the stage.

What Kuleshov meant by montage in this example was nothing other than the editing technique that D. W. Griffith had perfected. Thus when Kuleshov said montage developed in America, he was speaking the truth. Pudovkin continued to explore the implications of montage, which at this stage still meant editing. He argued that the foundation of film art is editing and that a film is not "shot" but "built" from individual strips of celluloid. Pudovkin was intrigued by what happens when two different shots are combined within the same narrative context. For example, in Henry King's *Tol'able David* (1921), a tramp enters a house, sees a kitten, and immediately wants to drop a stone on it. Pudovkin read the scene in this way: Tramp + Kitten = Sadist.

To Eisenstein, Pudovkin was incorrect: The equation was not $A + B = C$, but $A \times B = Y$. Shots are meant to collide, not join together. With Eisenstein montage was no longer a matter of combining shots or of alternating them, but of making them collide with each other: $A \times B = Y$; fox $\times$ businessman = cunning. In *Tol'able David*, when King cuts from the tramp to the kitten, both the tramp and the kitten figure prominently in the same scene; in *Strike* (1924), when Eisenstein juxtaposes the face of a man and the picture of a fox, the fox is not an integral part of the scene the way the kitten is in *Tol'able David*. To King the kitten is a character; to Eisenstein the fox is a metaphor.

## The Grammarians

As new terms (montage, dissolve, wipe, etc.) entered the vocabulary of film, definitions became necessary to explain their functions. In 1935 Raymond Spottiswoode published *A Grammar of the Film*, whose purpose was "to make as precise as possible the language and grammar of film."[1] Spottiswoode was critical of some of the ways in which film expressed itself. He had little use for the wipe because, unlike the cut, which is imperceptible, the wipe calls attention to itself. He believed that while dissolves could be justified, they generally interfered with the film's rhythm because they slurred over the bridge between shots and altered the tone of a scene. Although *A Grammar of the Film* was a serious attempt to analyze film techniques, much of it is passé by today's standards. One no longer speaks of "credit titles," and what were once known as "strip titles" are now "subtitles."

## The Apologists

Spottiswoode combined a study of film terminology with a defense of the medium, arguing that movies can only become an art if they first become part of a nation's cultural life and that critics must help film develop a national character. He was forced to defend film, as Sidney was forced to defend poetry 350 years earlier, against its detractors, who called moviegoers "celluloid nitwits." However, few defenses of the film maker are as eloquent as Rudolf Arnheim's in *Film as Art:*

> [The film maker] shows the world not only as it appears objectively but also subjectively. He creates new realities, in which things can be multiplied, turns their movements and actions backward, distorts them, retards or accelerates them. . . . He breathes life into stone and bids it move. Of chaotic and illimitable space he creates pictures . . . as subjective and complex as painting.[2]

To Arnheim the fact that photography is limited is precisely what makes film an art. Because photography is incapable of perfect reproduction, film ceases to be a mere replica of reality and becomes reality's ally or enemy but never its equivalent. Film is the art of partial illusion, the same illusion that exists on the stage, where we accept a room with only three walls. In a silent film we accept characters who speak but cannot be heard; in a black and white film we tolerate the absence of color.

Because film is capable of distortion, it is not a purely realistic medium. To the doubters who think the camera reproduces the object as it is, Arnheim explains how the camera's ability to approach an object from different and unusual angles creates effects that are ordinarily found in great painting. "Art begins where mechanical reproduction leaves off,"[3] and Arnheim had no doubts that film was art.

## The Realists

Since the first film critics based their theories on the silents, they were more sympathetic to montage than the critics who came of age with the talkies. Sound brought spoken dialogue, and once the pictures learned to talk, they were not so docile as they were when they were silent. Russian montage was not well suited to the narrative sound film, in which the combination of happy face and flowing brook could break the dramatic continuity or destroy verisimilitude.

"There are cases in which montage far from being the essence of cinema is indeed its negation," wrote André Bazin,[4] whose early death in 1958 was an irreparable loss to film criticism. What bothered Bazin about montage was its inability to offer more than a limited and frequently distorted view of reality. Bazin discerned two main traditions in film: montage and *mise-en-scène*, or the cut as opposed to the long take. It was *mise-en-scène* that he championed, and it was the *mise-en-scène* directors (Jean Renoir, William Wyler, Orson Welles, etc.) whom he favored.

*Mise-en-scène*, a term derived from the theater, is difficult to translate because it signifies a variety of things. It means staging a film with the same feeling for style and detail that a theater director *(metteur-en-scène)* brings to a play; it means that the director stages the action, positions the actors within the frame, dresses them in costumes suitable to the era and mood of the film, provides them with décor that is similarly evocative—in short, blends all the elements of film making, from acting and make-up to the composition of the shots, into a whole to give as close an approximation of reality as he or she can.

Directors who work within the *mise-en-scène* tradition achieve a high degree of realism by shooting certain scenes in long take. In fact, some of the finest camera work in film is a result of the long take. The opening of Welles's *Touch of Evil* (1958) derives its power from being an uninterrupted tracking shot (see chapter 2). The long take was particularly evident in Wyler's *The Best Years of Our*

10–1  *In the celebrated long take from* The Best Years of Our Lives *(1946),
William Wyler brings all the principals into the frame for the wedding of Homer
(Harold Russell) and Wilma (Cathy O'Donnell). Courtesy Samuel Goldwyn
Productions.*

*Lives* (1946), a 172-minute movie with under 200 shots; the average
film has between 300 to 400 per hour. Wyler filmed several scenes
without making a single cut, creating action and reaction within
the same shot. Bazin justly admired the famous ending: the wedding of Wilma (Cathy O'Donnell) and Homer (Harold Russell), the
double amputee. All of the principals are present: Al and Milly
Stephenson (Fredric March and Myrna Loy); their daughter Peggy
(Teresa Wright); and Fred Derry (Dana Andrews), Homer's best
man. Fred and Peggy are in love, but his inability to find a job has
prevented their marriage. As Homer and Wilma exchange vows,
Fred turns in the direction of Peggy, who is standing with her
parents. At that moment Wyler brings everyone into the frame.
The vows seem equally applicable to Fred and Peggy; the result is
the illusion of a double wedding. A cut at any point during the
scene would have shattered that illusion.

  Another scene Bazin praised was the one in which Fred
phones Peggy to terminate their relationship. Fred, Al Ste-

phenson, and Homer are in a bar. Homer is playing the piano with his hooks. In one unbroken movement the camera goes from the piano to the phone booth, pausing only for a quick look at Al. Another director might have used several cuts or allowed us to overhear the conversation between Fred and Peggy. The fact that Wyler did neither reinforces Bazin's thesis that Wyler did not have imitators, only disciples.

Bazin wanted film to encompass as much reality as possible, but *mise-en-scène* cannot produce realism by itself; it needs *deep focus*, a technique in which background and foreground are in focus at the same time. Thus *mise-en-scène* and deep focus are allies. Deep focus has three other advantages for Bazin: (1) It brings spectators into closer contact with the image; (2) it is intellectually more challenging than montage, which manipulates spectators and annihilates their freedom of choice by making them see only what the film maker wants them to see (deep focus, by contrast, presents spectators with the whole image, from which they may choose to see only a part, such as the foreground); (3) it allows for ambiguity, which is absolutely essential to works of art, whereas montage reduces a scene to one meaning (smiling face + babbling brook admits of only one interpretation).

Bazin never expressed his theory of film in a full-scale critical work, but only in the form of essays and articles, not all of which have been translated into English. Yet it is clear that he was moving toward an aesthetics of realism. Bazin was especially impressed by the neorealistic Italian films that appeared after World War II—for example, Roberto Rossellini's *Open City* (1945) and *Paisan* (1946), and Vittorio De Sica's *The Bicycle Thief* (1949). He saw these films as showing the same respect for reality that Welles showed in the deep-focus shots in *Citizen Kane* (1941). Neorealism and deep focus have the same purpose: to keep reality intact. In a neorealistic film, Eisensteinian montage is impossible; nothing can be added to the existing reality. The cutting must follow the script, which cannot tolerate juxtapositions.

Initially, it was film's realism that caused its adversaries to regard it as a copy of nature. To Siegfried Kracauer film's ability to capture reality, far from being a handicap, is its greatest asset. Just as in the *Poetics* Aristotle determined the nature of art before he discussed the nature of tragedy, Kracauer began his epochal *Theory of Film* not with film itself, but with its parent—photography.

Kracauer is unwilling to call photography an art for the same reason he is unwilling to call film an art: The photographer lacks the artist's freedom to create his or her own inner vision. Both the photographer and the film maker are more dependent on the material world than either the painter or the poet. In art the raw material of nature disappears; in film it remains.

Kracauer's reluctance to elevate film to an art form follows inevitably from his belief that film is better equipped to record physical reality than any other medium. Consequently, film should stay on the surface of reality, for when it tries to penetrate the surface, it becomes uncinematic. Parker Tyler challenged Kracauer's thesis by showing that film has successfully explored such themes as split personality (Ingmar Bergman's *Persona*, 1966) and the impossibility of certitude (Michelangelo Antonioni's *Blow-Up*, 1966) by moving from the surface into the realms of human consciousness, where the camera once feared to tread. Kracauer would probably agree with Tyler but then add: "*Persona* and *Blow-Up* are uncinematic," meaning not that they are inferior films (quite the contrary), but that they deal with a form of reality that is better suited to the novel. Kracauer's position is thoroughly classical: Each form reaches its highest stage of development when it accomplishes what no other form can.

To Kracauer films are either cinematic or uncinematic. The more they reflect the material world, the more cinematic they are; as soon as they forsake physical reality for spiritual reality, they become less cinematic. Thus he would call the following genres uncinematic by nature: (1) the historical film because it is an artificial reproduction of a bygone age; (2) the fantasy film because of its otherworldliness; (3) the literary adaptation because in a novel or a drama the physical world is not the only one that matters; there is the inner world of the characters, which the camera has difficulty entering.

Because film evolved from photography, it shares with it four characteristics: (1) an affinity for unstaged reality, (2) a penchant for the fortuitous and the random, (3) a sense of endlessness, and (4) a preference for the indeterminate. A fifth characteristic is peculiar to film alone: an ability to capture the open-ended flow of life as it appears in the stream of situations and occurrences that constitute human existence. Kracauer is not saying that film must never attempt to stage reality or that it must always deal with such themes as chance encounters and unpredictable events. He means only that film favors nature in the raw and resists the artificial; thus, film balks at being made to resemble a play. As we have seen, shooting a film from the point of view of a spectator in an orchestra seat is entirely different from shooting it from the point of view of the camera eye, which can look up, down, around, over, under, and beyond what it sees. Naturally photography favors the fortuitous; some of the most memorable pictures ever taken were the result of the photographer's being in the right place at the right time, as the first chapter of this book demonstrates.

When Kracauer says that film has a liking for the fortuitous, he does not mean that the camera will record whatever passes in front of its lens; he does mean that a good many movies involve chance occurrences on streets, in the badlands of the West, on ships, in airports, railroad stations, hotel lobbies, and so forth. Film tends toward the endless because physical reality is seemingly without end; thus, in a movie a change of scene may be a change of continent. The film maker had to learn how to bridge vast distances by creating transitions such as the fade and the dissolve.

Film is indeterminate because physical reality is indeterminate. The juxtaposition of laughing face and flowing brook evokes the same response the world over. But what of the meal of wild strawberries and milk that Mia offered the Knight in *The Seventh Seal* (1957)? Bergman has not falsified reality by making the strawberries and milk other than what they are. The context of the scene changes the strawberries and milk from picnic food to food for a eucharistic meal; it also changes those eating the food into communicants. Reality's indeterminacy is one of the glories of film, where an object can be both itself and a symbol at the same time. The strawberries and milk never cease to be what they are: a means of sustenance. The scene determines the *kind* of sustenance: spiritual as well as physical.

Toward the end of *Theory of Film* Kracauer distills the essence of his thesis into a myth. It is not an original myth but the old one of Perseus and Medusa's head. Because the sight of Medusa's head turned men to stone, Athena warned Perseus not to look directly at her but only at the reflection on his shield:

> Now of all the existing media the cinema alone holds up a mirror to nature. Hence our dependence on it for the reflection of happenings which would petrify us were we to encounter them in real life. The film screen is Athena's polished shield.[5]

Hence the complete title of Kracauer's book: *Theory of Film: The Redemption of Physical Reality*. Kracauer does not believe that film deals only with nature in the raw as opposed to nature transfigured. Nature in the raw, of course, is film's starting point, as it must be; for nature in the raw—physical reality—is to film what language in the raw—words—is to literature: the means by which the work comes into being. Yet how does film redeem physical reality? The very fact that Kracauer speaks of holding a mirror up to nature, a polished mirror at that, provides the answer. A polished mirror will not catch a reflection of the physical universe as it is, but as something better than it is; it catches a higher form of reality, one that is no less real than what we see around us, but superior to it. How can art imitate nature and improve it? Aristotle never tells us. How can film mirror reality and redeem it? Kracauer never tells us. For the answer we must examine the works of artists who knew the secret of working within the material universe without becoming mired in it.

## The Auteurists

It was in the late 1950s that the cult of the director arose and resulted in a spate of books on the great and not so great *auteurs*. These books fall into three categories: the interview, the popular biography, and the critical study.

Because of the growing interest in film, particularly among the young, commercial publishers and university presses alike began bringing out monographs on directors, including the major figures (Orson Welles and Jean Renoir, Billy Wilder, Alfred Hitchcock) and the minor ones (Douglas Sirk, Samuel Fuller, Otto Preminger, Don Siegel). Interviews also became increasingly popular. Of course, interviews were always a part of criticism, and even the literary quarterlies featured them. The value of an interview depends upon how knowledgeable the interviewer is and how much information he or she can extract from the subject. François Truffaut's *Hitchcock* is a unique interview book; because Truffaut respects Hitchcock, knows his films intimately, and is a critic as well as a director, he was able to ask the right questions; because Hitchcock is an intelligent man who can speak incisively about his craft, he was receptive to Truffaut's questions. Consequently, Truffaut obtained information from Hitchcock that other interviewers could not.

The popular biography keeps interpretation to a minimum; it concentrates on the director's career and the people who were part of it—from the stars to the dialogue coaches. Mitchell Leisen was an interesting director at Paramount, and David Chierichetti's *Hollywood Director: The Career of Mitchell Leisen* is a treasure-trove of information, right down to the fact that Olivia de Havilland used four different colognes to match the four ages of her character in *To Each His Own* (1946). However, as criticism, *Hollywood Director* has little value.

The critical study interprets a film maker's work within a context that is considerably broader than his or her career. The best critical studies—Joel E. Siegel's *Val Lewton: The Reality of Terror*, Leo Braudy's *Jean Renoir*, Lotte H. Eisner's *Fritz Lang*—not only analyze the films but also note recurring themes and images, sources and influences, and similarities with the films of other directors. The true critical study includes an assessment of the director's worth and his or her contribution to world film.

## The Mythographers

Parker Tyler was the first film critic to understand how mythic the movies are. In *The Hollywood Hallucination* Tyler explained the extraordinary appeal of stars like Greta Garbo and Marlene Dietrich: They were mystery women, phantom ladies, moon goddesses like Diana. Their inaccessibility made them more desirable than they really were. If they ever loved a man, they could love him only in myth, where they would never have to yield their maidenhood. Even when a man would break down their resistance, we could never believe these goddesses could offer him anything more than fairy tale love.

To Tyler even Mickey Mouse cartoons had mythic underpinnings. Intelligent moviegoers watch an animated mouse without feeling their intelligence has been insulted because they instinctively recognize some myth, some universal pattern of experience behind the cartoon. Tyler identified it as the Frankenstein myth, which is based on an even older myth of the artist who creates a human being out of inert matter (e.g., Prometheus who molded man from earth; Pygmalion who carved Galatea out of marble). We understand intuitively that Mickey Mouse is someone's creation. Tyler cited other similarities between Mickey Mouse and the Frankenstein monster: Both are mechanized beings; both are factory products (Mickey, the product of the Disney factory; the monster of Frankenstein's laboratory); both obey their masters. There is also a difference between them: In James Whale's *Frankenstein* (1931) the monster turns on his maker, but Mickey always remains an amiable mouse.

We identify with the underdogs in animated cartoons because

they have the same problems we do. We forget they are ducks, mice, or pigs and think of them as humans running the same obstacle course as ourselves and encountering the same frustrations. Yet, Tyler asks, is it not the same situation in gangster films? Don't we empathize with the Little Caesars, the Dillingers, the Bonnies and the Clydes? Many moviegoers find gangsters sympathetic for various reasons: They are nonconformists who flaunt morality; their lives are colorful; they are upwardly mobile, often beginning at the bottom with petty crime and moving up the ladder of notoriety to bank heists and bloodbaths. Hollywood tends to humanize its gangsters, and to Tyler humanization equals glorification. Interestingly, Tyler made no distinction between Superman and the gangster. Who gave Superman the right to take the law into his hands? He is only a newspaper man, not a policeman. Yet we look the other way when Clark Kent ducks into a phone booth and emerges as Superman; or rather, our unconscious looks the other way as a reporter becomes a disrupter of the normal order.

In *Magic and Myth of the Movies* Tyler continued to explore the ways in which the unconscious sees films and to show how we accept certain actions in a movie that we would not tolerate in real life. Physical pain is never humorous, yet we laugh when the comic slips on a banana peel or gets a pie thrown in his face. We do not laugh because we are sadistic; the comic gives us the right to laugh by becoming a scapegoat for our sake and suffering indignities on our behalf. It is the same with the comedienne who distorts her face and mocks her body: She laughs at herself first so that we can laugh with her. Yet if we read her actions correctly, the rubber-faced lady is really asking for our approval, our love. She humiliates herself to win our applause.

Tyler saw the stars of the 1930s and 1940s as gods and goddesses. Because the screen made them immortal, they could not die; they only underwent a ritual death, like the vegetation deities who die in winter and are resurrected in spring. A star can never really die because divinity makes death impossible. The almost universal interest in films of the past supports Tyler's thesis. Humphrey Bogart will live as long as his films are shown, and there is little likelihood that the world will call a moratorium on movies. To see Bogart in Michael Curtiz's *Casablanca* (1943) is to see a man in his prime, not a man who died of cancer in 1957. In Richard Brooks's *The Happy Ending* (1969), the heroine's husband accuses her of mooning over *Casablanca* whenever it is on television. When he reminds her that practically the entire cast is dead, she replies that Humphrey Bogart, Peter Lorre, Sidney Greenstreet, and Claude Rains are more alive than either of them.

Tyler was instrumental in shaping the thinking of critics and educators such as Richard Schickel, Leo Braudy, and Amos Vogel. At Tyler's memorial service in the fall of 1974, drama critic Eric Bentley and art historian Meyer Schapiro also expressed their indebtedness to him.

## The Semioticians

*Semiotics,* the newest branch of film criticism but actually one of the oldest, emphasizes the way a film transmits its meaning through signs and codes.[6] Its approach is similar to that of the myth critics, who search out universal patterns and archetypal themes. Semiotics is also the theoretical side of structuralism, which is not so much a new discipline as a new approach to older disciplines such as linguistics, anthropology, psychoanalysis, and rhetoric, disciplines that are more concerned with signs than with objects. Thus structuralists are invariably attracted to myth because myths are the first structures, the first messages of a culture.

But myths are coded; they are invisible patterns, "offstage voices," as Roland Barthes might call them. The structuralist tries to bring the voice from the wings to center stage. Myths remain coded until they become transparent; then society discards them as clichés. The reason myths were such unifying forces in ancient societies is that they resisted decoding. Frequently they appeared in binary form, reflecting the dualism inherent in human beings (spirit/matter, male/female, life/death) and in their culture (urban/rural, endogamy/exogamy, freedom/imprisonment). The great myths are inexhaustibly bipolar; they resist any attempt to reduce them to a single meaning. Oppositeness is at the heart of Greek mythology which is one reason why it is constantly being reinterpreted. The Oedipus myth, for example, embodies the polarities knowledge/ignorance, wife/mother, old order/new order, rationalism/mysticism, sight/blindness. Myths such as this are deathless because they are founded on natural, not artificial, opposites.

It is understandable that semiotics would be in such vogue today. Semiotics is studied in the university and in Adult Education centers, where "Semiotics for the Layperson" teaches students to translate the signs they encounter in daily life: the TV commercials that promise a world where young and old, white and black will stand together if they drink Pepsi or chew Juicy Fruit gum; the clothing ads that build sexual potency into their product; the body language that is spoken at parties but not always understood.

In *Mythologies* Roland Barthes sees signs everywhere. A person's hair style can designate the class and era to which he or she belongs. In Joseph L. Mankiewicz's *Julius Caesar* (1953), the fringed hair of the characters was a sign of their "Roman-ness." Wrestling abounds in signs. The wrestler with the fleshy, sagging body telegraphs certain messages to the spectator: repulsiveness, cruelty, cowardice. The wrestler's body determines the way he acts in the ring. The conventions of wrestling (the armlock, the twisting of the leg) are all parodies of tragedy. Just as the mask of tragedy is an exaggeration of the human face, so too is wrestling an exaggeration of human suffering. The opponent who lies flat on his back with his arms outstretched has been crucified. In wrestling defeat reaches the nadir of humiliation—crucifixion.

Even our detergents speak to us, according to Barthes. Chlorinated detergents proclaim they are absolute; as liquid fire, they blaze a path through the dirt and annihilate it. Powdered detergents are more selective; they liberate the dirt. Foam detergents, on the other hand, are useless. They are luxury items, airy and immaterial, as impractical as a bubble bath.

If detergents talk, so does food. Fish 'n chips speak of nostalgia, of the British bearing up under the Blitz; steak speaks of virility, and if it is served rare and swimming in blood, of ambrosia that produces godlike strength. (In Jacques Tourneur's *Experiment Perilous, 1944*, a woman on a train orders steak for a male passenger because she assumes steak is a man's dish.)

The striptease is a coded message, although it is doubtful that grind-house patrons will accept Barthes' thesis that there is nothing sexual about stripping. The burlesque queen who peels down to her spangled G-string transforms her groin into a triangular shield, thus preventing the spectator from seeing her genitals as they really are. The G-string is a No Trespassing sign; it is a barrier between the stripper's organs and her public.

On the surface, semiotics seems rather easy to understand. There is the signifier (say, a gold band) and the signified (marriage); there is denotation, by which a word keeps its literal meaning ("He lit the *fire*"), and connotation, by which it takes on other meanings ("She was consumed by the *fire* of passion"); there is *langue*, language system that can be verbal (English, German, etc.) or nonverbal (the "language" of poker, falconry, etc.), and there is *parole* (speech), the actual practice of a language system.

The problems begin when one attempts to apply this terminology to film. In film what are the signifiers? Can a movie denote and connote, or in film does denotation become connotation? There is also the haunting question: Is film a language system? To Christian Metz, the best known of the film semioticians, film is not *langue*.[7] In language, a word can acquire a different meaning merely by the addition of a single letter—for example, "d" or "r" added to "love." But film has no words. Metz rightly rejects the shot-as-word theory and compares the shot to the sentence. Like a gifted child, film skipped the parts of speech and moved to a higher grade. But if film has no parts of speech, then it has no grammar. We know "He see the man" is ungrammatical; but what is ungrammatical in a movie? Using a dissolve instead of a cut?

Another difference is that in words there is a distance between the signifier and the signified. "Sadness" can be broken up into its signifier (the sound săd'něs) and its signified (the concept of unhappiness). But in film the signified cannot be disengaged from the signifier. In a movie the sound of sadness is not săd'něs, but a child weeping, a man wailing, an American secretary sitting alone in an outdoor café in Venice while couples stroll past her. In a movie sadness is not a concept but an actual situation (a sad family) or an attribute of a specific person (a sad man). For the same reason denotation and connotation are not distinct in film. A movie denotes and connotes at the same time. When Isak Borg raises a glass of wine in Bergman's *Wild Strawberries*, he is Isak Borg who at that moment is having lunch with his daughter-in-law and some young hitchhikers; he is also Isak Borg the priest-figure officiating at a communion service and elevating not a wine glass but a chalice.

Metz claims that film is "like" language because it communicates. But how does it communicate? In two ways: syntagmatically and paradigmatically. A *syntagm* is a unit of actual relationship; thus *syntagmatic relationships* result when the units of a statement or the units in a filmic chain follow each other in order. If we analyze the way the subplots of Robert Altman's *Nashville* (1975) interconnect or trace the rise of a character such as Mildred Pierce from housewife to restaurant owner, we are approaching the film syntagmatically.

A *paradigm* is a unit of potential relationship; thus *paradigmatic relationships* are associative, not sequential. They are not concerned with the order of the links in the chain but with the meanings we associate with them. If we associate Frank Serpico with Jesus

Christ or the madness that erupted at the Hollywood premiere in John Schlesinger's *The Day of the Locust* (1975) with the outbreak of World War II, we are approaching the film paradigmatically. Because paradigmatic relationships are independent of the order in which the events occur, they can also exist between scenes taking place at different times within the film. Shane's ride of vengeance at the end of George Stevens's film of the same name should, by its horizontal movement, recall the first appearance of Wilson the gunfighter, who also rode horizontally across the frame; yet it also contrasts with the way Shane rode down into the valley at the beginning of the film. If we associate descent with something positive (the desire to reform) and horizontal movement with something negative (the desire to murder), then we have made a paradigmatic connection.

It is not enough for the semiotician simply to isolate syntagmas and paradigms; the movie relays its messages through codes that the film maker used and that the semiotician must now reconstruct. There are all kinds of codes: codes of dress, color, lighting, and so forth. In certain simplistic westerns we may discover that white and black attire mean hero and villain respectively; in other westerns the dress code will yield to a landscape code, in which the signifier (Monument Valley) becomes the signified (America in microcosm).

Transportation codes are particularly meaningful in discovering a film maker's intentions. Karl Reisz saw the car as a vehicle charged with associations of death in *Isadora* (1969); in *Two for the Road* (1967), Stanley Donen related the particular car the couple was using to a particular stage in their marriage. In Laslo Benedek's *The Wild One* (1954), the motorcycle is the embodiment of raw virility, fascism, and arrested sexuality; but in Dennis Hopper's *Easy Rider* (1969), the motorcycle epitomized young, disenchanted America in the late 1960s.

Sometimes codes are not quite so easy to decipher. Whenever Marlene Dietrich wore a tuxedo in a movie, as she did in Josef von Sternberg's *Morocco* (1930) and *Blonde Venus* (1932), audiences were at first taken aback at the sight of such a sensuous woman in men's clothes. A dress code was operating, but what did it mean? In *Morocco* it meant that a strange form of defeminization had taken place by which Dietrich had become the essence of Hollywood Woman (seductive, smoldering) decked out with the trappings of Hollywood Man (debonair, aggressive). Thus the Dietrich figure in a tuxedo became double-sexed, androgynous.

Semiotics is to film what linguistics is to literature. A knowledge of linguistics can be extremely helpful in reading dialect literature or in interpreting poetry since poets coin new words and use old ones in startlingly new ways. Similarly semiotics can enhance our perception of a film by disclosing the way signs and codes operate in it.

## The Reviewers

### The Beginnings of Movie Reviewing

At the turn of the century the public was hungry for some type of film criticism, even if it consisted of plot summaries or naïve accounts of the wonders of celluloid. By 1904 the *Philadelphia Inquirer* was reviewing movies; the *Inquirer*'s review of Edwin S. Porter's *The Great Train Robbery* (1903) was superficial ("There is a great amount of shooting"), but at least it was a beginning. By 1906 the first film journals had been started. In 1909 the *New York Times* ran its first movie review, an archly written piece on D. W. Griffith's *Pippa Passes;* from that time on, film reviewing became a regular department in the *Times.* Since there were no special qualifications for reviewing films, anyone could write about them, and often did. Frank Woods, an advertising salesman for *The New York Dramatic Mirror,* wrote a movie column in the *Mirror* under the pseudonym of "The Spectator" from 1908 to 1912; later he went on to become a leading screenwriter.

Before he became a major playwright, Robert E. Sherwood served as film critic for *Life* magazine from 1920 to 1928. Men of letters such as Edmund Wilson, Joseph Wood Krutch, and Mark Van Doren also wrote occasional film criticism. However, Wilson, Krutch, and Van Doren made their reputations in literary criticism, not movie reviewing. The first writer to achieve a national reputation for movie reviewing was James Agee, who between 1941 and 1948 reviewed for both *Time* magazine and *The Nation.* In addition to being a critic, Agee was also a novelist, a poet, and a screenwriter; thus his reviews had a literacy not generally found in movie columns. Agee could be vicious, but generally he was honest and regarded himself as an amateur conversing with his readers.

Agee's early death at forty-five prevented his leaving behind a fully developed theory of film; yet he demonstrated in outline, if not in detail, what a critic should be. It is clear from his review of

Michael Curtiz's *Mission to Moscow* (1943), made when Russia was an American ally, that he sensed the film's importance, not as art but as pro-Soviet propaganda. Although *Mission to Moscow* justified Stalin's purge trials, Agee was unmoved by the film's rationalizations. Instead he wrote:

> About the trials I am not qualified to speak. On surface falsifications of fact and atmosphere I might, but on the one crucial question, whether Trotsky and Trotskyists were or were not involved with Germany and Japan in a plot to overthrow the government and to partition the country, I am capable of no sensible opinion. I neither believe it nor disbelieve it.[8]

One imagines Agee would have been the kind of critic who could take a film on its own terms, however political those terms may be. His charge that *Mission to Moscow* indulges its audience is more damning than five paragraphs of invective. Agee was not the kind of critic who catered to prejudices and yearned to make his audience a reflection of himself, but the kind who believed that readers have the right instincts within them and only need the proper guidance to bring them forth.

Whether Agee would have become an *auteurist* is problematical. He was certainly conscious of the role of the director, as is evident from his review of Preston Sturges's *Hail the Conquering Hero* (1944). Sturges's mother was a bohemian who gave her son a charmed life: private schools and early exposure to opera, theater, and ballet. Sturges's foster father was a down-to-earth Chicago millionaire. Agee saw Sturges as a man torn between his mother's love of the arts and his foster father's success in business. Thus in his films Sturges was always floundering between art and popular entertainment, tending more to the latter than to the former. Agee realized he was doing something quite unusual when he invoked a director's life as background for his films. Here is one of those tantalizing glimpses into the kind of critic Agee might have become. He seemed to be on the right track with Sturges. In *Sullivan's Travels* (1941), John L. Sullivan (Joel McCrea), a liberal director who may well be Sturges's persona, abandons social consciousness films for comedies because "there's a lot to be said for making people laugh." In *The Palm Beach Story* (1942), Sturges was completely ambivalent toward money, satirizing the gold diggers and the frivolous rich alike but resolving their problems before the fade-out.

Agee was not afraid to express admiration for B films. He must have known Val Lewton's movies would someday be classics, for he hailed *The Curse of the Cat People* and Mark Robson's *Youth Runs Wild,* also a Lewton production, as the best "fiction films" of 1944. Agee also wrote favorably of Robert Siodmak's *Phantom Lady* (1944), now regarded as a model of *film noir.*

Another important reviewer was Bosley Crowther.[9] Of all the newspaper reviewers of his era, he carried the greatest weight because from 1940 through 1967 he wrote for the *New York Times.* Since Crowther reviewed for the most prestigious paper in America, he did not waste his time on what he deemed "junk." Whereas Agee saw more in Val Lewton films than calculated fright, Crowther saw nothing in them. Jacques Tourneur's *Cat People* (1942) was "labored and obvious"; and although he found *The Curse of the Cat People* sensitive, it did not make his Ten Best list.

Crowther wrote for that anomaly known as the *New York Times* reader: someone who was educated but not pedantic, conservative but not a book burner, liberal without endorsing every cause as right, a believer in human values without being a teary sentimentalist. Crowther had these qualities himself. When the National Legion of Decency condemned Roberto Rossellini's *The Miracle* (1948) as an affront to the Virgin Birth, Crowther praised it as a work of art. But in the 1960s, his influence began to wane. The movies were changing and so were audiences. One of the last reviews Crowther wrote before his retirement was of Arthur Penn's *Bonnie and Clyde* (1967). The review gave no indication of the sane judgments of which he was capable. Unable to see the film as a commentary on the Great Depression, he branded it as cheap, pointless, and marred by violence.

## Movie Reviewing Today

There is more to criticism than expressing opinions. Dwight Macdonald, who devoted over forty years of his life to movie reviewing, has summarized the threefold function of the critic: (1) to judge the film's quality, (2) to prove the film's quality, and (3) to compare the film with other films, giving it its proper place within the history of art.[10] Three contemporary reviewers—Andrew Sarris, John Simon, and Pauline Kael—seem to fit the model of Macdonald's ideal critic.

Since Andrew Sarris popularized *auteurism* in America, one would expect him to excel at writing about directors. In *The American Cinema* he ranked directors according to specific categories, evidencing a knowledge of both their films and their style. His monographs on Josef von Sternberg and John Ford also reflect his ability to see a director's output as a totality, not as a series of unrelated movies. In his weekly columns for *The Village Voice* he rarely expresses opinions without substantiating them. Although he admired the beginning and the end of Robert Altman's *Nashville* (1975), he found the middle deficient because the interrelationships between the twenty-four characters seemed more suited to a big, sprawling novel than to a film. Because Sarris is an *auteurist*, he was not content merely to pass judgment on *Nashville*; instead, he related *Nashville* to Altman's other movies, comparing Barbara Jean's slaying with ritual deaths in *That Cold Day in the Park* (1969), *Images* (1972), *The Long Goodbye* (1973), and *Thieves Like Us* (1974).

Of all his colleagues John Simon has the most impressive credentials. The Yugoslavian-born, Harvard-educated critic holds a Ph.D. in comparative literature and had taught at such institutions as the Massachusetts Institute of Technology and Bard College before he made criticism his profession in 1960, when he began writing drama criticism for the *Hudson Review*. Three years later he started reviewing films for *The New Leader*. Although Simon still writes film criticism, he is also known as the drama critic for *New York Magazine*.

Since he expects every film at least to aspire to the level of art, he deals severely with those that do not. Unlike Sarris, who wears his learning gracefully, Simon tends to overwhelm the reader with his erudition. Simon was never a fan of Hitchcock, but he was familiar enough with Hitchcock criticism to know the French theory that the director's Roman Catholicism was partly accountable for the themes of guilt and salvation that run through his films. Instead of just panning *Family Plot* (1976), Simon decided to show his readers that he too was familiar with the Hitchcock question:

> Do you know what breaks the impetus of that car hurtling toward disaster? A large wooden cross. . . . And when are the miscreants apprehended? When their victim is a bishop, kidnapped from a cathedral. . . . And what is the name of the chief malefactor? Adamson, the son of Adam and inheritor of his curse.[11]

While John Simon believes in film as art, Pauline Kael believes in movies as entertainment. Kael is one of the most knowledgeable reviewers in America today. Because of her love of the medium and her identification with the moviegoer, she has been forced at times to assume an egalitarian, even an anti-intellectual pose. She constantly laments the teaching of film in the university, claiming that an overly academic approach will kill the "movies" (her favorite term for the medium because in America we never say, "I'm going to the films," but "I'm going to the movies"). She scorns pretentiousness, believing that films like Resnais' *Last Year at Marienbad* (1961) will drive moviegoers out of the theaters. She champions American movies, yet she is not chauvinistic; she merely feels they come closer to what movies ought to be than most European films. Although she scorns *auteurism*, she sometimes comes to the aid of beleaguered directors like Altman and Sam Peckinpah as if they were her children; she even tried to justify Peckinpah's *The Killer Elite* (1975). Although she writes for *The New Yorker*, there is no worldliness in her style; but there is wit, which may explain her association with that magazine.

Kael's style is deceptive; it has a thick hide but a tender underbelly. When she feels strongly about a film, she becomes hyperbolic, rating it more highly than she probably should. She compared the evening Bernardo Bertolucci's *Last Tango in Paris* closed the 1972 New York Film Festival with the evening Igor Stravinsky's *The Rite of Spring* had its premiere, calling each date a cultural landmark.

Yet Pauline Kael has a vision, if not a philosophy, of film: It is a people's art form, and she, as their representative, is a higher form of the average moviegoer. Moviegoers loathe sham; they prefer "movies" to "cinema"; they want theorizing kept to a minimum; they cannot bear to see their values mocked. Thus Kael was repelled by Stanley Kubrick's *A Clockwork Orange* (1971) because it argued that the human capacity for evil is never exhausted. Kael, who believes in people (or at least in moviegoers), could not accept Kubrick's thesis. Consequently, she was forced into taking an almost irrational stand against the film, downgrading its art and accusing its director of "sucking up to the thugs in the audience."[12]

Since Pauline Kael enjoys considerably more space than most reviewers, she can write about films at greater length. Her method is to reconstruct the film, incorporating into that reconstruction her own impressions, comparisons with other movies, and frequently comparisons with other art forms. Those who dislike her essay-reviews claim that in reconstructing the film, she creates an antifilm that bears little resemblance to the original. She began her review of Francis Ford Coppola's *Godfather II* (1974) by noting that at the end of his *The Godfather* (1972), Michael's face looked as if it were beginning to rot. One might accept "petrify," but "rot" seems inappropriate. Yet Michael's face must rot for her review to be valid.

Kael excels at historical criticism not only because she knows movies but also because she knows the movie industry. "Raising Kane," the introductory essay to *The Citizen Kane Book*, is a defense of screenwriter Herman J. Mankiewicz as the real author of *Citizen Kane* although the credits attribute the screenplay to Welles and Mankiewicz. Kael naturally has her blind spots: She fails or refuses to see how Welles impressed his personality on *Citizen Kane* by drawing on his stage and radio experience to combine the best of both media in the film. However, her purpose in writing "Raising Kane" was to solve the authorship problem of *Citizen Kane*, not to enhance the reputation of Orson Welles.

One reads Pauline Kael for her vast knowledge of film and for her style that is colloquial but polished. Few writers can provide pleasure and knowledge at the same time.

## PRACTICAL CRITICISM

True critics in any medium are rare, a fact that Alexander Pope recognized in the eighteenth century, perhaps the greatest period of literary criticism:

*In Poets as true Genius is but rare,*
*True Taste as seldom is the Critic's share.*
—An Essay on Criticism, I, 11–12

Pope knew that the impressionable can lose their way in the "maze of schools," each of which claims to have the only key to the house of criticism. However, if fiction is a house with many windows, as Henry James alleged, then criticism is a house with many doors, each with its own key. No school of literary criticism has a monopoly on interpretation; each offers its own peculiar access to the work: The New Criticism stresses the text; historical criticism places the text within its time; biographical criticism, within the context of the author's life; Marxist criticism, within the framework of the class struggle; psychoanalytic criticism, within the workings of the unconscious; myth criticism, within the universal dreams of human beings.

Criticism is an applied art. The truth of this becomes evident by comparing the interpretations of *Citizen Kane* that four different critics—a film historian, an *auteurist*, a myth critic, and a Marxist—might undertake.

## The Film Historian's Interpretation

Thanks to Pauline Kael's epochal "Raising Kane," *Kane* has indeed been "razed," reduced to its prenatal nakedness before Orson Welles dressed it in his own garb. Kael singles out two of Welles's collaborators—screenwriter Herman J. Mankiewicz and cinematographer Gregg Toland—as deserving credit for the film's success. The script was Mankiewicz's; it was not coauthored as the credits imply. And the *mise-en-scène* that the *auteurists* call "Wellesian" owes more to Gregg Toland's cinematography than to Welles's direction. Compare *Kane* with *Mad Love* (1935), a Peter Lorre "mad doctor" film, which Toland photographed, and some striking similarities emerge: gothic sets, a physical resemblance between the bald Lorre and the bald Welles, cavernous rooms, and even a white cockatoo. Toland obviously taught Welles the fundamentals of German Expressionism.

Although Mankiewicz was an excellent screenwriter, he was not the first to attempt a rags-to-riches script. There is a definite kinship between *Citizen Kane* and the script Preston Sturges wrote for *The Power and the Glory* (1933), which dealt with a Kane-like railroad magnate, Thomas Garner (Spencer Tracy), who was as enigmatic as the master of Xanadu. There are points of contact between both scripts: the Horatio Alger theme, the flashbacks following the tycoon's death, violations of chronology, and the extremes of admiration and contempt that the Great Man inspired in others.[13]

As for the overpraised gothic atmosphere of the opening sequence, that owes much to the style of RKO Studios; the spooky Xanadu bears an uncanny resemblance to castles in earlier RKO films such as Ernest B. Schoedsack's *The Most Dangerous Game* (1932) and Walt Disney's *Snow White and the Seven Dwarfs* (1938). RKO knew how to use a good thing: The famous staircase in Welles's next film, *The Magnificent Ambersons* (1942), ended up in the brownstone where Irena lived in *Cat People*, just as the fireplace in John Ford's *Mary of Scotland* (1936) turned up in *Citizen Kane* as one of Xanadu's more impressive features.

Moreover, before crediting Welles with the actual assembling of the film, it might be well to recall that *Citizen Kane* was edited by Robert Wise and the unbilled Mark Robson. Both of these men were considerably more knowledgeable about film than Welles, and both went on to become directors in their own right.

*Citizen Kane* is the quintessentially American film because Mankiewicz's screenplay, originally entitled *American*, explores the typically American theme of success and its consequences.

## The Auteurist's Interpretation

Like every first film *Citizen Kane* contains within it Orson Welles's major themes and preoccupations, chiefly his ambivalence toward wealth and his fascination with corruption. Welles's world is full of potentates, of men larger than life: Kane, Bannister of *The Lady from Shanghai* (1948), Gregori Arkadin of *Mr. Arkadin* (1955), and their alter egos in the director's Shakespearean films (*Macbeth*, 1947; *Othello*, 1952; and *Chimes at Midnight*, 1967).

Wealth assumes various forms in Welles's films: Kane's Xanadu, the Amberson mansion in *The Magnificent Ambersons*, the yacht in *The Lady from Shanghai,* the castle of Dunsinane in *Macbeth,* the castle at San Tirso in *Mr. Arkadin,* and Henry IV's court in *Chimes at Midnight.* Conversely, symbols of squalor also recur: Mary Kane's boarding house, the boarding house to which George and Aunt Fanny retreat in *The Magnificent Ambersons,* the Mexican fleabag in *Touch of Evil* (1958), K's flat in *The Trial* (1963).

There are certain Wellesian artifacts that characterize the rich, the corrupt, and the guilty: mirrors *(Kane, The Lady from Shanghai, Othello);* corridors *(Kane, Macbeth, The Trial);* staircases *(Kane, The Magnificent Ambersons);* chauffeured cars *(Kane)* and private planes *(Mr. Arkadin).*

Another Wellesian theme is the war of the worlds. The extraordinary world encroaches on the ordinary, and the fortuitous and the irrational confront the stable and the orderly. In *Kane* Susan Alexander gives up a secure but mediocre existence to enter Kane's erratic world in which she clearly does not belong. In Welles's other films the two worlds are reflected in various ways: the automobile confronts the horse and buggy in *The Magnificent Ambersons;* Nazism brings disorder to a quiet Connecticut town in *The Stranger* (1946); an Irish sailor is exposed to the idle but murderous rich in *The Lady from Shanghai;* an ordinary couple is thrown into a nightmarish world of drugs and violence in *Touch of Evil;* the little man is introduced to fascist bureaucracy in *The Trial.* Even in the Shakespearean cycle, worlds collide: Macbeth's and Lady Macbeth's, Macbeth's and Macduff's *(Macbeth);* Othello's and

Iago's, Othello's and Desdemona's *(Othello)*; Falstaff's and Henry's, Falstaff's and Hal's *(Chimes at Midnight)*.

The Wellesian king-figure dies as he lived—in style: Kane's arms solemnly folded on his breast, Othello's bier carried aloft, Henry IV expiring on his throne. Even the Wellesian villain goes out in the grand manner: from the top of a tower *(The Stranger)*, in a maze of mirrors *(The Lady from Shanghai)*, plunging through space *(Mr. Arkadin)*.

*Citizen Kane* is not quintessentially American; it is quintessentially Wellesian.

## The Myth Critic's Interpretation

Every leading character in *Citizen Kane* is the incarnation of a mythological figure. Kane himself is a Zeus type. Zeus never had a childhood but was whisked off to Crete by his mother so that his wicked father, Cronus, would not devour him as he had his other children. Charles Foster Kane was also deprived of a normal boyhood; when he was a child, his mother entrusted him to a guardian so that he could have the life she could never give him, and equally important, so that he would not be exposed to the influence of his unsuccessful father.

Zeus's marriage to Hera may have been made on Olympus but it was not blessed with tranquillity. Hera's shrewish nature made Zeus turn to other women. Kane's marriage to the cool, patrician beauty Emily Norton was no different; a president's niece, Emily was socially superior to her husband and showed it by her demeanor. Like Zeus, Kane was forced to look for love elsewhere, to women who were mortal and vulnerable—specifically to an aspiring but monumentally untalented singer, Susan Alexander. Zeus rarely appeared to women as himself; he would either assume another form (a bull, a swan, a husband away at war) or else he would visit them by night. At the beginning Kane conceals his importance from Susan because he wants her to love him for himself: "I run a couple of newspapers. How about you?"

When Kane tries to make Susan into an opera star, he steps out of the role of Zeus and into that of Pygmalion; but he becomes a Pygmalion in reverse. The sculptor Pygmalion fell in love with his own creation, which miraculously came to life. Welles inverts the myth, making Kane into an anti-Pygmalion who fashions a puppet for himself out of a living woman.

Zeus replaced his father's tyranny with the enlightened rule of the Olympians. Kane must fight his surrogate father, Thatcher, his guardian, who embodies the worst qualities of the privileged class. When Thatcher asks Kane what he would like to have been, Kane replies, "Everything you hate." In fact, Kane is always fighting Cronus in some form: Thatcher, the elderly owner of *The Inquirer* that he takes over, the political boss Jim Gettys. When he is not clashing with Cronus, he is battling Prometheus in the person of Leland, who sees Kane for what he is: "You don't care about anything except you."

Ultimately, Zeus became another Cronus: authoritarian, misanthropic, vindictive, fearful of having his power usurped, and finally aloof. Kane gradually grows more and more like Thatcher-Cronus; although he wants to benefit humanity, he has become too corrupted by wealth to do so. In the *Iliad*, Zeus, weary of all the infighting among the Olympians, frequently retired to the topmost peak of Mount Ida; Kane, disillusioned by political defeat, broken friendships, and Susan's failure as an opera star, retires to the seclusion of Xanadu.

*Kane* is not quintessentially American; it is quintessentially mythic.

## The Marxist Interpretation

*Citizen Kane*, more than any other film, exposes the roots of American capitalism, which thrives on sheer luck and the misuse of the benefits that luck may bring. As Machiavelli noted in *The Prince*, half of our affairs are governed by fortune *(fortuna)*; the other half, by personal endeavor *(virtù)*. So it is with the captitalist system.

It was by pure chance that Mary Kane, a mere boardinghouse owner, acquired the Colorado Lode. A boarder, unable to pay his rent, gave her a deed to an abandoned mine shaft that turned out to be the world's third richest gold mine. Once *fortuna* places something in our path, *virtù* must take over. Unfortunately, Mary Kane's *virtù* was diseased; married to a failure, she did not want her son Charles to become a replica of his father. Therefore, she entrusted the boy to the care of Walter P. Thatcher, a noted financier; in so doing, she deprived Charles of a normal childhood so that he could enjoy a life befitting a millionaire.

The American dream is essentially a nightmare. A victim of capitalism, Charles Foster Kane first tries to redeem himself. When he assumes control of the *New York Inquirer*, he begins exposing

10-2 The Three
Faces of Kane.

10-2A The Republican
Kane flanked by Leland,
his drama critic (Joseph
Cotten), and Bernstein,
his managing editor
(Everett Sloane).
Courtesy Janus Films.
Photo courtesy Museum
of Modern Art/Film Stills
Archive.

10-2B The Democratic
Kane as Man of the
People. Courtesy Janus
Films. Photo courtesy
Museum of Modern
Art/Film Stills Archive.

10-2C The Imperial
Kane as Master of
Xanadu. Courtesy Janus
Films. Photo courtesy
Museum of Modern
Art/Film Stills Archive.

trusts and slumlords. He tells his guardian: "It is my duty—I'll let you in on a secret—it is also my pleasure—to see to it that decent hard-working people of this community aren't robbed blind by a pack of money-mad pirates!"

Kane may be a muckraker, but he is a principled one. He also refuses to run the newspaper as if it were his private enterprise; instead, he delegates authority. He even writes a Declaration of Principles, promising his readers an honest newspaper. However, while he is writing it, his face is shrouded in darkness. Kane is clearly irredeemable.

There is no salvation for Kane because he is heir to his mother's belief that the purchasing power of money is infinite. Just as his mother bought him a privileged life, Kane buys his second wife an operatic career as well as an opera house, forcing her into a role for which she has no talent. Finally, to achieve the seclusion he requires, he buys a pleasure dome on the Florida Gulf Coast.

Who is Charles Foster Kane? After his death, the press called him a plutocrat; his guardian branded him a Communist; the Union Square demagogues labeled him a fascist. Then there is Kane's view of himself: "I am, always will be, and always have been one thing: an American."

The popular conception of Kane, confused and contradictory, is no different from the popular conception of America: the republic to which we pledge allegiance, the democracy we claim we are, the empire we have become. The three faces of America become Kane's three faces. First he is the republican editor who delegates authority to his representatives; then he is the democratic leader, promising in his Declaration of Principles to be a champion of human rights; finally, he is the imperialist, bald and gowned, an Oriental potentate living in splendor at Xanadu.

*Citizen Kane* forces us to watch the transformation of the country through the transformation of one man. If *Citizen Kane* is the quintessential American film, it is because it has uncovered the origins of the fundamental American evil: capitalism.

## GUIDELINES FOR FILM CRITICISM

There is no one way to criticize film. After a lifetime of reviewing, Dwight Macdonald wondered whether the norms that had once served him were still valid. Since Macdonald's guidelines are among the best that a contemporary critic can offer a student of film, it is worthwhile to repeat them here. They represent ways of approaching film, however, not ironclad laws. Thus there will be exceptions; some of the guidelines may not be applicable to a particular film, as Macdonald is the first to admit. Still, it is easier to deal with exceptions when one has standards by which to measure them than if one has no standards at all. The following excerpt from Macdonald's work, *Dwight Macdonald on Movies*, summarizes his guidelines succinctly:

I know something about cinema after forty years, and being a congenital critic, I know what I like and why. But I can't explain the *why* except in terms of the specific work under consideration, on which I'm copious enough. The general theory, the larger view, the gestalt— these have always eluded me. Whether this gap in my critical armor be called an idiosyncrasy or, less charitably, a personal failing, it has always been most definitely there.

But people, especially undergraduates hot for certainty, keep asking me what rules, principles or standards I judge movies by—a fair question to which I can never think of an answer. Years ago, some forgotten but evidently sharp stimulus spurred me to put some guidelines down on paper. The result, hitherto unprinted for reasons which will become clear, was:

(1) Are the characters consistent, and in fact are there characters at all?

(2) Is it true to life?

(3) Is the photography cliché, or is it adapted to the particular film and therefore original?

(4) Do the parts go together; do they add up to something; is there a rhythm established so that there is form, shape, climax, building up tension and exploding it?

(5) Is there a mind behind it; is there a feeling that a single intelligence has imposed his own view on the material?

The last two questions rough out some vague sort of meaning, and the third is sound, if truistic. But I can't account for the first two being there at all, let alone in the lead-off place. Many films I admire are not "true to life" unless that stretchable term is strained beyond normal usage: *Broken Blossoms, Children of Paradise, Zéro de Conduite, Caligari, On Approval,* Eisenstein's *Ivan the Terrible.* And some have no "characters" at all, consistent or no: *Potemkin, Arsenal, October, Intolerance, Marienbad, Orpheus, Olympia.* The comedies of Keaton, Chaplin, Lubitsch, the Marx Brothers and W. C. Fields occupy a middle ground. They have "consistent characters" all right, and they are also "true to life." But the consistency is always extreme and sometimes compulsive and obsessed (W. C., Groucho, Buster), and the truth is abstract. In short, they are so highly stylized . . . that they are constantly floating up from terra firma into the empyrean of art, right before my astonished and delighted eyes. [14]

If philosophy begins with wonder, as Plato claimed, so too does film criticism—with a sense of amazement that pictures can move and the desire to explain how the moving picture can be a work of art.

## NOTES

[1]Raymond Spottiswoode, *A Grammar of the Film: An Analysis of Film Technique* (Berkeley: University of California Press, 1969), p. 29.

[2]Rudolf Arnheim, *Film as Art* (Berkeley: University of California Press, 1974), p. 133.

[3]Ibid., p. 57.

[4]André Bazin, *What Is Cinema?*, trans. Hugh Gray, Vol. I (Berkeley: University of California Press, 1967), p. 50.

[5]Siegfried Kracauer, *Theory of Film: The Redemption of Physical Reality* (New York: Oxford University Press/Galaxy Books, 1965), p. 305.

[6]The most lucid treatment of film semiotics is in J. Dudley Andrew, *The Major Film Theories: An Introduction* (New York: Oxford University Press, 1976), pp. 212–241. Also recommended is the structuralism issue of *College English* (October 1975), especially Dorothy B. Selz's bibliography and glossary for the nonspecialist, pp. 160–166.

[7]Christian Metz, *Film Language: A Semiotics of the Cinema*, trans. Michael Taylor (New York: Oxford University Press, 1974), p. 105.

[8]*Agee on Film: Reviews and Comments by James Agee* (New York: Grosset & Dunlap, 1969), p. 39.

[9]On Crowther's career, see Frank E. Beaver, *Bosley Crowther: Social Critic of the Film* (New York: Arno Press, 1974).

[10]Dwight Macdonald, *Dwight Macdonald on Movies* (Englewood Cliffs, N.J.: Prentice-Hall, 1969), p. 471.

[11]John Simon, "Old Man Out," *New York Magazine* (April 19, 1976), p. 85.

[12]Pauline Kael, *Deeper into Movies* (Boston: Atlantic-Little, Brown, 1974), p. 378.

[13]For a more detailed comparison, see Richard Corliss, *Talking Pictures: Screenwriters in the American Cinema* (New York: Penguin Books, 1975), pp. 26–34.

[14]*Dwight Macdonald on Movies*, pp. ix–x.

# Selected
# Bibliography

## GENERAL

### Film Theory

Andrew, J. Dudley. *The Major Film Theories: An Introduction.* New York: Oxford University Press, 1976.

Arnheim, Rudolf. *Film as Art.* Berkeley: University of California Press, 1974.

Bazin, André. *What Is Cinema?* Translated and selected by Hugh Gray. 2 vols. Berkeley: University of California Press, 1967, 1971.

Eisenstein, Sergei. *Film Form: Essays in Film Theory.* Translated and edited by Jay Leyda. New York: Harcourt Brace & World, 1949.

———. *The Film Sense.* Translated and edited by Jay Leyda. New York: Harcourt Brace & World, 1942, 1947.

Kracauer, Siegfried. *Theory of Film: The Redemption of Physical Reality.* New York: Oxford University Press, 1960.

Kuleshov, Lev. *Kuleshov on Film: Writings by Lev Kuleshov.* Translated and edited by Ronald Levaco. Berkeley: University of California Press, 1974.

Mast, Gerald, and Marshall Cohen, eds. *Film Theory and Criticism: Introductory Readings.* New York: Oxford University Press, 1974.

Metz, Christian. *Film Language: A Semiotics of the Cinema*. Translated by Michael Taylor. New York: Oxford University Press, 1974.

Murray, Edward. *Nine American Film Critics: A Study of Theory and Practice*. New York: Frederick Ungar, 1975.

Pudovkin, V. I. *Film Technique and Film Acting*. Translated by Ivor Montagu. New York: Grove Press, 1970.

Tudor, Andrew. *Theories of Film*. New York: Viking Press, 1973.

Tyler, Parker. *The Hollywood Hallucination*. New York: Simon & Schuster, 1970.

————. *Magic and Myth of the Movies*. New York: Simon & Schuster, 1970.

————. *The Shadow of an Airplane Climbs the Empire State Building: A World Theory of Film*. Garden City, N. Y.: Doubleday, 1972.

Wollen, Peter. *Signs and Meaning in the Cinema*. 3rd ed. Bloomington: Indiana University Press, 1972.

## Film Practice

Agee, James. *Agee on Film: Reviews and Comments by James Agee*. New York: Grosset & Dunlap-Universal Library, 1969.

Kael, Pauline. *Deeper into Movies*. Boston: Little, Brown, 1972.

————. *Going Steady*. Boston: Little, Brown, 1970.

————. *I Lost It at the Movies*. Boston: Little, Brown, 1965.

————. *Kiss Kiss Bang Bang*. Boston: Little, Brown, 1968.

————. *Reeling*. Boston: Atlantic-Little, Brown, 1976.

Macdonald, Dwight. *Dwight Macdonald on Movies*. Englewood Cliffs, N. J.: Prentice-Hall, 1969.

Sarris, Andrew. *The American Cinema: Directors and Directions 1929–1968*. New York: E. P. Dutton, 1968.

————. *Confessions of a Cultist*. New York: Simon & Schuster, 1970.

————. *The Primal Screen*. New York: Simon & Schuster, 1973.

Simon, John. *Acid Test*. New York: Stein & Day, 1963.

————. *Movies into Film*. New York: Dial, 1971.

————. *Private Screenings*. New York: Macmillan, 1967.

## BIBLIOGRAPHY OF SELECTED DIRECTORS

### Robert Altman

Dempsey, Michael. "Altman: The Empty Staircase and the Chinese Princess." *Film Comment*, 10 (September–October 1974), 10–17.

Jameson, Richard T. "*Nashville*." *Movietone News*, No. 43 (September 4, 1975), 1–24. The most detailed analysis of the film available.

Rosenbaum, Jonathan. "Improvisations and Interactions of Altmanville." *Sight and Sound*, 44 (Spring 1975), 90–95.

### Michelangelo Antonioni

Cameron, Ian, and Robin Wood. *Antonioni*. New York: Praeger, 1969.

Epstein, Renee. "Antonioni Speaks—and Listens." *Film Comment*, 11 (July–August 1975), 6–8.

Peploe, Mark, Peter Wollen, and Michelangelo Antonioni. *The Passenger*. New York: Grove Press, 1975.

Perry, Ted. "Men and Landscapes in Antonioni's *The Passenger*." *Film Comment*, 11 (July–August 1975), 2–5.

## Ingmar Bergman

Bergman, Ingmar. *The Seventh Seal*. Translated by Lars Malmström and David Kushner. New York: Simon & Schuster, 1960.

———. *Wild Strawberries*. Translated by Lars Malmström and David Kushner. New York: Simon & Schuster, 1960.

De Nito, Dennis, and William Herman. *Film and the Critical Eye*. New York: Macmillan, 1975. Excellent on *The Seventh Seal* and *Wild Strawberries*.

Simon, John. *Ingmar Bergman Directs*. New York: Harcourt Brace Jovanovich, 1972.

Steene, Birgitta. *Ingmar Bergman*. New York: Twayne, 1968.

———, ed. *Focus on The Seventh Seal*. Englewood Cliffs, N. J.: Prentice-Hall, 1972.

Wood, Robin. *Ingmar Bergman*. New York: Praeger, 1969.

## Bernardo Bertolucci

Arcalli, Franco, and Bernardo Bertolucci. *Bernardo Bertolucci's Last Tango in Paris: The Screenplay*. New York: Dell, 1973.

Haskell, Molly. *From Reverence to Rape: The Treatment of Women in the Movies*. New York: Holt, Rinehart and Winston, 1974.

Mellen, Joan. "Sexual Politics and *Last Tango in Paris*." *Film Quarterly*, 26 (Spring 1973), 9–19.

## Luis Buñuel

Buñuel, Luis. *Three Screenplays: Viridiana, The Exterminating Angel, Simon of the Desert*. New York: Grossman, 1969.

Durgnat, Raymond. *Luis Buñuel*. Berkeley: University of California Press, 1968.

Taylor, John Russell. *Cinema Eye, Cinema Ear: Some Key Film-Makers of the Sixties*. New York:Hill and Wang, 1964.

## Francis Ford Coppola

Rosen, Marjorie. "Interview with Francis Ford Coppola." *Film Comment*, 10 (July–August 1974), 43–49.

Vogelsang, Judith. "Motifs of Image and Sound in *The Godfather*." *The Journal of Popular Film*, 2 (Spring 1973), 115–135.

## Delmer Daves

Higham, Charles, and Joel Greenberg. *Hollywood in the Forties*. New York: Paperback Library, 1970.

Sennett, Ted. *Warner Brothers Presents*. Secaucus, N. J.: Castle Books, 1971.

### Sergei Eisenstein

Barna, Yon. *Eisenstein: The Growth of a Cinematic Genius*. Bloomington: Indiana University Press, 1973.

Mayer, David. *Eisenstein's Potemkin: A Shot-by-Shot Presentation*. New York: Grossman, 1972.


### John Ford

Baxter, John. *The Cinema of John Ford*. New York: A. S. Barnes, 1971.

French, Warren. *Filmguide to The Grapes of Wrath*. Bloomington: Indiana University Press, 1973.

McBride, Joseph, and Michael Wilmington. *John Ford*. London: Secker & Warburg, 1974.

Sarris, Andrew. *The John Ford Movie Mystery*. Bloomington: Indiana University Press, 1976.


### D. W. Griffith

Geduld, Harry, ed. *Focus on D. W. Griffith*. Englewood Cliffs, N. J.: Prentice-Hall, 1971.

Henderson, Robert M. *D. W. Griffith: His Life and Work*. New York: Oxford University Press, 1972.

Silva, Fred, ed. *Focus on The Birth of a Nation*. Englewood Cliffs, N. J.: Prentice-Hall, 1971.


### Alfred Hitchcock

Durgnat, Raymond. *The Strange Case of Alfred Hitchcock, or The Plain Man's Hitchcock*. Cambridge, Mass.: M.I.T. Press, 1975.

LaValley, Albert J., ed. *Focus on Hitchcock*. Englewood Cliffs, N. J.: Prentice-Hall, 1972.

Naremore, James. *Filmguide to Psycho*. Bloomington: Indiana University Press, 1973.

Truffaut, François. *Hitchcock*. New York: Simon & Schuster, 1967.

Wood, Robin. *Hitchcock's Films*. New York: Paperback Library, 1970.


### Stanley Kubrick

Geduld, Carolyn. *Filmguide to 2001: A Space Odyssey*. Bloomington: Indiana University Press, 1973.

Houston, Penelope. *"Barry Lyndon." Sight and Sound*, 45 (Spring 1976), 77–80.

Kagan, Norman. *The Cinema of Stanley Kubrick*. New York: Grove Press, 1975.

Kubrick, Stanley. *Stanley Kubrick's A Clockwork Orange*. New York: Ballantine Books, 1972.


### Mitchell Leisen

Chierichetti, David. *Hollywood Director: The Career of Mitchell Leisen*. New York: Curtis Books, 1973.

**Joseph Losey**
Leahy, James. *The Cinema of Joseph Losey*. New York: A. S. Barnes, 1967.

**Sidney Lumet**
Luciano, Dale. *"Long Day's Journey into Night*: An Interview with Sidney Lumet." *Film Quarterly*, 25 (1971), 20–29.
Petrie, Graham. "The Films of Sidney Lumet: Adaptation as Art." *Film Quarterly*, 21 (Winter 1967–1968), 9–18.

**Terence Malick**
Johnson, William. *"Badlands." Film Quarterly*, 27 (Spring 1974), 43–46.

**Rouben Mamoulian**
Milne, Tom. *Rouben Mamoulian*. Bloomington: Indiana University Press, 1970.

**Max Ophuls**
*Film Comment*, 7 (Summer 1971). One-third of the issue is devoted to Ophuls.

**Sam Peckinpah**
*Film Heritage*, 10 (Winter 1974–1975). Devoted exclusively to Peckinpah.

**Sir Carol Reed**
Greene, Graham, and Carol Reed. *The Third Man*. New York: Simon & Schuster, 1968.
Phillips, Gene. *Graham Greene: The Films of His Fiction*. New York: Columbia Teachers College Press, 1974.

**Alain Resnais**
Duras, Marguerite. *Hiroshima Mon Amour*. Translated by Richard Seaver. New York: Grove Press, 1961.
Ward, John. *Alain Resnais, or The Theme of Time*. Garden City, N. Y.: Doubleday, 1968.

**John Schlesinger**
*Film Comment*, 11 (May–June 1975). Articles and background on *The Day of the Locust*, including West's Hollywood years.

**Martin Scorsese**
Patterson, Patricia, and Manny Farber. "The Power and the Gory" (review of *Taxi Driver*). *Film Comment*, 12 (May–June 1976), 27–30.
Rosen, Marjorie. "Martin Scorsese Interview." *Film Comment*, 11 (March–April 1975), 40–46.

**George Stevens**
Richie, Donald. *George Stevens: An American Romantic*. New York: Museum of Modern Art, 1970.

**Robert Stevenson**
Riley, Michael. "Gothic Melodrama and Spiritual Romance: Vision and Fidelity in Two Versions of *Jane Eyre*." *Literature/Film Quarterly*, 3 (Spring 1975), 145–159.

**Preston Sturges**
Mast, Gerald. *The Comic Mind: Comedy and the Movies*. Indianapolis, Ind.: Bobbs-Merrill, 1973.
Ursini, James. *Preston Sturges: An American Dreamer*. New York: Curtis Books, 1973.

**Jacques Tourneur**
Higham, Charles, and Joel Greenberg. *The Celluloid Muse: Hollywood Directors Speak*. Chicago: Henry Regnery, 1969.
Siegel, Joel E. *Val Lewton: The Reality of Terror*. New York: Viking, 1973.

**François Truffaut**
Crisp, C. G. *François Truffaut*. New York: Praeger, 1972.
Petrie, Graham. *The Cinema of François Truffaut*. New York: A. S. Barnes, 1970.
Truffaut, François. *Day for Night*. Translated by Sam Flores. New York: Grove Press, 1975.
————. *The Story of Adele H*. New York: Grove Press, 1976.
Truffaut, François, and Jean Gruault. *The Wild Child*. Translated by Linda Lewin and Christine Lémery. New York: Washington Square Press, 1973.
Truffaut, François, and Marcel Moussy. *The 400 Blows*. New York: Grove Press, 1969.

**Raoul Walsh**
Canham, Kingsley. *The Hollywood Professionals: Michael Curtiz, Raoul Walsh, Henry Hathaway*. New York: A. S. Barnes, 1973.
*Movietone News*, No. 45 (November 9, 1975). A Raoul Walsh issue with articles on *High Sierra* and *Colorado Territory*.

**Orson Welles**
Carringer, Robert L. "Rosebud, Dead or Alive: Narrative and Symbolic Structure in *Citizen Kane*." *PMLA*, 91 (March 1976), 185–193.
*The Citizen Kane Book*. Boston: Atlantic-Little, Brown, 1971. Includes Pauline Kael's "Raising Kane," the shooting script, and the cutting continuity of the actual film.

*Film Reader*, 1 (1975). Articles on semiotics and *Citizen Kane*.

Gottesman, Ronald, ed. *Focus on Citizen Kane*. Englewood Cliffs, N. J.: Prentice-Hall, 1971.

————. *Focus on Orson Welles*. Englewood Cliffs, N. J.: Prentice-Hall, 1976.

Higham, Charles. *The Films of Orson Welles*. Berkeley: University of California Press, 1971.

**Billy Wilder**

Farber, Stephen. "The Films of Billy Wilder." *Film Comment*, 7 (Winter 1971–1972), 8–22.

McBride, Joseph, and Michael Wilmington. "The Private Life of Billy Wilder." *Film Quarterly*, 23 (Summer 1970), 2–9.

Madsen, Axel. *Billy Wilder*. Bloomington: Indiana University Press, 1969.

Wood, Tom. *The Bright Side of Billy Wilder, Primarily*. Garden City, N. Y.: Doubleday, 1970.

Zolotow, Maurice. *Billy Wilder in Hollywood*. New York: G. P. Putnam's Sons, 1977.

**William Wyler**

Madsen, Axel. *William Wyler*. New York: Crowell, 1973.

# Rental Sources for Films Discussed

The abbreviation appearing after each title designates the current 16mm distributor of the particular film. To be certain that the rental source has not changed or that the film has not been withdrawn, consult the latest catalogue.

AB  Audio Brandon
34 MacQuesten Parkway, South
Mount Vernon, New York 10550

CW  Cine World
13 Arcadia Road
Old Greenwich, Conecticut 06870

CON  Contemporary/McGraw-Hill
Princeton Road
Hightstown, New Jersey 08520

FI  Films Incorporated
440 Park Avenue South
New York, New York 10016

I  Ivy Films
165 West 46 Street
New York, New York 10036

JAN  Janus Films
745 Fifth Avenue
New York, New York 10022

MOMA  Museum of Modern Art
11 West 53 Street
New York, New York 10019

SWA  Swank Motion Pictures, Inc.
393 Front Street
Hempstead, New York 11550

UA    United Artists 16
729 Seventh Avenue
New York, New York 10019

UNI    Universal 16
445 Park Avenue
New York, New York 10003

WAR    Warner Bros., Inc.
Non-Theatrical Division
4000 Warner Boulevard
Burbank, California 91522

**A**

| | |
|---|---|
| *Accused, The* (William Dieterle, 1948) | UNI |
| *Act of Murder, An* (Michael Gordon, 1948) | UNI |
| *All the President's Men* (Alan J. Pakula, 1976) | SWA |
| *Apartment, The* (Billy Wilder, 1960) | UA |
| *Arise, My Love* (Mitchell Leisen, 1940) | UNI |
| *Avanti!* (Billy Wilder, 1972) | UA |

**B**

| | |
|---|---|
| *Badlands* (Terence Malick, 1973) | WAR |
| *Ball of Fire* (Howard Hawks, 1941) | AB |
| *Barry Lyndon* (Stanley Kubrick, 1975) | SWA |
| *Beau Geste* (William Wellman, 1939) | UNI |
| *Best Years of Our Lives, The* (William Wyler, 1946) | AB |
| *Big Carnival, The* (*Ace in the Hole*) (Billy Wilder, 1951) | FI |
| *Birth of a Nation, The* (D. W. Griffith 1915) | MOMA |
| *Blackboard Jungle, The* (Richard Brooks, 1955) | FI |
| *Blue Dahlia, The* (George Marshall, 1946) | UNI |
| *Bonnie and Clyde* (Arthur Penn, 1967) | AB |
| *Breathless* (Jean-Luc Godard, 1959) | CON |
| *Brief Encounter* (David Lean, 1946) | CON |
| *Broken Blossoms* (D. W. Griffith, 1919) | MOMA |
| *Brute Force* (Jules Dassin, 1947) | I |
| *Butch Cassidy and the Sundance Kid* (George Roy Hill, 1969) | FI |

**C**

| | |
|---|---|
| *Cat People* (Jacques Tourneur, 1942) | FI |
| *Caught* (Max Ophuls, 1948) | I |
| *Chien Andalou, Un* (*An Andalusian Dog*; Luis Buñuel, 1928) | MOMA, JAN |
| *Children's Hour, The* (William Wyler, 1962) | AB |
| *Citizen Kane* (Orson Welles, 1941) | FI, JAN |

*Clockwork Orange, A* (Stanley Kubrick, 1971)     WAR
*Colorado Territory* (Raoul Walsh, 1949)     UA


**D**
*Dark Passage* (Delmer Daves, 1947)     UA
*Day for Night* (François Truffaut, 1973)     WAR
*Day of the Locust, The* (John Schlesinger, 1975)     FI
*Diary of a Country Priest* (Robert Bresson, 1950)     AB
*Dog Day Afternoon* (Sidney Lumet, 1975)     SWA
*Double Indemnity* (Billy Wilder, 1944)     UNI
*Dr. Jekyll and Mr. Hyde* (Rouben Mamoulian, 1932)     FI
*Dracula's Daughter* (Lambert Hillyer, 1936)     UNI
*Duel in the Sun* (King Vidor, 1947)     AB

**E**
*Easy Living* (Mitchell Leisen, 1937)     MOMA, UNI
*8 1/2* (Federico Fellini, 1963)     AB
*Emperor Waltz, The* (Billy Wilder, 1948)     UNI
*Enchantment* (Irving Reis, 1948)     AB

**F**
*Family Plot* (Alfred Hitchcock, 1976)     UNI
*Five Graves to Cairo* (Billy Wider, 1943)     UNI
*Foreign Affair, A* (Billy Wilder, 1948)     UNI
*Foreign Correspondent* (Alfred Hitchcock, 1940)     AB
*Fortune Cookie, The* (Billy Wilder, 1966)     UA
*400 Blows, The* (François Truffaut, 1959)     JAN
*Front Page, The* (Billy Wilder, 1974)     UNI

**G**
*Godfather, The, Part II* (Francis Ford Coppola, 1974)     FI
*Grapes of Wrath, The* (John Ford, 1940)     FI
*Greatest Story Ever Told, The* (George Stevens, 1965)     AB
*Great Expectations* (David Lean, 1947)     AB

**H**
*Hennessy* (Don Sharp, 1975)     SWA
*High Sierra* (Raoul Walsh, 1941)     UA
*Hiroshima Mon Amour* (Alain Resnais, 1960)     AB
*How Green Was My Valley* (John Ford, 1941)     FI
*Hustle* (Robert Aldrich, 1975)     FI

**I**
*I Confess* (Alfred Hitchcock, 1952)     WAR
*Intolerance* (D. W. Griffith, 1916)     MOMA, AB

*Irma la Douce* (Billy Wilder, 1963)                                    UA
*It Happened One Night* (Frank Capra, 1934)                             SWA
*I Walked with a Zombie* (Jacques Tourneur, 1943)                       FI

**J**

*Jane Eyre* (Robert Stevenson, 1944)                                   FI

**K**

*King and Country* (Joseph Losey, 1964)                                 AB
*Kiss Me, Stupid* (Billy Wilder, 1964)                                 UA

**L**

*Lady and the Monster, The* (George Sherman, 1944)                      I
*Lady Eve, The* (Preston Sturges, 1941)                                UNI
*Last Picture Show, The* (Peter Bogdanovich, 1971)                     SWA
*Last Tango in Paris* (Bernardo Bertolucci, 1972)                      UA
*L'Atalante* (Jean Vigo, 1934)                                         AB
*Laura* (Otto Preminger, 1944)                                         FI
*Letter from an Unknown Woman* (Max Ophuls, 1948)                      I
*Long Day's Journey into Night* (Sidney Lumet, 1962)                   AB
*Lost Weekend, The* (Billy Wilder, 1945)                              UNI

**M**

*M* (Fritz Lang, 1931)                                                JAN
*Macbeth* (Orson Welles, 1947)                                        AB
*Magnificent Ambersons, The* (Orson Welles, 1942)                     FI
*Major and the Minor, The* (Billy Wilder, 1942)                       UNI
*Medium Cool* (Haskell Wexler, 1969)                                  FI
*Mr. Arkadin* (Orson Welles, 1955)                                    CON
*Mr. Skeffington* (Vincent Sherman, 1944)                             UA
*Mr. Smith Goes to Washington* (Frank Capra, 1939)                    SWA, AB
*Mrs. Miniver* (William Wyler, 1942)                                  FI
*Murder on the Orient Express* (Sidney Lumet, 1974)                   FI
*My Darling Clementine* (John Ford, 1946)                             FI

**N**

*Naked City, The* (Jules Dassin, 1948)                                I
*Nashville* (Robert Altman, 1975)                                     FI
*Next Voice You Hear, The* (William Wellman, 1950)                    FI
*Nickelodeon* (Peter Bogdanovich, 1976)                              SWA
*Night of the Hunter, The* (Charles Laughton, 1955)                  UA
*North by Northwest* (Alfred Hitchcock, 1959)                        FI
*Notorious* (Alfred Hitchcock, 1946)                                 AB

**O**

*One Flew over the Cuckoo's Nest* (Miloš Forman, 1975)               UA
*One, Two, Three* (Billy Wilder, 1961)                               UA

**P**

| | |
|---|---|
| *Passenger, The* (Michelangelo Antonioni, 1975) | FI |
| *Penny Serenade* (George Stevens, 1941) | AB |
| *Potemkin* (Sergei Eisenstein, 1925) | MOMA, AB |
| *Private Life of Sherlock Holmes, The* (Billy Wilder, 1970) | UA |
| *Psycho* (Alfred Hitchcock, 1960) | UNI |
| *Public Enemy* (William Wellman, 1931) | UA |

**Q**

| | |
|---|---|
| *Queen Christina* (Rouben Mamoulian, 1933) | FI |

**R**

| | |
|---|---|
| *Rebecca* (Alfred Hitchcock, 1940) | AB |
| *Revolt of Mamie Stover, The* (Raoul Walsh, 1956) | FI |

**S**

| | |
|---|---|
| *Saboteur* (Alfred Hitchcock, 1942) | UNI |
| *Sea of Grass* (Elia Kazan, 1947) | FI |
| *Searchers, The* (John Ford, 1956) | WAR |
| *Serpico* (Sidney Lumet, 1973) | FI |
| *Seventh Seal, The* (Ingmar Bergman, 1957) | JAN |
| *Shane* (George Stevens, 1953) | FI |
| *Shock Corridor* (Samuel Fuller, 1963) | CW |
| *Some Like It Hot* (Billy Wilder, 1959) | UA |
| *Song of Bernadette, The* (Henry King, 1943) | FI |
| *Stage Fright* (Alfred Hitchcock, 1950) | WAR |
| *Stalag 17* (Billy Wilder, 1953) | FI |
| *Sting, The* (George Roy Hill, 1973) | SWA |
| *Story of Adele H., The* (François Truffaut, 1975) | FI |
| *Stranger Knocks, A* (Johan Jacobsen, 1963) | AB |
| *Sullivan's Travels* (Preston Sturges, 1941) | UNI |
| *Sunset Boulevard* (Billy Wilder, 1950) | FI |

**T**

| | |
|---|---|
| *Tale of Two Cities, A* (Jack Conway, 1935) | FI |
| *Taxi Driver* (Martin Scorsese, 1976) | SWA |
| *Tea and Sympathy* (Vincente Minnelli, 1956) | FI |
| *These Three* (William Wyler, 1936) | AB |
| *They Shoot Horses, Don't They?* (Sydney Pollack, 1969) | FI |
| *Thin Man, The* (Woody Van Dyke, 1934) | FI |
| *Third Man, The* (Sir Carol Reed, 1949) | CON |
| *Three Days of the Condor* (Sydney Pollack, 1975) | FI |
| *Through a Glass Darkly* (Ingmar Bergman, 1962) | JAN |
| *Tol'able David* (Henry King, 1921) | MOMA |
| *Topaz* (Alfred Hitchcock, 1969) | UNI |
| *Touch of Evil* (Orson Welles, 1958) | UNI |
| *Two Flags West* (Robert Wise, 1950) | FI |

| | |
|---|---|
| *Two for the Road* (Stanley Donen, 1967) | FI |
| *Two Mrs. Carrolls, The* (Peter Godfrey, 1947) | UA |

**V**

| | |
|---|---|
| *Viridiana* (Luis Buñuel, 1961) | AB |

**W**

| | |
|---|---|
| *Wild Bunch, The* (Sam Peckinpah, 1969) | CON |
| *Wild Child, The* (François Truffaut, 1970) | UA |
| *Wild One, The* (Laslo Benedek, 1954) | AB |
| *Wild Strawberries* (Ingmar Bergman, 1957) | JAN |
| *Witness for the Prosecution* (Billy Wilder, 1957) | UA |
| *Woman in White, The* (Peter Godfrey, 1948) | UA |
| *Women in Love* (Ken Russell, 1970) | UA |
| *Wrong Man, The* (Alfred Hitchcock, 1957) | WAR |

# Index*

*Page numbers in italics refer to illustrations.

narrative device
music as, 105
*See also* Literary devices; Print;
Voice-over
narrator-agent, 78–80
narrators
reliable and unreliable, 79–80
self-conscious, 78–79
*Nashville*, 47–51, 69, 75, 134, 173
Negulesco, Jean, 104
neorealism, 160
New Critics, 155
Newman, Alfred, 136
newspaper headlines, 53
New Wave films, *101*, 102
*New York, New York*, 39
*New York Times*, 170
*Next Voice You Hear, The*, 69
Nichols, Mike, 54
Nicholson, Jack, 94–96, *95*
*Nickelodeon*, 4, 39
*Night Must Fall*, 39
*Night of the Hunter, The*, 29
*Night Porter, The*, 107
*Ninotchka*, 138
*North by Northwest*, 20, 26, 32, 33,
37, 140
*Notorious*, 4, 10, 14, 24, 25, *25*, *31*,
31–32, 69

objectivity, myth of, 127
objects, unifying, 24–26
Odessa Steps sequence, in
*Potemkin*, 4, 42–43, 142, *143*
*Odyssey* (Homer), 72, 114
Oedipus myth, 166
*The Passenger* and, 125–126
Olivier, Laurence, 79
omniscient author, 75–76
*One, Two, Three*, 139, 140
*One Flew over the Cuckoo's Nest*, 94–
96, *95*
O'Neill, Robert, 1, *2*
opening-credit prologues, 71
Ophuls, Max, 21, 32, 60
*Othello*, 177–178

overlapping voice, 66

pace (rhythm), editing and, 44–51
Pacino, Al, *92*, 92–93
Pakula, Alan J., 17, *18*, 53, 65, 71
*Palm Beach Story, The*, 171
pan shot, 18–20
paradigmatic relationships, 168–
169
*Paradise Lost* (Milton), 72
parallel cutting (crosscutting), 29–
30, 49–51, 73, 98
Paramount, 137, 145–146, 148
*Passenger, The*, 19–20, 115–128, *122*
assumed identity theme in, 115–
117, 128
existential implications of, 124–
125
limitations of film's ability to
record reality and, 123, 126–
127
mistaken identity theme in sub-
text of, 123–124
mythic elements in, 125–126
subtext of, 123–128
text of, 117–123, **128**
as total film, 127–128
Pater, Walter, 111
Peckinpah, Sam, 41, 71, 174
Penn, Arthur, 41, 137, 149, 172
*Penny Serenade*, 39, 72
*Persona*, 161
*Petrified Forest, The*, 91
Petronius, 83
*Petty Girl, The*, 36
*Phantom Lady*, 172
*Philadelphia Inquirer* (newspaper),
170
*Philadelphia Story, The*, 105
photography
Arnheim on, 157
Kracauer on, 160–162
*Picture of Dorian Gray, The*, 55
Pidgeon, Walter, 27, 31
Pierson, Frank, 8, 23
place-time introductions, 55

plot (text), 82–83, 111
music and, 105, 106
of *The Passenger*, 117–123, 128
poems, epic, 72
point of view, 74–80
implied author, 76–77
narrator-agent, 78–80
omniscient author, 75–76
reliable and unreliable narrators, 79–80
self-conscious narrator, 78–79
Pollack, Sydney, 53, 66, 73
Pope, Alexander, 131, 175
*Poseidon Adventure, The*, 132
*Potemkin*, 4, 42–43, 142, *143*
Powell, Michael, 105
*Power and the Glory, The*, 176
prefatory remarks, 55–56
*See also* Prologue
*Prelude, The* (Wordsworth), 32–33
Preminger, Otto, 69
Print (printed material), 52–57
*Private Life of Sherlock Holmes, The*, 107, 139, 140, 151
producer, 132
collaboration between director and, 137
Wilder on, 150
prolepsis, 73–74
prologue, 54–56, 61
dramatized, 70–71
opening-credit, 71
precredit, 71
*Psycho*, 15, 36–37, 55, 66
*Public Enemy*, 133
Pudovkin, V. I., 40, 42, 155–156
*Purple Heart, The*, 109
*Pygmalion, Citizen Kane* and, 178
Pynchon, Thomas, 72

*Queen Christina*, 15

Rachmaninoff, Sergei, 106
radio, 105–106
Raft, George, 90, *91*, 92
range of shot, 14–16

Rapper, Irving, 105
realism, 158–163
reality, limitations of ability to know, 157–158
*The Passenger* and, 116, 123, 124, 126–127
*Rebecca*, 26, 36–37, 57, 65, 136
recapitulation, 34, 65–66
*Red Shoes, The*, 105
Reed, Sir Carol, 113
reflectors, 76, 78, 79
Reis, Irving, 56–57
Reisz, Karel, 39, 41, 169
remake, relationship between original and, 103–105
Renoir, Jean, 55, 79
repetition of motifs, 140
repetitive voice, 65–66
Resnais, Alain, 68
*Return of a Man Called Horse*, 53
reviewing, 170–175
beginnings of, 170–172
today, 172–175
*Revolt of Mamie Stover, The*, 13
*Rhapsody in Blue*, 105
rhythm (pace), editing and, 44–51
Richie, Donald, 86
Rimsky-Korsakov, Nikolai, 110
RKO studios, 176
Robson, Mark, 137, 172, 176–177
"roll up," 56
Rossellini, Roberto, 172
Rossen, Robert, 21*n*
Rossini, G., 110
Rosza, Miklos, 106, 107
Rota, Nino, 136
*Rules of the Game, The*, 55, 79
Russell, Ken, 23
Russian criticism, early twentieth-century, 155–156
Russian montage, 156, 158
Ryan, Sheila, *95*

*Saboteur*, 14, 29, 74, 136, 140
*Sabrina*, 138–140
Sarris, Andrew, 131–132, 172–173